CULTIVATING VICTORY

Cultivating Victory

THE WOMEN'S LAND ARMY AND THE VICTORY GARDEN MOVEMENT

Cecilia Gowdy-Wygant

UNIVERSITY OF PITTSBURGH PRESS

Published by the University of Pittsburgh Press, Pittsburgh, Pa., 15260
Copyright © 2013, University of Pittsburgh Press
All rights reserved
Manufactured in the United States of America
Printed on acid-free paper
10 9 8 7 6 5 4 3 2 1

Library of Congress Cataloging-in-Publication Data

Gowdy-Wygant, Cecilia.
    Cultivating victory : the Women's Land Army and the Victory Garden
movement / Cecilia Gowdy-Wygant.
        p.   cm.
    ISBN 978-0-8229-4425-6 (hardback)
    1. Women's Land Army (Great Britain)—History.   2. Women's Land
Army (United States) —History   3. Victory gardens—Great Britain—
History.   4. Victory gardens—United States—History.   I. Title.
    S455.G754 2013
    635.09—dc23   2012047728

CONTENTS

v

ACKNOWLEDGMENTS

The cultivation of this book has been a long and at times arduous process. In recognition of the process, there are many individuals who helped in the planting of ideas, the sowing of the research and writing, and the harvesting of the publication process.

I wish to thank the University of Pittsburgh Press for the opportunity to publish this broad-reaching international story of cultivation as identity. Thanks go to Cynthia Miller, Kelley Johovic, and Alex Wolfe for their professional editorial support. I wish to thank the two anonymous reviewers of the press for their careful scrutiny and guidance of the story. Your insight helped provide a richer and more concrete story than I initially imagined possible. I also wish to thank Maria Sticco for her work in the publicity of the book. I also extend thanks to the dozens of other behind-the-scenes UPP editorial staff members that helped in the publication process.

Certainly this book would not be possible without the guidance of Mark Stoll of Texas Tech University in his mentorship and teaching of environmental history. His standards of excellence and his genuine dedication to his students toward graduation and beyond make him a model mentor and historian. Justin Hart, Aliza Wong, and Julie Willett provided support beyond imagination and countless hours of reading. Their guidance shaped the various iterations of the manuscript to the very end. I thank you for a wonderful foundation upon which this story was cultivated.

I wish to thank the many archivists and staff of the National Archives of the United States, the Library of Congress, the National Archives of the

United Kingdom, and the Imperial War Museum for their help and guidance in obtaining records and permissions to bring the wonderful historic images to the public through this book.

Thanks go to the many wonderful friends and family who supported me and my work. Though there are too many supportive friends and family to list, I want you all to know your support meant the world to me and provided me with the stamina to keep moving forward. Thanks to my parents who taught me the value of commitment and sacrifice; and thanks go to my parents-in-law who provided unending moral support. I wish to thank my husband, David L. Wygant, for his support, encouragement, and assistance in the organization of research, and for being a terrific colleague and friend. I am sure that he read more copies of this manuscript than he ever dreamed of or ever wanted to. Last, I want to express my gratitude to my children, Whitney and Grace. Thanks for showing interest in the topic and for your encouragement in the publishing process. This book is for you.

CULTIVATING VICTORY

Introduction
GARDENING IN THE NEW CENTURY

There'll be tomatoes where the roses used to grow,
Potatoes where petunias used to grow.
No more sunflow'rs waving high 'til the pole beans reach the sky,
Then you'll serve a vict'ry dinner bye and bye.

. . . [R]emember as ye sow, so shall ye reap,
Come on and hoe a row and dig it deep,

Ev'ry seed is goin' to grow into victory I know
with tomatoes where the roses used to grow.

—Gilbert Mills, Ted Rolfe, and Billy Faber,
   "There'll Be Tomatoes Where the Roses Used to Grow," 1945

THROUGHOUT THE TWENTIETH CENTURY, the seeds of victory were sown on farms, vacant lots, in backyards, rooftops, and window boxes. Intentionally selected, meticulously planted, and carefully harvested, these seeds provided food in times of scarcity and a political ideological focus for warring nations. While allied nations shared agricultural strategies, women across three continents shared common goals of liberation, survival, and adventure. As the U.S. and British governments used propaganda and agricultural programs to cultivate both victory and identity, national and international women's organizations promoted women's place and space within the farm labor force and society through waged farm work. Regardless of national intent and the programs participated in, women who cultivated the land during wartime not only cultivated victory, but also participated in spreading a new political and social culture of abundance focused on the production and distribution of food.[1]

For both nations, gardening was a cultural statement about national identity. For the English, ornamental gardens were part and parcel of the expression of leisure; families expressed their wealth and stature in society through the elaborate ornamental plants and design of the landscape. For many of England's elite, garden parties were the center of social gatherings, and the elaborate gardens were as much a part of their homes as the dining halls or salons. The "English garden" as it became known around the world, was a place of natural splendor where the elite took time to contemplate, socialize and, as the decades passed, even to organize reform movements. For those of lesser means and stature, gardens were the bridge between the middle class and the elite. Knowledge of ornamental gardening was seen as a genteel trait, as opposed to farm labor, which carried with it a stigma of peasant labor and strife. Thus garden training for women focused more heavily on flower cultivation and garden design rather than nutritive needs of the nation, and many saw this training as preparation for a life of leisure. Though many English women tended to kitchen gardens where they produced basic foods for their families, women's magazines and journals of the day focused on the aesthetic nature of those gardens rather than on the labor involved in them or the importance of the production of food. The national focus on these small food-based gardens began to change, however, as wartime food shortages demanded a shift away from the aesthetic to the utilitarian.

Americans shared much of the same cultural identity of their English ancestors, though the cultivation of food held both gender and racial stigmas. Built on a history of slavery, agriculture in America significantly altered Americans' perceptions about who cultivated and why. Thus, American women's sphere in gardening included ornamental plantings and landscape design much like their English counterparts. It was not uncommon for the upper classes in America to grow food, however, as many held significant orchards or owned commercial farms. Even President Andrew Jackson turned an old building left to ruins adjacent to the White House into a great orangery during his tenure in office in the 1830s to provide citrus fruits for the White House dinner table for decades to come. Full-scale food production though, held social and gendered lines of stratification: white women were often excluded from the labor of food production in efforts to maintain the roles of white men as food production leaders and the working classes, including minority men and women, as laborers. Thus training for American women focused on the ornamental rather than the utilitarian just as it did in England. Although kitchen gardens were less popular in America among the working classes than they were in England, many American women did attempt them but found little support for urban gardens outside of the aesthetic. Women's magazines and journals in America also focused on the ornamental as a hallmark of social status and as a representation of a life of leisure for white women. Just as in England, the focus on gardening began to change as wartime food needs of the Allies signaled a new strategy for success. Although the focus did shift from the aesthetic to the utilitarian, cultural struggles ensued as traditional roles of the management of food production moved from men to women.

The cultivation of land in the first half of the twentieth century brought monumental changes in the way the Western world observed the interrelationship of women, labor, and abundance. In response to food shortages and with intense longing for change, women cultivated both victory and identity. Though this particular kind of cultivation centered on the actions of urban middle- and working-class women, the governments of the United States and Great Britain practiced their own forms of cultivating both victory and identity. Through propaganda, imagery, and educational programs focused on food and the cultivation of land, nations attempted to form national identities and achieve international victories during both the First World War and Second World War. Although some women responded to the national propaganda and official calls for change by engaging in homefront food campaigns, much of the agricultural labor women provided for their nations stemmed from a historical interest on the part of both national and international women's organizations in promoting women's place and space within both the labor force and society. This agricultural labor marked a transformation in political and social culture and in the identity of both the cultivators and those who promoted cultivation.

During the First and Second World Wars, nations sought victory by many means. Economies mobilized for war, and governments urged citizens to contribute to and sacrifice for the war in various ways. The creation of Women's Land Armies and victory gardens were just two of the various ways citizens across national borders, most especially and significantly middle-class women, were able to contribute to the war effort. The following chapters analyze the formation of these efforts, outline the key persons involved in the organization, and illustrate the lasting social, political, and cultural effects of the movements. This story, positioned at the intersection of histories of cultivation, nationalism, and the production and consumption of food, offers unique perspectives on the impact of cultivation on shaping political and personal identities during the first half of the twentieth century.

For over a century, women around the world and their governments used cultivation to create new identities that shaped not only the way women saw their role in agriculture and homefront wartime experiences, but also how nations viewed the importance of women and the cultivation of food as tools of diplomacy. During the First World War, at a time when American women had yet to attain suffrage, the United States urged women to create war (later termed "victory") gardens in their own backyards but was not as active as other nations in persuading women to leave the home and join their nation's agricultural labor program, known as the Women's Land Army of America (WLAA). The evidence of female agricultural work in the United States showed the societal preference toward domestic gardening during wartime over formal rural occupations. Though American women participated in the cultivation of an estimated 3.5 million war gardens by 1918, approximately 15,000 women worked on farms as part of the WLAA. Undoubtedly the late entry of the United States into the war affected its homefront campaigns, though the cultivation and production of food reigned as a vital symbol in promoting both an Allied victory and an American identity as a land of abundance. The culture of abundance in turn shaped national and international identity in the interwar and postwar years as nations used food no longer as a weapon, but as a tool of diplomacy.[2]

Composed of primarily white, middle-class women, many women's political and social organizations did not accurately represent their nation's female laborers, but rather served as avenues for middle-class women to obtain careers and leadership roles. As many African American and immigrant women needed employment before either of the wars began, wartime employment did not change much for them. Many women did not seek wartime employment in agriculture but found career opportunities in industrial work, leaving domestic employment to pursue higher-paying jobs in the factories. As a result, white middle- and upper-class women were left with household management duties that included gardening, canning, and shopping. Due to the dire economic and security situations the British experienced during war, women of all races and economic classes in England had to make changes to their lifestyles as they experienced altered relationships with food. Regardless of nationality, American and British white middle-class women used the opportunity to forge new identities through new career options and forms of household management.

Britons differed from Americans in their attitudes about women's wartime roles because the British food situation differed from that of the United States. The experience of firsthand attacks on British soil promoted a stronger sense of obligation and eagerness to fight in any way they could, and, although in 1914 approximately 50 percent of the food Britain needed to maintain its population of 36 million was the result of importation, the British government and citizens alike quickly organized plans to replace agricultural workers with a team of women eager to prevent hunger caused by enemy import blockades. As a result, British urban middle-class women responded to the national agricultural need and drove the movement of women war workers during the First World War by creating the Women's Land Army (WLA). During the war, around 80,000 British women served as nurses, cooks, ambulance drivers, or in other service roles as part of the Women's Army Auxiliary Corps (WAAC) either on the home front or the Western Front to aid the war effort. Additionally, the British WLA attracted approximately 23,000 women seeking both adventure and opportunity to serve their country.

Casualties of the First World War included many of the social and political gains of the Progressive Era in America and the progressive movements of the Labour and Liberal Parties for the advancement of women's rights in Great Britain. The movement for women's rights and suffrage that spread across the Western world stalled due to the international wartime focus, but at the same time in many ways benefited from the opportunities women found to prove their ability to contribute economically and politically. These patriotic homefront contributions aided the movement somewhat by diminishing concerns about socialist influences in women's actions toward equality. The female workforce on the home front in both the United States and Great Britain received appreciation at the end of the war for assistance in maintaining stability during the war. Some recognition grew into political and social gains as a result of continued connections between homefront efforts and political organizations that existed before the war began. These efforts remained in the memory of political leaders in the decades to come, and when the threat of war seemed imminent a mere two decades later, nations called upon their women to contribute to the effort a second time.

In the era of the Second World War, the United States fully promoted *both* the Victory Garden and the WLAA campaigns. Due to advances in women's rights and position in labor and society as well as the advancements in technology that made industrial food production more efficient, the nation looked to women's production of food as symbolic of the abundance of America and gave soldiers a visual representation of a nation worth fighting for. At the end of the war and into the postwar era, the United States and its consumer culture attempted to utilize this socially and politically constructed wartime connection to the land and production of food to (re)domesticate women.

The Second World War marked a profound change in cultural identity for the British people. Stemming from increased air raids, shortages of food, and considerable threat to national survival, the domestic situation of England differed immensely from that in the United States. One thing that the two nations had in common, however, was the intense desire to motivate women to do all they could to help achieve victory.[3] For England, however,

the nation realized that merely creating backyard gardens or canning vegetables was not enough to sustain the nation so dependent upon agricultural
imports. Importing nearly 70 percent of its food supply when it entered the
war, Britain's need in the face of German blockades was great. Nonetheless,
English women across class boundaries gardened in existing urban and rural
plots or helped cultivate on urban land allocated for gardening as part of the
Grow More Food (GMF) or "Dig For Victory" campaign. In addition to these
efforts, urban middle- and working-class women of England responded to the
anticipated food crisis that a second global war might bring by reestablish-
ing the WLA three months before Britain declared war in September 1939. In
the months leading to war, the British WLA acquired over 10,000 female recruits for training and service. Though accurate records are difficult to obtain
because the British government eliminated records of the WLA after the end
of the war, we do know that at its peak in 1945, the British WLA contained
approximately 77,000 members.

Much of the interest in developing the WLAs in multiple nations stemmed
from wide-scale women's organizations that held close ties with their international wartime sisters like Lady Gertrude Denman and Harriot Stanton
Blatch. Lady Denman served as assistant director of the British WLA in the
First World War and later as director of the British WLA in the Second World
War. Before her work with the WLA, she was an international activist for
women's issues and was also wife of Thomas Denman, the fifth governor-general of Australia. Lady Denman held many positions of leadership in women's
organizations, both national and international, and represented a growing
international exchange of progressive ideas about women's place in labor and
society. Harriot Stanton Blatch, daughter of the famed American suffragist
Elizabeth Cady Stanton, spent two decades in England fighting for women's
equality in labor and brought her connections and ideas back to America and
became the director of the WLAA in 1917. Blatch dedicated her book *Mobilizing Woman Power* to the women of Great Britain and France, realizing the
importance of using foreign examples and ideas to encourage the American
people to make the best use of their female workforce. Blatch argued that a
WLAA, modeled on the WLA of Great Britain, would change societal expectations of spheres for women and claimed,

> But facts remain facts in spite of prejudice, and the Woman's Land Army
> with faith and enthusiasm in lieu of a national treasury, are endeavoring to
> bring woman power and the untilled fields together. The proved achieve-
> ment of the individual worker will win the employer, the unit plan with
> its solution of housing conditions and dreary isolation will overcome not

only the opposition of the farmer's wife, but that of the intelligent worker. When the seed time of the movement has been lived through by anxious and inspired women, the government may step in to reap the harvest of a nation's gratitude.[4]

This female patriotic *agri*-culture grew stronger in the postwar years. When the Second World War began, nations organized many of their home-front campaigns around strengthening the efficiency of the so-called weaponry of nature. Denman, director of the British WLA in the Second World War, claimed the German people and especially Hitler were out to "starve the British people into submission."[5] Whether urban or rural, young or old, single or married with children, women in the first half of the twentieth century found political, social, and inner voices through laboring with and against nature for their nations. Mothers, daughters, and sisters found that though their nations needed them to cultivate victory, their experiences and hard labor on the land brought them deep empathy, compassion, and understanding of class and racial perspectives that they might not have otherwise been privy to. The "land girls" of the Western world set out to transform nature into victory, but in the end, found themselves transformed.

Addressing how women viewed their roles and how those views compared with and contrasted to those of other workers, domestics, the general public, and their national governments, then, is a difficult task that is best achieved by first analyzing individually the kind of labor performed and then comparing and contrasting the overarching themes that transcend geographic location, culture, and time. Agricultural labor, whether domestic or commercial, urban or rural, served as a solution to the myriad of social, political, and gendered struggles women faced in the decades leading up to the First World War as such labor often agitated the social order. Political and personal liberation of women was not the result of a few acts of the "great" thinkers and reformers of the day, but a culmination of many, many acts of resistance and change that took place over decades. Women at the end of the nineteenth century found little or no hope of a profession or access to political and social equality; and those women in Western societies born of working-class status either married or became a servant of some measure, or both. Women of somewhat higher social stature, however, had the option to marry or to remain single in the family's household if financial responsibilities allowed. Society did not encourage these women to think of employment as an option—socially it was seen as a sign of financial weakness and denigration to their attractiveness in "society with a big S." Therefore, women of strong minds and limited opportunities involved themselves in philanthropic adventures and thus sought the non-wage-earning career of social activism to find fulfillment. These "small acts" in many ways led to dramatic changes in social acceptance of women as laborers, political equals, and vital contributors to the strength of their nations.

Female activists did not fight alone in their quest for political, social, and economic reform; many other groups or movements of the day sought change in the workplace, living conditions, and political equity. Activists for the advancement of women and their organizations were more diverse than perhaps any other group of the nineteenth and early twentieth centuries because they did not merely focus on one goal or even a small group of goals. For women, gender alone determined their lot in life, though arguably class and race complicated it even further. The nature of discrimination and prejudice against their sex dictated that they were unequal in every aspect of life; therefore, female activists and reformers sought not to change just one or a few situations, but all areas needing improvement. Areas of concern and reform included education, politics, and labor; and though there existed a complicated internal battle between upper-class and working-class reformers, it is worth noting and exploring further that, regardless of social orientation, many of the programs and reformers benefited from and benchmarked each other's platforms and strategies. For example, some English members of the International Council of Women (ICW) were also members of the Women's Agricultural and Horticultural International Union (WAHIU) and brought with them ideas about women's place in agriculture when they helped form and joined the membership of the WLA during the First World War. It is in this light that we must view the development of agricultural education and organized labor for women during the late nineteenth and early twentieth centuries, for, through the lens of the small acts of various international women's agricultural labor reformers, we observe how a stronger societal appreciation of women's place in the nation emerged.

This book follows two unique and at times imposing storylines as it narrates two fields or perspectives of history—women and the environment—and observes each through the lens of cultural and national identity to the point where the two intersect, and where the narrative of each myopic view takes on the patina of the other. Throughout, I analyze how British and American government agencies utilized the images and memory of women and of their lives to tie both the mental and physical images of women to the land and to forge a connection of women and nature as voiceless symbols of nationalism. I utilize newspapers and government propaganda found in formal and informal collections of various national archives, libraries, and war memorial organizations to offer the reader a sense of what governments expected of their female citizens during wartime and how those governments viewed food as a tool of diplomacy. Then I compare and contrast how women's organizations and actions provided outlets for the creation of imagined communities and opportunities to voice their ideas, though at times those voices went unrecognized publicly. Exploring the transnational exchange of ideas of women's organizations and leaders gives new insights into the interconnectedness of environment, gender, and nationalism. Here I utilize organizational records, personal memoirs, letters, and manuscripts of women who found expression of their patriotic activities through the printed word. Images of propaganda, labor, and popular culture complement this exploration and provide a visual example of the evolving image of cultivation spanning an entire century.

Divided into three parts, this book explores the urban and rural campaigns of the First and Second World Wars and the cultural memory associated with them. Part I explores the origins of, as well as the working structure of, the various limited national support campaigns of the war garden and WLA movements by charting the philanthropic adventures of early reformers of the late nineteenth century. It is the work of these women, connected by international communication and interest, that solidifies the resolve of women in the early twentieth century to get involved in helping win the First World War. Women's organizations filtered information and activity between the government agencies and the laborers themselves and vice versa. Through such progressive organizations both national and international, important relationships formed that helped forge a coalition of women eager to make a place for themselves in international, national, and local political realms. Women's organizations helped administer information and support as well as womanpower for wartime consumption, conservation, and recycling programs. Activists in many of these organizations during the First World War later served to create and lead the WLAs of England and the United States during the Second World War, when nations called upon these women's organizations for the support and mobilization of agricultural employment once the threat of war appeared imminent.

The development and lasting impact of war gardens stemmed from a growing awareness and interest in progressive social reform. In America, previous agricultural activities based upon urban societal improvement such as urban cultivation programs, school gardens, and civic beautification programs, provided the ease of opportunity to create war gardens during the First World War. Women who formed agricultural movements did so to aid the war effort out of a desire to promote social and political reform, whereas women who actually served in such wartime agricultural programs did so out of a desire to express their patriotism or to find employment or simply out of a desire to escape the clutches of chaperonage. From a broader perspective still, we must examine the role governments played in such movements. Though the reformers were responsible for inspiring public approval of women's place in agriculture, it was government-sanctioned wartime programs that would eventually take over the women's agricultural labor movement. Though the elimination of records of the WLA at the end of the First World War make it somewhat difficult to obtain official images and records from the period, those that do remain offer rich details about the importance of the image of women laboring on the land.

Part II discusses the role of war gardens and WLAs during the Second World War as well as the political diplomacy associated with them. After the First World War, war gardens acquired the label of victory gardens, and the wartime food campaigns of the Second World War called upon urban culti-vators once more. Building upon the success of the WLAs in the First World War, nations turned to urban women to fill the labor gap once war claimed male farm laborers and left work available. Despite the growing acceptance of women as farm laborers, the members of the WLA continued to face preju-dice and lack of recognition. Here it is necessary not only to examine personal memoirs of members, laborers, and leading figures in the development of the victory garden and WLA movement, but also to explore the significance of images used in wartime propaganda of victory gardens. The role of image (in propaganda posters, pamphlets, and other mass media) in setting standards and suggestions for domesticity and youth is crucial in understanding the role of the victory garden and WLA in shaping both gender and age roles as well as social and political behaviors in a modern society.

Part III examines the postwar cultural memory of the rural and urban agricultural movements. As Britons expressed their admiration for the land girls of the WLA, Americans nearly erased the farmerettes from their cultural memory, adopting instead a wartime ideal of urban women working in fac-tories and planting victory gardens in efforts to display the abundance of the nation. In the postwar years, many attempts at urban gardening movements recalled the successes of the wartime gardens, though the motives for and at-titudes about gardening changed significantly. Britons and Americans alike found that their cultural memory, like the soil, could be cultivated to achieve personal and political gain.

I conclude by analyzing how the public recognition, or lack thereof, at the end of the Second World War profoundly shaped the cultural memory of women's role and place in agriculture. More than just the individual memo-ries of the women who cultivated victory are important here; national and cultural memories are also profoundly significant. Women and cultivation be-came symbols of nationalism and wartime nostalgia through both a consumer culture and through foreign relations of the United States and Great Britain. While women transitioned from wartime to a postwar society and economy, nations looked at food as a tool of diplomacy and symbol of democracy. Thus governmental propaganda, personal letters, and newspapers help to convey the governmental and personal perspectives on the history of the movements, while an examination of the modern world of consumption provides nuanced perspectives that illustrate how popular and cultural memories about the war efforts penetrated the consumer industry.

With recognition of and respect to the various avenues by which one could explore this history, this perspective is unique. This narrative, in an attempt to illustrate the international connections and collaboration, is de-signed to provide an overarching view of the projects and people involved. At the same time, it also explores the narrative of the individual in an effort to find commonality among the international programs and to analyze their significance to the people they served. Without the texts and inspirations of many histories previously written, perhaps this story could be told, but with less direction and seasoning. This book is not an attempt to present one his-tory better, but rather to serve as a bridge to many histories within which the previously published stories reside. In many ways the subtle methodologies of this book complement yet complicate the existing narrative of nations, na-ture, and gender in the twentieth century; for, although this is a transnational, comparative story, nations and individuals cultivated identities unique to their own wartime experiences—thus comparison is at times difficult to present in one neat and linear narrative.

This book aims to explore national and transnational interconnections and variances in the creation of, motivation for, and methods of operation of the Victory Garden and WLA campaigns of the First and Second World Wars as well as their cultural transcendence through time. Histories of the indi-viduals serving in the WLAs grow in number as the cultural memory grows regarding wartime service. The story however will mark new territory in both historiography and analysis of victory gardens and the WLAs from envi-ronmental, gendered, and cultural perspectives and representations, as it will explore the varying perspectives of the United States and England and the similarities and differences in their respective wartime food campaigns. Thus this story attempts to bridge existing narratives by providing more inclusive and international narrative of social, cultural, and environmental connections to the events of war in the first half of the twentieth century than those pre-ceding it, for no study to my knowledge has told the story of *both* the Victory

Garden and WLA campaigns in a single volume and looked at the significance of these topics from an international perspective. The perspective taken here is admittedly broad, yet necessary for analyzing the change of political and personal identity over time.

Whereas many other previous works of published literature (personal memoirs, photographic journals, etc.) all focus on one aspect or nation in their scaled perspectives, this study attempts to use sources that bridge the two campaigns and illustrate the significance of internationalism in shaping such nationalistic behavior as "digging for victory." Elements and examples of the textual and visual imagery of women found in government propaganda, news media, and advertising offer unique perspectives on gender, domesticity, and nationalism during these significant periods of wartime food production. Recognizing that one cannot analyze variances in identity without observing the personal perspectives on such programs by women who took part in them, I find editorials, interviews, diaries, and books written by women agriculturalists or in reference to women's place in agriculture are crucial to examining the transformation and complexity of how food and cultivation shaped women's identity in the first half of the twentieth century. These sources bring new perspectives on varied histories of the complex relationships women had with the land, each other, and their governments.

The twentieth century brought significant change in the relationships women and their governments had with agriculture. In the midst of struggles for political voice and recognition, women found opportunity in cultivation both for social, community, and political recognition as well as for broader personal and societal perspectives that ultimately altered their self-identification. *Who* cultivated for victory is significant. *Why* and *what* they cultivated for victory are significant. *Why* nations wanted them to grow and *what* nations did to get women to do it are significant. *How* we remember these women and their actions of cultivating victory is significant. In the history of Western society, the phrases "victory garden" and "Women's Land Army" are cultural legacies that have transcended time and connotation. How and why this happened is perhaps the most significant aspect of all.

Part I.

THE FIRST WORLD WAR

Ladies of leisure—and women of action. Time hangs heavily on their hands. They decide to join the women who are helping so much. . . . They go to work on land to counteract the U-boats' work at sea. Weeds, like U-boats, must be exterminated.

—Women's Land Army recruiting film, 1918

CHAPTER 1

Ladies of Leisure and Women of Action

The war has called women over the top. Since that fateful August, 1914, four provinces of Canada and the Dominion itself have raised the banner of votes for women. Nevada and Montana declared for suffrage before the war was four months old, and Denmark enfranchised its women before the year was out. And when America went forth to fight for democracy abroad, Arkansas, Michigan, Vermont, Nebraska, North Dakota, Rhode Island, began to lay the foundations of freedom at home, and New York in no faltering voice proclaimed full liberty for all its people. Lastly Great Britain has enfranchised its women, and surely the Congress of the United States will not lag behind the Mother of Parliaments!

—Harriot Stanton Blatch, *Mobilizing Woman-Power*, 1918

ACROSS TWO CONTINENTS amid the dawn of a new age of social change, the First World War called women over the top. The war called women to climb out of the parapet of the protective trenches of leisure and over the top into a world of political and social service. Like men on a battlefield, women on two continents fought for cultural and social values, honor, and patriotism. Their duty to both their country and themselves drove their desire to climb out of the trenches and into the battlefield of social change. Their mission was to achieve victory for their countries and victory over an age-old cultural tradition of women's place and space in labor, politics, and society. As a result, the rhetoric of women's sphere, steeped in the cultural traditions of the nineteenth-century Western world, met great opposition at the turn of the twentieth century. Female political and social activists such as Harriot Stanton Blatch, Countess Frances Evelyn "Daisy" Maynard Warwick, and Lady Gertrude Denman utilized agricultural labor shortages in Great Britain and the United States to improve the position of women in labor and to increase the momentum of the global female suffrage movements. The achievement of these tasks, while varied in outcomes, successfully turned the tide of a cultural and political sphere for women from one of leisure and subservience to one of action and influence.

Women's Political Voice in the Early Twentieth Century

The late eighteenth century was ripe for political change for women. That change, through social and political struggle, often met fierce resistance. Centuries-old social and cultural traditions in both Great Britain and the United States left women limited opportunities within the socially accepted female sphere of influence. A woman's "sphere" dictated the social and political path of her life and both British and American societies referred to this sphere as a sacred set of values based upon national and cultural traditions. This sphere, much like a social caste, left little room for personal growth or identity outside of societal expectations. As a result, many women fought to find acceptance outside of this sphere and instead forged their own positions in labor and politics.

At the turn of the twentieth century the movement for women's suffrage was international in scale. Suffrage movements in both Great Britain and the United States epitomized the struggle for women's political voice and equity in labor. Prior to the First World War, women in Great Britain and the United States did not have complete suffrage. Without the vote, women on both continents found little opportunity for recognition and equal opportunities in labor. By means of intense and at times deadly action, suffragists in England achieved a limited right to vote in 1918, although universal suffrage was not granted until 1928. Though some American women held rights to vote in state or local matters, for many, universal suffrage for women seemed impossible to obtain in the face of federal resistance. The United States was world renowned as a land of democracy; however, the movement for suffrage lagged behind the successes of movements in the United Kingdom, New Zealand, Finland, Norway, the Kingdom of Denmark, Canada, Australia, the Netherlands, Southern Rhodesia, the Azerbaijan Republic, the Republic of Estonia, the Democratic Republic of Georgia, the Hungarian Democratic Republic, Latvia, Lithuania, Union of Soviet Socialist Republics, Austria, Czechoslovakia, Poland, Sweden, Germany, and Luxembourg. After nearly a century of work toward gender equality, American women turned to strategies found in international political organizations for ideas and support for their own movement.

Women's Place and Space in Labor

Women's place in labor was a major topic of interest within the international and national suffrage movements. Activists argued that once women received the opportunity to work in occupations previously closed to women, public perceptions of their abilities to contribute to society would change. They also argued, however, that until women received fair wages, no progress could ensue. In Great Britain, women looked to areas of agriculture and degreed professions as areas for economic opportunity. Historians debate the accuracy of the numbers of women who actively participated in the British labor system, as there are no comprehensive sources that include married and unmarried women as well as farm families. Some estimates claim that by 1851 women made up 11 percent of the agricultural workforce, while making up a paltry 3 percent of the medical field and more than 85 percent of the domestic service industries. As the farmers of England placed women into lower-paying agricultural jobs, women earned nearly one-half of the agricultural wages that men did near the mid-nineteenth century. As a result, a movement grew to find greater career opportunities for women in agricultural labor and management.

Women in Great Britain held few rights, despite support from the Labour Party. Suffragists maintained a politically active presence, though that presence only seemed to harden the resolve of many opposed to women's equality in society. In the latter half of the nineteenth century, British women increasingly argued for political equality by means of the vote and in education so that they might gain entrance into occupations previously denied to them. In 1870, Queen Victoria attempted to calm the tensions associated with a movement to include women in education by stating quite simply, "To tear away all the barriers which surround a woman, and to propose that she study with *men*—things which could not be named before them, certainly not in a mixed audience—would be to introduce a total disregard of what must be considered as belonging to the rules and principles of morality. Let women be what God intended, a helpmate for man, but with totally different duties and vocations."[1] Such sentiment only escalated previously emerging feminist movements in England. In the years that followed, the intense political activism and hunger strikes of activists like Sylvia Pankhurst frightened many British men and women from voicing support for the movement or for women's equality in general.

Women in America found that the position of women in labor mirrored that of their British sisters. At the end of the Civil War, women made up an unmeasured percentage of agricultural labor due to the transition from slave to free labor and due to no governmental reporting of farm family labor as an occupation. In other occupations, however, women held nearly 7 percent of positions in agriculture, while comprising 5 percent of the positions in the medical fields and nearly 85 percent of paid domestic work. In America in the nineteenth century, women often found themselves left out of labor unions and, as a result, formed unions of their own to voice their needs. As a new century dawned and the voices of women demanding suffrage grew, however, many labor organizations began to acknowledge women as laborers, albeit in different classes of labor. Some unions accepted the voice of women and a few allowed women to serve as leaders and organizers of regional efforts. Though women made great strides in organizing unions in areas such as the needle trades, the textile industry, as well as laundry and service industries, areas such as metalworking, woodworking, printing, and agriculture held strong gendered cultural norms that stymied the position of women as equal laborers. During the late nineteenth century, a time termed the "Gilded Age" due to rapid industrial and economic growth, women's role in labor increased significantly, growing from 2.6 million women working in 1880 to 8.6 million in 1900. Unions discouraged women from entering the workforce, as they competed for male labor and were paid less than male workers. There is not a consensus on the amount or type of agricultural labor American women performed. Women on farms often did not report their labor as paid labor and therefore are not factored into the statistics on agricultural labor. Formal recognition of the occupation of self-employment left many women without a space in labor because their husbands and fathers claimed the work of the family farm as their own in reports to the government. This discrepancy has racial implications as well, for as many as half of the black women in America in 1900 lived in households engaged in agricultural labor; however no clear consensus exists for their role as workers on family farms. Perhaps a better understanding of what women did on farms, and why they continued or rejected it during wartime will give clearer indications of why white women dominated the labor force of the Women's Land Army (WLA) in the United States.

From 1750 to 1900, British agriculture underwent a series of rollercoaster booms and busts, and as a result became the subject of many reexaminations, revisions, and changes in the labor distribution and cultural norms of the English "rural idyll." Whereas English tradition held that villages often reserved *common land* for people to cultivate without fees or ownership, population increases dictated a need for increased agricultural production and that need, when combined with new farming technologies, led to a movement where farm *enclosures* replaced the common land opportunities, leading to an increased urban migration for many English people. As farming changed, so did the need for and roles of farm laborers; yet one element that remained unchanged was the contribution of the farm wife and family of the rural areas. Just as in decades past, farm women at the turn of the twentieth century aided their husbands in the management of the farm and were vital to the success of the dwindling occupation of farming.

Rural life in America, however, faced different challenges for women. Based on a standing tradition of minority agricultural labor, women did not have a place in agriculture in the decades after 1870. Though American urban society often dictated women's sphere as excluding manual labor, married farm women often found themselves in a lifelong joint business partnership, as the financial success of the farm depended upon the contribution of all family members regardless of gender. However, gendered divisions of labor on the farm dictated what roles women played in the business. The farm was much like the diminishing cottage industry in that while men performed most of the production of raw agricultural materials, the farm wife and children often turned those raw materials into products both for use by the family and for sale to the public. The financial success of the farm depended upon each member's contribution to the family business. In America, married women held a stronger place in labor than single female laborers, as they found greater access to political voice through farmers' alliances and the Grange movement. Often these organizations provided refuge from the tedious and often solitary life of farmers. These organizations, both fraternal and political in nature, also provided opportunities for farm women to form their own groups within and adjunct to male groups that provided education, social support, and occasionally a political voice for women.

England's wartime food shortages paved the way for women's place in agricultural labor. As the war progressed, people internationally began to realize that food was the key element in national survival and it became the focus of various homefront campaigns (see fig. 1.1). England was the first nation among many to establish a national agricultural plan for homefront assistance in the war effort, creating the Ministry of Food in 1915. Eventually such plans centered on the recruitment of young women to take the place of workers leaving to fight in the war. To win the war Britain needed male soldiers, but to keep the nation and its people alive and strong they needed women to work in factories, at clerical jobs, and most significantly, on farms. The recruitment and enlistment of female agricultural workers, easily the most vital civilian effort in the fight against hunger on the home front, not only helped feed a nation at war but also provided opportunities for social and political movements to-

FIGURE 1.1. *The Kitchen Is the [Key] to Victory Eat Less Bread*, poster issued March 1917. Imperial War Museum, London.

ward female equality. Steeped in nationalistic rhetoric, women's organizations provided an international platform from which to share ideas for social and political change.

Women's Organizations and the Social and Political Climate

Women's assistance in the solution to the growing wartime agricultural problem stemmed from a longer period of social and political reform. Internationally, reform movements grew in the last few decades of the nineteenth century, and inclusive in such movements was the international movement for women's rights. International events in the transatlantic world in the late nineteenth century forged transnational political and social ideological connections among the leaders of the Western world, and these ideas influenced women's goals toward organization. As national social, political, and economic leaders shared ideas and examples of progress, these transnational connections shaped not only the goals of the Progressive Era in America, but also the political cultures of England as well, as many English political activists were termed the "progressive forces of England."[2] One political issue of transnational importance, women's equal rights in labor, inspired women to create and expand both international and national movements despite the fact that women's arguments for suffrage and equality often met intense verbal and often violent opposition. Though the governments of England and the United States often encouraged male leaders to share progressive successes, they often treated women activists as troublemakers. Female activists raised public consciousness about women's ability and place in labor, however many people deemed such behavior part and parcel of a broader era of unrest.[3] Opponents labeled the women "suffragettes" as a way to both express their disdain and to diminish the work of the suffragists. In turn, British and American women took ownership of the label and used it to define the role of women in an unequal labor market.

In the years leading up to the granting of suffrage, British and American women sought ways to carve out a place for themselves in society; as part of that strategy, they participated in organizations with progressive ideas and goals. By joining and participating in social organizations, they established for themselves a sphere of identity separate from that in which they lived. Young unmarried women of this period rejected the task-oriented employment of their mothers that confined them to the household. In place of the constraints of such employment, women turned to urban employment such as factory and retail work.[4] Leisure time for these urban working-class women consisted of a variety of social activities surrounding work and amusement; joining women's clubs and organizations, whether for social or political reasons, is one such example.

Women who did not work outside of the home, as well as those looking to improve their position in labor, found opportunity in these political organizations. Led mostly by educated "ladies of leisure," these organizations provided humanitarian work for their members. Organizations on an international scale focused on the broader political issues of suffrage and reformed female labor and often sought to lead the working urban and rural classes in the movement for new identities for women in society. The women of these national and international organizations discovered commonalities that transcended borders: women's roles as mothers, the protection of women from exploitation in the workplace, as well as the core debates of suffrage and equality. Despite their humanist efforts, these female activists were elitist. Exclusions based upon race, class, language, and religion left the leadership and often the membership of the organizations full of wealthy white Christian women from North America and Western Europe, determined to speak for women as a whole.[5] Despite the apparent class and racial conflicts, however, many women in these organizations worked diligently toward their common goals and in many cases these "ladies of leisure" became "women of action," providing significant aid to their nations during wartime and beyond.

At the end of the nineteenth century, British agriculture was a topic of interest for England's elite as they looked for areas to concentrate their efforts at societal reform. Efforts at grabbing the attention of farm women through the national media resulted in the publication of several journals depicting a new ideal of the modern farm woman. Women's organizations, often composed of urban elite women, worked together with leaders in the rural communities to address the needs of farm women and provide both information and inspiration for the changing demands of modern rural life. In response to the growing demand to address the needs of the rural populations, the Women's Institute (WI) took on the challenge as leaders in the production and dissemination of information to the rural women of England.

These wealthy white women from England argued for change in women's place in society by focusing on labor issues. Responding to as much as a 75 percent drop in female agricultural laborers during 1850–1872, activists considered improved agricultural labor as a potential avenue for the advancement of women.[6] As a result, these women developed a variety of agricultural education structures and collectives of trained women before the First World War began. Though the evolution of the WLA involved many women, certain women's and organizations' contributions stand out as significant in understanding the social and political climate surrounding women's agricultural labor. The International Council of Women (ICW) and the Women's Agricultural and Horticultural International Union (WAHIU) as well as the many women associated with these organizations shaped the landscape of female agricultural labor profoundly in the years leading to war.

In 1883 a call for an ICW came forth from political activists in the United Kingdom, the United States, and France. Founding leaders included famed American suffragist Elizabeth Cady Stanton, a representative of the American office, and her daughter, Harriot Stanton Blatch, a representative of the London office. Commemorating the fortieth anniversary of the American Seneca Falls Convention in 1848, the international group formalized their allegiance in Washington, D.C., in 1888. Members of the ICW asserted that women of all classes or positions in society should have as equal an opportunity as men to create lasting career opportunities. When a constitution was created in 1898, the council stated the intent of the organization was to form a collective of women to find ways to serve as stewards of both the family and their individual nations. Deciding to table the position on suffrage to appease more conservative members, the organization focused more generally on women's position within society and in labor. Critics to an official position on suffrage argued that only after women made their worth known through dedicated service to their nations would suffrage be granted.

Though deferring the issue of suffrage was disappointing to many members, it did not deter leaders such as Stanton and her daughter Harriot from actively participating. Harriot assisted her mother in various social reform movements and carried on her legacy through her own lectures, writing, and activism. After her American childhood she earned an M.A. at Vassar that concluded with a study on the working conditions of English women. Harriot then readied herself for a life of international activism. Through her travels she met her husband, English businessman William Harry Blatch Jr., and continued to travel and lecture in both countries for years to come. She lived in London with her husband for nearly twenty years prior to the First World War where she was active in the Women's Local Government Society, the Fabian Society, and the Women's Franchise League (see fig. 1.2). As a social reformer in England, she worked as a supporter of the Labour Party and of women's rights. This international experience explains much of her passion about bringing information back to American women of the successes of British and French wartime agricultural work. Blatch returned to America in 1902 but retained her international connections and work in both countries.

As an activist for suffrage, Blatch brought with her the methods of British suffragettes and the more militant strategies associated with them. In the years leading to war, Blatch continued her work toward suffrage by encouraging

FIGURE 1.2. *Harriot Stanton Blatch, half-length portrait, seated, facing slightly right, writing.* George Grantham Bain Collection, Library of Congress. Photo by Montauk, from the Gilliams Press Syndicate, LOT 11052-5.

American women to demand their place in labor. Recruiting working-class women into the movement for suffrage, Blatch revived the stagnating suffrage movement in America by leading suffrage parades and public displays of protest like the famous suffrage parade in 1910 in New York City. As part of the National Women's Party, a militant American group poised for direct action, Blatch called on American women to picket the White House each day holding banners proclaiming "MR. PRESIDENT, WHAT WILL YOU DO FOR SUFFRAGE?" and "MR. PRESIDENT, HOW LONG MUST WOMEN WAIT FOR LIBERTY?" Blatch called for these "silent sentinels" to stand guard every day so that the president and the public had no choice but to remember their domestic fight for liberty. Focused on presenting these silent sentinels as a domestic army for justice, the group inadvertently struck fear into the hearts of many Americans resistant to change. This feared image of a female "army" remained in the collective mind of Americans as discussions ensued about a female land army to replace male agricultural workers.

When the United States joined the war, Blatch, just as many other reformers, turned her attention toward assisting the nation in its time of need. Because Blatch held a reputation for international leadership among women and excellent oratory skills, she was appointed as head of the Food Administration Speakers Bureau. Blatch contributed her lectures and worked with the Food Administration to report on international efforts at food production and to assist developing agricultural plans for wartime. Additionally, she worked with reformers in training women to serve as agricultural workers; as a result she was named director of the Women's Land Army of America (WLAA) in

1917.[7] Though her family lineage certainly benefited Blatch when it came to her place in reform movements, much of the political platform she acquired in both England and the United States came from initial connections and opportunities found in the initial years of the ICW. Those connections and experiences inspired Blatch to bring the political and social strategies for success to her work toward suffrage and agricultural labor in the United States.

When the ICW convened in London in 1899, delegates from across the world attended to discuss matters related to the advancement of women through such topics as education, legislation, and politics as well as establishing women in professions. A session addressing female professions established an agriculture and horticulture subsection in which delegates discussed the role of women in such areas as dairy farming, ostrich farming, beekeeping, and the harvesting of silk.[8] One paper, "Farming in Its Various Branches as an Occupation for Women," and another on the role of female agricultural education and training addressed the roles women could play in agriculture and foreshadowed future British concepts of female agricultural training and commented on the suitability of women in certain areas of agricultural employment.[9] Some speakers commented on the successes already achieved by women in agriculture at Swanley College and encouraged the growth of new programs and the opening up of existing programs to women. The Horticulture College at Swanley, which opened its doors in 1892, was part of a movement to bring horticultural education programs to women seeking a profession in botanical or agricultural service. Social reformers promoted this school and others as part of a larger plan to give English women avenues to occupations, other than domestic service, that included work in both flower and food production. Though the educational systems aimed at the English working classes, many of the wealthy classes promoted the programs and focused perhaps as much on their own opportunities for change through leadership of the programs as they did on the workers they intended to train.

Britain's Prince of Wales, in some circles known as "Edward the Caresser," and his mistresses took on social reform and farm education for women as their courtly hobbies at the turn of the century. Edward's mistress and long-time friend Frances Evelyn Maynard Grenville, the Countess of Warwick otherwise known to the English public as "Daisy," became one of the forerunners for the organization of women in agriculture that made the WLA possible because of her involvement in the promotion of female agricultural education and training. As one of the foremost "beauties" in the period of English society coined the "Society Beauty Age," Lady Warwick held a unique position to use her influence on polite society as a springboard for women's labor and educational reform.[10] An active supporter of the Labour Party, Warwick organized a program called the Agricultural Scheme for Women and a news journal titled *Women's Agricultural Times*.[11] Warwick was quite the socialite and attempted to stay central in the public eye above other ladies the prince fancied by throwing herself into the cause of female educational reform and working as an advocate for women of minor social standing.[12] Some accounts claim, however, that it was her background and interest in the British Labour Party and socialism that cost the countess her public relationship with Prince Edward, who moved on to a mistress of more conservative political sensibilities, Mrs. Alice Keppel.[13]

This does not mean that the relationship between the prince and the countess ceased; letters between the two reveal that even though she tried to distance herself from him in a way that would not damage her position in society, he suggested they involve themselves in some philanthropic project in which they could both find interest. Soon after that Lady Warwick committed herself to the full-scale development of women's agricultural education programs.[14] She made use of her social connections as well as her reputation as both a reformer and public beauty to bring her messages to the people of England. In a speech to members of the "Pleasant Sunday Afternoon Brotherhood" in May 1900, Warwick gave a lecture that the *Daily News of London* referred to as a "sermon" on "Man's Opportunity." She asked the male audience, "Was there ever a man . . . who wished he was a woman?" and then added that she was one of many women who "would give everything in the world to be a man," for men held the right to choose their own career opportunities and held the power to influence political change whereas women did not have such opportunity due to the inferior social standing they obtained at birth.[15] She argued for "complete 'Emancipation of Womanhood'" and for a political awakening of those with the power to vote. She argued that men take such power for granted and that if they used it wisely, "they would use their votes to return only those men to Parliament and governing bodies who had the welfare of the workers at heart. Talent and welfare often struggled at enormous odds because there was no money to develop them. Yet these two attributes should be the only test. We fear we are still a long way from the ideal, but such a message from the castle to the cottage is one well worth remembering and applying."[16] According to her argument, "the castle," or rather the ruling classes, should promote such talent and character to the cottages of the nation by means of agricultural training for women. In the months and years to come, Lady Warwick helped influence and develop agricultural training programs for women to help combat the issue of limited opportunities for female labor by means of education and awareness.

Warwick immersed herself in the cause of female agricultural education, coordinating with such agricultural colleges as the Oxford University Extension College at Reading and Swanley College to organize programs that would admit female students for educational purposes in a program designed specifically for them. As a result of increased public awareness of the need for women's agricultural training, ideological changes in college administrations allowed women as students of agriculture. Other programs at Seale Hayne College and elsewhere followed, admitting women into their programs, often for the first time. Warwick also proposed an Agricultural Training College built specifically for and tailored to women.[17] Agricultural training program developers and their advocates hoped that graduates of such a program could help build farming communities by learning the business of selling fresh flowers, fruit, milk, eggs, poultry, and so forth and, at a minimum, completing training in the practical aspects of the "lighter branches of agriculture" such as picking flowers and fruit as well as packing produce for market.[18]

Three months after the congress of the ICW met in London, the Lady Warwick Agricultural Association for Women developed on a national scale, though Lady Warwick hoped to bring the organization into an international level. Lady Warwick designed this association specifically for those who had already obtained some level of education about managerial agricultural positions that were not too physically challenging. Philosophically, the organization was designed to recruit and place women into farm worker positions, but many who joined this organization had a more educated and genteel background and desired to teach and train the working classes to do basic farm work such as milking cows, feeding poultry, collecting eggs, and tending to basic flowers and herbs. One member, physician Elizabeth Garrett Anderson, argued that the Lady Warwick Agricultural Association should promote the placing of "duly qualified" women with advantages of "full fellowship in scientific and other learned societies."[19]

Women had long fought the battle with academe over control and nomenclature when it came to horticulture, and here it was no different. For centuries, male-dominated academe removed the nomenclature of plants and herbs from women's sphere of knowledge, power, and management and in the process made women's interest in plants and herbs and use of the old terminologies seem superstitious and vulgar. The year 1899 was the precise moment when women attempted to reclaim that space, not by doing something different than men but by entering the academe that had shut them out for so long; agricultural labor was the guise for the larger goal of the reclamation of space. This is apparent from the kind of people that made up the Lady Warwick Agricultural Association: a female medical doctor, a male professor and secretary of the London University Extension Society, and several other philanthropic women and men all of a professional class. The association was established to *join* academe in some way, not merely to find a place for women to *settle* because they could not have a first-class education. There was no talk of the significance of labor in general; the talk was of building hostels for women *studying* horticulture and farming industries.

Undoubtedly these initial attempts at agricultural education significantly furthered women's roles in British agriculture as paid laborers, but a publicized debate in newspapers ensued over exactly what *kind* of women the programs should recruit. Lady Warwick designed her programs to target the educated, genteel class of women and publicly noted that programs should target such women. The scheme thus developed, with the daughters of professional men who would come into smaller inheritances in mind, so that the women might maintain their properties while obtaining additional income.[20] Still other reformers argued that working- and lower-class women needed training in skills that were both practical and morally superior to work as barmaids or prostitutes. From this perspective, one can infer the intent of educational reform for the working classes was to use residential agricultural training programs to spread political and social ideas about what standards of middle- and lower-class morality and households should conform to. Amid this push for conformity, however, many working-class women participated in female agricultural programs as a refuge from the stifles of European chaperonage reminiscent of the Victorian era.

Regardless of ideological differences between Lady Warwick and the ICW, their educational programs for women derived from related theoretical and moral frameworks. Many proponents of such programs noted that potential agricultural jobs outnumbered available graduates of such training. Graduates still faced social resistance to the idea of women in agriculture because farmers remained prejudiced against even educated women. So few women graduated from these programs in the prewar years that placement of all graduates into agricultural positions resulted in no real visible change in the percentage of women in agriculture.[21] Many graduates were upper-class women who wanted education and training as a means to teach others and who avoided labor such as dairy work or other specialized labor-intensive jobs. In fact, many organizations such as the Women's Agricultural and Horticultural International Union (WAHIU), a movement created in 1900 by inspired attendees of the ICW meeting in London, urged their members to stop thinking of teaching as the only participation for the "cultured" woman. The WAHIU claimed in an explanatory leaflet, "All want to become lecturers, and if this mania continues the lecturers will have to hold forth to each other."[22] Thus educated women were more likely to promote themselves in leadership roles than to claim women's space in the general labor force. Mrs. Chamberlain, a member of the WAHIU, delivered a paper at a conference sponsored by the WI in London in November 1900. She claimed: "Social movements spread from the top downwards. If, presently, girls and women of the less educated classes find that a country life, and work on farm or garden is not without charm for the more educated classes, they will not be so anxious to get away to towns and shops. . . . When it is seen that *ladies* are healthy, happy and contented working on the land, the rustic damsel will begin to think it may be worthwhile to acquire knowledge of the primitive industries they have so neglected."[23]

The WAHIU focused more on its international profile than on women's agricultural education and labor, however. The WAHIU was perhaps overly concerned with maintaining its internationalism at times, but that internationalism brought great opportunity for the sharing of ideas about women and agriculture. The WAHIU gained international support and recognition from such members as Adelaide Hoodless, the Canadian founder of the Women's Institute movement in 1897, as a way to form a collective of wives of members of Canada's Farmers' Alliance.[24] This association proved pivotal in establishing a WI in England. The WI of England served as an umbrella organization or hub of information for women's organizations and provided just the structure England needed to recruit women farm laborers in 1917.

Recognizing the need for a united collaboration of women in wartime, the regional chapters of the WIs formed a National Federation of Women's Institutes (NFWI), and Lady Gertrude Denman took the lead as the first president. Though Denman, known as "Trudie" in English society circles, came to the WI a lady of leisure, she worked harder than perhaps any British reformer to provide support for programs of agricultural assistance while advancing the position of women in British society. She emerged as a leader of social reform as a young woman of twenty-four when she was elected to the Executive Committee of the Women's Liberal Federation (WLF), a position similar to that her mother held years earlier. She worked diligently with the group to raise the question of women's suffrage and promote Liberal candidates who vowed their support of it. Married to Lord Thomas Denman, a Liberal peer, Lady Denman forged her own sphere in British politics by combining her position in English society with the organizational goals of the WLF.

Just as Denman settled into her leadership role in the WLF, waves in British politics sent her husband to Australia where he served as governor-general from 1911 to 1914. Though she kept her position as president of the NFWI, she also found time to focus on women's local issues in Australia like bush nursing and work with the Australian National Councils of Women, a regional group of the ICW. Though Lady Denman continued to travel back to England to escape the demands as wife of the governor-general, upon Lord Denman's resignation in 1914, she returned permanently to England to continue her work with the NFWI and the ICW, this time taking up the work of organizing women to assist England as it prepared for war. Working within these organizations, she helped to organize and recruit for the first Women's Land Army (WLA) and served as director of the WLA during the Second World War.

Several sources suggest that Denman's work in these organizations helped fill time to compensate for a strained marriage. In that light, reform work was more than help for society, it was personal liberation and solace as well. For many women, leadership of these organizations provided opportunity to focus their attention on things outside of the home and the realm of what many deemed appropriate for wealthy women of society. For Harriot Stanton Blatch, leadership of the WLA and work with the Food Administration provided her focus after the death of her husband. For Lady Warwick, work in women's agricultural training also provided both liberation and solace from a life of failed relationships and social demands, while for Lady Denman, reform work and the organization of agricultural labor provided refuge from the demanding social and political world associated with her husband. Though the leadership involved in the reform work may suggest increased stress on the leaders of such organizations, the writings of these three women suggest that this work energized them and in some ways provided for each of them what American suffragist Elizabeth Cady Stanton termed "the solitude of self."

Regardless of the complexity of issues presented by their members, the ICW, the WAHIU, and the NFWI understood the need for agricultural labor and thus needed motivated educational program directors to continually seek additional funding and to focus on growth and the potential for social reform through the *agrarian myth*: the idea that labor on the land was not only good for one's character, but also made people loyal to the land and better citizens. Part of a long tradition in Western society, it specifically shaped the Empire of Great Britain's theories on colonization and imperialism. In this way, women's organizations sought to reform society *and* forge new identities for themselves through labor on the land. Those organizations that focused more on agriculture as a solution to a growing labor problem modified Warwick's agricultural scheme. One of the more publicly visible members of the WAHIU, Cambridge-trained Louisa Wilkins, argued after the outbreak of the First World War that the WAHIU had a responsibility to aid the war effort by recruiting and supplying farm labor to England. Wilkins's background included lecturing as an agricultural authority and as the only woman chosen to serve as governor of the Agricultural Organisation Society (AOS), a forerunner of the National Farmers Union and composed primarily of male agriculturalists. Wilkins's expertise and drive to improve opportunities for women in agriculture brought both credibility and visibility to the groups of trained women eager to cultivate victory. Though some members of the organization disliked the idea of removing the international focus of the organization, once war broke out in Europe, English members took steps to reshape the organization from national perspectives. Americans rallied around the formation of a national Women's National Horticulture and Garden Association (later renamed Women's National Farm and Garden Association) in 1914. The British national movement formed in May 1915 and officially changed the name of the organization to the Women's Farm and Garden Union (WFGU). Both of these groups, composed of many of the prominent members of the ICW, served as the regional foundation for promoting increased agriculture production across two continents as the First World War threatened food supplies.

Over the Top

As the war called women over the top, women left the nineteenth-century social and political traditions that held them in a sphere of confinement and looked for opportunity to forge new personal and political identities. National and international organizations led women to national service and recognition through labor and political action. Once ladies of leisure, many women including the Countess of Warwick, Blatch, and Lady Gertrude Denman showed women of all classes what it meant to be "women of action." They led the way out of the sphere of confinement by encouraging and inspiring young women to serve their countries in their time of need and to display their thoughts and desires for equality in the professions through actions instead of mere words. For themselves, this service offered refuge and solace from a gendered world of leisure and an opportunity to contribute to the betterment of society. In the decades to come, these women not only shaped the structures of wartime rural agricultural labor, but also influenced the perceptions of wartime contributions in urban agricultural settings.

The women of England and the United States, through social and political ties, joined together in a movement of transformation in agricultural labor at the turn of the twentieth century. This movement, though intended to improve women's place and space in labor, unintentionally formed the basis for a new wave of nationalism based upon agriculture. Though this movement came out of a broader movement for social and political change, what manifested from it was a path for many women to shape their own personal and national identities. In the decades to come, Great Britain and the United States focused less on the acknowledgment of women's contributions to solving national need and instead turned more to the rhetoric of nationalism and devised strategies to use agricultural labor as a way to cultivate their own national identities. For the women who cultivated the land, however, the motivation to serve was both personal and political.

CHAPTER 2

The Land Girls

*I had been out shopping and I came in and mother was clustered . . . in the
dining room with two of her chums, and I heard her say, . . . "There's a war,
yes, it won't last very long," but she said "Mary will do everything for us, she's
just left school, it's alright. She'll do the shopping and the cooking." So I thought
"Blow me you will not! Mary's not going to do the cooking and the shopping!"
So I went straight to the post office, I took out my savings, I wrote in, I had a
very wonderful godfather . . . and I went straight out to see him and I said "Look
here, you're going to do something for me!" He knew the director at Seale Hayne
College. I said "I want to get out; I want to go in the first lot of people who are
going out on the land."*

—Mary Lees, British land girl, oral interview, 30 November 1974,
Imperial War Museum, catalogue number 506

MARY LEES NEEDED TO get out of the house. Just shy of her eighteenth
birthday, she was one of 23,000 English land girls and the 15,000
American farmerettes who left the familiarity of their homes to aid their countries and seek adventure. For many urban women, getting out of the house
and "going out on the land" provided unprecedented opportunities.[1] By migrating from the urban to more rural areas of England and the United States
to take the place of male agriculturalists during the First World War, women
left their homes seeking adventure, employment, and a chance to gain public
respect for their acts of patriotism. Once the agricultural threats of war increased for Great Britain and the United States, urban women responded to
the need through the formation of labor organizations known as the Wom-
en's Land Armies (WLAs). Understanding how and why the WLAs of both
Britain and the United States developed, as well examining the challenges
and successes of its members, provides nuanced perspectives on the changing

33

identities and roles of women in labor and agriculture in the first decades of
the twentieth century.

Britain was not the first victim of food shortages during the First World
War. Britons waged a war of hunger against the Germans in 1914 by block-
ing German ports from receiving supplies, depleting Germany's economy,
and spreading famine and starvation across Germany.² Germany retaliated
initially with a cruiser blockade and then with U-boat threats to American
ships bringing supplies to their political ally. Since the structure of the British
economy in 1914 necessitated the importation of nearly 50 percent of all its
foodstuffs, German prevention of such imports threatened to starve the British into defeat. Germany endangered crucial supply lines between the United
States and England in 1915 with the sinking of the U.S. passenger ship *Lusita-
nia*; and though diplomatic relations between Germany and the United States
produced a German agreement not to attack additional passenger ships, Germany broke that agreement with a policy of unrestricted submarine warfare
in 1917. Not until the German U-boat threat to British imports increased in
severity in 1917 did English efforts begin to organize a national movement
to assist in the production of food. In 1917 at the height of the threat, England estimated it only had about three weeks' supply of food in reserve. In
response, Lord Selbourne, the British minister of agriculture, appointed Miss
Meriel Talbot as director of the women's division of the Food Production Department. Though discussion and proposals occurred prior to this, it was not
until 1917 that real progress toward an official organization of female agricultural workers began.

Once the war began, England and later the United States established propaganda and economic controls over civilian supplies to battle the war on the
homefront and keep the economy and agricultural needs of the civilian populations stable. While the young and able British and American men fought
on the battlefronts, women, children, and older, less able men fought on the
homefronts to ensure the survival of their nation's population and soldiers'
success. Despite the variety of homefront soldiers, propaganda and economic
controls directed toward the people of England and the United States, both
nations had two things in common: women and abundance (or lack thereof).
Both Britain and the United States encouraged their civilian populations to
produce more and consume less in the name of victory; however, the propaganda and support programs directly appealed to and featured women. As
the primary consumers of their nations, women naturally were the subjects of
economic control programs, but during the war nations encouraged them to
rethink old patterns of consumption and instead focus on production, a tactic
so successful that agencies used it again in the Second World War.³

The British WLA

Faced with dire need, women volunteered in large numbers to prevent food shortages during the First World War. From the start of the war women advocated an organization of agricultural laborers to fill the positions men left behind. During reorganization the Women's Agricultural and Horticultural International Union (WAHIU) changed its name to Women's Farm and Garden Union (WFGU); however, it remained a leader in the recruitment and training of women in agriculture at the dawn of war. In July 1914, leaders of the WFGU met with Roland Prothero, a Conservative member of Parliament and author of several texts on the history of English agriculture, to discuss the position of agricultural labor and how women could help in the coming months. The WFGU saw themselves as the experts on agricultural training and as such they felt they were best poised to take on the issue of labor shortages. Prothero told the group that England had previously relied on borrowing money for food supplies and that they must be cautious not to acquire too much debt as a result of the war. He urged that every effort be made to assure successful increased agricultural production on their own soil, and though labor shortages were not evident at that time, he did foresee a need for help in the future and felt that this was women's opportunity to assist. Last, he warned the women to be cautious not to "antagonise the male worker" by accepting lower wages just to get employment and not to leave farmers discouraged by sending out poorly trained workers. Members of the WFGU expressed that they had worked for sixteen years to educate women in the areas of agriculture and horticulture and that their efforts at training had already placed 109 women on the land in 1914, and that of those 109, only 6 "had proved failures."[4]

Though some women's international organizations may have worked individually or even at odds before the war began due to stances on suffrage and internationalism, once the war began, they put aside their differences and worked together in common goals of patriotism and service. The WFGU joined together with other women's political and social organizations to further discuss the "land question" and invited international members and experts to local garden parties and teas to discuss the possibilities for women as workers on the land. Together with local agricultural colleges and schemes such as the Lady Warwick Agricultural Association, the WFGU established a precedent of trained, skilled workers ready to take the place of farm men who joined the military. Just as men served their country by going to the battlefield, these women were eager to place women on the farm fields, to serve as a female army on the land.

In the initial years of war, government support for women's efforts was

FIGURE 2.1. Cowman to new recruit of the Women's Land Army: "You get behind that there water-butt. Mebbe cows won't come in if they see you in that there rig." *Punch, or the London Charivari* 152 (30 May 1917): 359.

minimal at best. Although the British government agreed to compile a *Register of Women*, which listed those willing to volunteer for wartime work as part of the call for the civilian National Service, it hesitated to call women to work on farms. Viscount Milner, part of David Lloyd George's five-member War Cabinet and later appointed secretary of state for war in 1918, led a committee in 1915 to analyze the food production of England and Wales. The committee proposed that the government turn to an organization of women such as the WFGU to recruit additional farm labor and suggested that the government fund such an endeavor. The proposal went through a series of revisions until late in 1916, when Prime Minister Henry Herbert Asquith accepted a weakened version that mentioned only in passing the need to organize women's labor. Recognizing the need to organize agricultural labor, the new Prime Minister David Lloyd George named agricultural expert Rowland Prothero as president of the Board of Agriculture in 1916. Prothero took action on the previous proposals of women's labor and named Meriel Talbot director of the women's branch of the Food Department. She proceeded with the recruitment of a body of female agricultural workers in 1917 by working with the WFGU and existing women's agricultural colleges as well as other international, national, and regional women's groups to further develop the organization proposed as the WLA.

As the leader of the new WLA, Talbot worked to expand the collaboration of women's agricultural associations into a unified movement. Through Talbot's association with the Women's Institute (WI), she recruited political activist Lady Gertrude Denman, wife of Australia's governor-general Thomas Denman, as honorary assistant director of the developing WLA. Denman's commitment to national service as well as her political and social connections made her an excellent fit for the position, and her leadership of the WLA would span three decades. After the birth of the WLA as an official organization, Talbot and Denman set out on a national drive for recruitment training and to battle societal prejudices about women as farm laborers (see fig. 2.1).

Recruitment and Training

The British WLA recruited young urban women seen as idle by county extension agents and offered them a choice of service in either agriculture, timber cutting, or animal feeding. Advertisements stressed the need for women agriculturalists, but cartoons, poems, songs, and newspaper editorials ridiculed women who dared take on agricultural labor.[5] The fact that young girls wanted to have a uniform (as male Army members did) inspired satire of women entirely focused on their appearance, to the detriment of their work (see fig. 2.2). Posters and pamphlets offered young women information about the WLA and encouraging messages to promote recruitment. Some of the posters displayed uniformed women happily working in the fields and encouraged young women to enlist in the WLA at their "local post office or employment exchange." One of the first posters designed to promote the WLA, originally labeled the National Women's Land Service, boasted "God Speed the Plough and the Woman Who Drives It" (see fig. 2.3). Short films depicting Britannia, the female personification of the nation, literally stepping out of the recruitment posters and onto the fields of England provided inspiration to women to get behind the plough. Other recruitment films depicted "ladies of leisure," riding horses under the watchful eye of well-dressed men, transforming into "women of action" by taking part in patriotic cultivation and farm work that was again encouraged by the image of Britannia walking the fields to inspect the work of the women. In later years, many of the women of the Land Army recalled feeling humored and even misled by the images of clean, attractive women having a good time basking in the sun in the fresh outdoors. They recalled instead days of muck, grime, and back-breaking labor that felt nothing like the sun-soaked adventure the posters promised.

FIGURE 2.2. *Lady Denman*, 1917.
Recruitment for the Women's
Land Army. Photographer
unknown. From Gervas Huxley,
Lady Denman, G. B. E.

Canadians, Australians, and New Zealanders looked toward their British
mother country for suggestions on how best to cope with the impending agricultural crisis resulting from the war. Though they faced shortages of their
own, perhaps their greatest political concern was how to aid England in her
fight against Germany. Maintaining adequate supplies of foodstuffs for the
mother country's people was not an easy task, but one many land girls in the
Empire took on as a patriotic duty. Following suit with England, Canadians
and Australians organized WLAs and kept close ties with their international
wartime sisters. Lady Gertrude Denman used her social and political position
as wife of Thomas Denman, past governor-general of Australia, to lead wom-
en's organizations and equal rights movements of both England and Australia in addition to her service with the WLA. She served as chairman of the
NFWI, an umbrella organization for women's activities—a position she held
until 1946. Connected by their own WIs and inspired by Lady Denman's
leadership and attention to enhancing women's role in agricultural production, many Canadian and Australian women served in their own WLAs. Some
women felt a need to contribute nearer the fighting and source of the struggle
and therefore left their homelands to serve in England's WLA.

Though the organizers of the movement were urban upper-class women
often from wealthy families and homes that encouraged a life of leisure, the

FIGURE 2.3. H. G. Gawthorn, *God Speed the Plough and the Woman Who Drives It*, D. A. and S. Ltd., London, 1917. Imperial War Museum, London, ART PST 21251.

women who fought in the fields of Great Britain, known as the land girls, were of a mixed variety. Ranging in age from eighteen to sixty, most volunteers were young, single females from middle-class families. The women earned eighteen shillings per week or the agreed upon local district rate, whichever was higher, plus housing during training and employment, and a hope for future employment on "carefully selected farms" with the possibility of promotion and advancement in pay for top performers. In 1917 the WLA advertised that it needed 5,000 milkers, 4,000 field workers, and 1,000 carters to meet the agricultural needs of the nation. While about 5,500 applied for service before April 1917 and 45,000 volunteers applied for service by the end of the war in November 1918, only about 23,000 worked because of the reluctance of farmers.[6]

Women chose to serve in the Land Army because it offered the opportunity not only to express patriotism and national duty (or to get them out of their parents' homes), but also to wear a uniform. The land girls wore a utilitarian uniform of khaki breeches, green v-neck sweater, overcoat, and hat. Overalls, gloves, and Wellingtons were optional depending upon the kind of work required and often were rare due to rationing. The WLA initially offered the uniform for free to women who volunteered for the work as an incentive to join the service.[7] The WLA uniform symbolized patriotism, public acceptance of the organization, as well as political and social equality with men who wore uniforms in the armed services. Though the farmers and general public might have found the women in uniform threatening in that they wore khaki breeches and came ready to take the place of male workers, for the women the uniform was a symbol of their hard labor and unity. Though lasting memories of the significance and sentimentality of land girls and their uniforms came in later years during the Second World War, when the British government demanded women return their uniforms upon disbandment, land girls of the First World War had considerably less animosity toward the government when it came to their uniforms. The WLA initially offered free uniforms but eventually required that new members personally bear all expenses including uniforms related to service in the Land Army. However, members received free transportation to and from the farms assigned.

Superintendents of the WLA encouraged women to wear the uniform and insignia of the organization at all times, even out in the field. Wearing the insignia signified the collective identity the organization wanted to promote: strong, educated British women doing their patriotic duty. For the women who wore the uniform, however, the insignia was not as important as the adventure and the liberation the life associated with it brought. In the photographs that remain from period, it is not uncommon to see women without official uniforms laboring in the fields along with women who did wear the uniform. Regardless of adherence to the uniform rules, in a time of clothing shortages many women who joined the WLA rejoiced in the opportunity to buy something new to wear. Though Britain discouraged the public from purchasing things like stockings and underwear, the government did allow its servicemen and servicewomen to obtain such items when needed. Many women did wear the uniform in the style and manner requested, but some opted to alter the standard uniform by removing items or rolling the breeches and shirtsleeves to the desired, albeit sometimes socially scandalous, level to cool themselves on hot days.[8]

Many colleges that provided training for WLA recruits developed dormitories for the women to reside in while enrolled at the schools. Just as in many other colleges of the day, these dormitories provided live-in chaperones—older educated women who attempted to set standards in behavior. This spirit of in loco parentis, quite common during the era, eased the minds of parents and others concerned about the respectability of such programs their daughters planned to attend so far away from home.[9] Once British WLA members completed training, they moved to hostels where large groups of women volunteers lived or to the farmhouses of individual families. The living conditions were not always what the WLA promised new recruits. One woman, eighty years old when she served as a land girl, had this to say about her first experiences in the Land Army in Yorkshire: "I found my little group of girls, some twenty in number, lodged in an old disused manor house which was in a very bad state—cracked floors, peeling walls, broken windows; the doors without handles. The kitchen was a huge bare room with an open fireplace, a Yorkshire oven, a cracked boiler, and useless firebars held in place by bits of wire. Imagine cooking meals for twenty hungry girls on such a stove!"[10]

For many, the WLA offered a chance to escape the restrictions of home and the chaperonage they had known their entire life. For them the war brought enormous opportunity and when the threat of food shortage brought the call for urban women to travel to the countryside, many English women saw it as a blessing of some sort. A threatened food shortage meant a social acceptance of women leaving their homes to respond to the national call. For many urbanites, a life on the land seemed a fitting response to the claustrophobic urban societal frameworks of acceptable behavior for young women. For these women, working on the land *was* the patriotic duty the nation made it out to be, but in the end it was much more than an act of patriotism. Women used the literal change in landscapes to paint new metaphorical landscapes of their life paths and futures; this is evident in the dozens of postwar oral interviews—women used their experiences as land girls as the springboard for the histories of adventures in their lives that came afterward. The recurring theme among the interviews is that labor on the land brought a sense of independence, personal responsibility, and self-assurance. English women from the middle and upper classes who participated in the WLA did not find wealth in the work, but rather a confidence in their abilities to do "men's work." Their brothers, fathers, and husbands were not the only ones with tales of triumph, tragedy, and adventure after the end of the war.

Societal Prejudice and Understanding

For Britain, recognizing the threat of a food crisis brought about by the war was one thing, but social acceptance of women as farm workers was quite another. Tied to this recognition and acceptance is a history of women and agriculture that tells a peculiar and entangled story of women's political, social, and class struggles.[11] Prior to the war, English women of higher social status tended to ornamental gardens composed of flowers and shrubbery. Many men doubted such women had the physical and emotional fortitude of men in agricultural management and farm work, and moreover deemed those who sought such a role socially inappropriate and unacceptable. British society regarded women of lower economic classes, however, as laborers first and foremost; so even though at least the social barrier was removed, these women still had to overcome the prejudice that they were physically and emotionally unfit for the "serious" business of agriculture.

Historians examine the significance of the relationship of British women to agriculture, observing how social reform in twentieth-century Britain brought immense changes in the social acceptance of women as legitimate farm workers. It took a considerable amount of cultural change for British society to alter their perspective of women in agriculture from that of a poor peasant worker to one of respectable, educated, and career-minded worker. Former WLA member Mary Lees recalled the social reluctance to send young women onto farms to help ease the agricultural crisis. Farmers hesitated and often bluntly refused to pay women to take the place of their lost male laborers. Newspaper articles of the day urged "obstinate farmers" to do as many other "intelligent and patriotic" farmers had and employ the thousands of trained and eager women waiting to serve on their farms.[12] As the nation's need increased and as word spread of the successes of women agricultural laborers, farmers began to employ more women, though many still held on to gender biases and prejudice. Nonetheless, news of the success of the WLA in alleviating the national food crisis spread among the national presses and among international women's groups, inspiring other nations to devise Land Armies of their own.

The WLA of America

Following the British call, many American women volunteered to serve in place of men leaving American farms for war in 1917. Though many considered Americans somewhat isolationist before their entrance into the First World War and though there was no threatened national food shortage for Americans to concern themselves with, many American groups from the philanthropic to the political urged their fellow countrymen to contribute as much as possible to the agricultural need of their political allies during the first years of war. When the United States joined the war in April 1917, however, the number of citizens realizing the importance of agricultural aid and labor increased exponentially. In August 1917 the Food and Fuel Control Act passed Congress and President Wilson created the Food Administration, naming Herbert Hoover as head of the division.[13] On September 29, 1917, Hoover called on American citizens to aid the war effort by producing more food with the slogan "Food Will Win the War."[14] The newly created Division of Pictorial Publicity of the Committee on Public Information, headed by George Creel, commissioned American artists to express the ideas and slogans of the nation through their art. Posters encouraging immigrants and women to conserve because "Food Will Win the War" served as vital elements in selling the American public on the importance of the food campaign.[15]

The Food Administration set out to find ways to both conserve what food American families had and to produce more. A series of speakers brought to discuss such topics started in 1917, and Hoover appointed international reform leader Harriot Stanton Blatch as head of the Food Administration Speaker's Bureau (see fig. 2.4). Though Stanton brought with her progressive ideas from international organizations she served in like the WAHIU and the ICW about training and placing women into agriculture labor, Hoover's Food Administration initially rejected these ideas and did not call for a federal registry of female agriculturalists as British allies did. Stanton realized that a WLA of America would have to organize through the work of nonprofit organizations and colleges and eventually through assistance from the U.S. Employment Service.[16]

In many of the same ways that British women organized agricultural programs for supporting the war effort, American women led homefront drives to recruit volunteers and encouraged all Americans to promote training programs to "Get Behind the Girl He Left Behind Him" (see fig. 2.5). In 1917 Barnard College geology professors Ida H. Ogilvie and Delia W. Marble turned their jointly owned 680-acre farm in New York into an agricultural training experiment for a dozen female students. Finding success in the training exper-

FIGURE 2.4. *Mrs. H. S. Blatch* (far right). George Grantham Bain Collection. Library of
Congress Prints and Photographs Division, LC-B2-2772-4.

iment, Ogilvie traveled across the nation over the following year to promote
the establishment of a WLA like Britain's that would provide both opportunity for female wartime work and patriotic service. Over the next year,
Ogilvie traveled the nation promoting the idea of a Women's Land Army of
America (WLAA). Working together with the American branch of the WFGU,
the Women's National Farm and Garden Association (WNFGA), the movement was so successful that women's groups and college campuses quickly
started creating agricultural training programs for women and recruited students to serve as replacement farm labor for the nation.[17]

Though less publicized and lauded than the domestic urban garden programs of the nation promoted by the Food Administration, the WLAA organized in June 1917 to aid the rural populations in need of agricultural laborers.
Due to the nature of its organization, the WLAA developed on more of a regional basis initially. Women inspired by the international women's organizations and the WLA of Britain sought to establish regional, self-sustaining
branches of the WLAA in eighteen states by April 1918 and twenty-seven
states by June of that year.[18] Members of the WNFGA, such as Mrs. Robert
Hill, joined the advisory council at the WLAA headquarters in New York
City.[19] In April 1918, President Woodrow Wilson expressed his encouragement and support of the development of a land army to a member of the

FIGURE 2.5. Guenther, *Get Behind the Girl He Left Behind Him Join the Land Army*, American Lithographic Co., New York, 1918. Library of Congress, POS-WWI-US, no. 156.

national board of directors of the WLAA, Mrs. Henry Wade Rogers: "I am gratified to hear of the plan of the Women's Land Army to help increase the food supply of our country and the Allies through enrolling active and patriotic young women in self-sustaining groups or units to aid in cultivating crops where the farmers have need of them. I trust that our farmers, like the farmers of Great Britain and Canada will avail themselves of this aid to the fullest extent practicable, and that the response of our loyal young women to this need, wherever it exists, will be generous and complete."[20] Though Wilson supported the idea of a land army, he did not support federal funding or supervision. Leaders of the WLAA disagreed on what role the government should play in leading the organization, and as a result no agreement ever formed between the government and the WLAA for federal organization. Since the American government did not fund the WLAA, many regional state WLAs filed certificates of incorporation and communicated with the national organization to varying degrees. Thus the success and structure of each state group differed throughout the war. For example, more state organizations developed in New England than in the southern part of the nation to aid local harvests. The national WLAA often met increased resistance in the southern and western states due to long-standing cultural traditions that discouraged white women from agricultural labor and as such some states refused the development of state WLAs.[21]

The Americans, like the British, were slow in their response to agricultural labor crises; that reluctance lasted until the war was nearly over. It was perhaps this lack of urgency to employ female volunteers that caused such great distress for WLAA Director Harriot Stanton Blatch, as evident in her speeches and writings. Even after the initiation of the program, the appointment of women laborers remained slow whereas the appointment of educated, married, middle-class women as administrators was more common. Examination of the structure of leadership revealed that three single ladies worked as directors of training and recruiting and as field secretary, but for the most part, only married women gained positions of power or authority within the organization. Additionally, the American farmer did not see the importance of hiring single urban women as full-time farmhands and often met the programs with resistance and prejudice.[22]

Recruitment and Training

In a style reminiscent of the ongoing suffrage movement, Blatch urged women to display their work in street parades across the country to recruit women and to gain public support for the new WLAA (see figs. 2.6 and 2.7). The WN-FGA, the New York City mayor's Committee of Women on National Defense,

FIGURE 2.6. *Farmerettes*, 1918. Library of Congress Prints and Photographs Division, LC-B2-4731-5, LOT 10969.

FIGURE 2.7. *The Women's Land Army*, date not recorded. Library of Congress Prints and Photographs Division, LC-B2-4877-11.

the Farm and Garden Clubs of America, and various other national and regional women's clubs played active roles in promoting female support of wartime employment and in doing so shaped the identity of the WLAA and its
members through agricultural education. By recruiting women to come train
for basic farm labor in 1917 at the Bedford Training Center, the New York
Women's Suffrage Party attracted many energetic young girls. These organizations took on the responsibility of setting up training programs for female
agriculturalists, and training spread across twenty states by the summer of
1918 recruiting 15,000 workers.[23] The WLAA developed state offices around
the country, with regional training facilities in New Hampshire, Vermont,
Connecticut, Rhode Island, New York, New Jersey, Pennsylvania, Maryland,
Virginia, Michigan, Nebraska, California, and the District of Columbia (see
figs. 2.8 and 2.9).

Training at the schools and estates varied as did the commitment required.[24] Recruitment of women for training and service in the WLAA depended upon a variety of programs designed by select state headquarters,
the national headquarters, local associations, and garden clubs. Large-scale
educational programs developed at Wellesley College and at the University
of Virginia; other smaller significant training programs developed on estates
used as training farms and also at Trenton Normal School in New Jersey,
Blackburn College in Illinois, the University of Wisconsin, Massachusetts Agricultural College, Cornell University, Pennsylvania State College, the Pennsylvania School of Horticulture, and the Peabody College for Teachers among
others. Other colleges and universities such as Smith College developed their
own units of the WLAA and worked together with the YMCA in creating agricultural programs of wartime assistance.[25]

The camp at the University of Virginia trained women in "Plowing, Har-
rowing, General Land Tillage, and Preparation of Land by Horse-Drawn Im-
plements" in either two-week or four-week courses. The university designed
the training as a residential intensive educational experience, and the fee was
$10.00 for the two-week course and $20.00 for the four-week course, both
including tuition and board. The fees for this kind of training prohibited all
but the middle and upper classes from attending, as the national average of
earnings for a day of farm labor varied from $1.56 to $2.08 depending upon
the time of year, while national earning averages for urban workers varied
from $2.00 to $6.00 per day depending upon skills and position. Thus working-class women, who often earned less than half of the national average for
men, often found it all but impossible to afford such training and thus took
other wartime jobs in industry. Some training facilities were free of charge
and recouped expenses through nominal fees and sales of produce to sur-

FIGURE 2.8. *Help! The Woman's Land Army of America, New Jersey Division, State House, Trenton*, 1918. Life Publishing Co., Library of Congress, POS-US.G52, no. 17.

FIGURE 2.9. Herbert Paus, *The Woman's Land Army of America: Training School, University of Virginia*, 1918. Library of Congress, POS-US.P38, no. 2.

rounding communities. Regardless of fees, the training programs were open to all women age eighteen and up, provided they passed a rigorous physical examination.[26] In addition to university-style intensive residential courses, working women could obtain training on a part-time basis. In the District of Columbia, for example, a large cooperative training farm developed right outside of Washington, D.C., so that "women who work in offices [can] register for late afternoons and night workers for the earlier hours."[27] The program trained as many as fifty women at one time for potential placement in surrounding farms during the harvest periods.

The national board of directors of the WLAA comprised fourteen women and, after nearly a year of work, set specific standards for both members and farmers participating in the program through publication of a *Handbook of Standards*. Standards of pay and treatment were important to the WLAA so that the women would not be treated differently from men or taken advantage of because of their gender. Mrs. William H. Schofield, president of the national board of directors of the WLAA, helped write its first handbook in 1919 with the endorsement of the U.S. Employment Service of the Department of Labor. The national board of directors recommended that WLAA recruits work in Community Units, in Single Farm Units, or in Individual Units, as the situation required. Community Units comprised ten to fifty women who lived under one roof with a WLAA supervisor, though the WLAA recommended most units range from twenty to thirty-five women. The Single Farm Units lived together in the residence of the farm under the supervision of a WLLA supervisor. The Individual Units were single workers stationed at small farms needing limited labor. The national board of directors discouraged Individual Units, however, and urged that no woman should be placed in this situation unless her "welfare can be satisfactorily safeguarded" and another woman resided in the farmer's household.[28]

The WLLA required those residing in Community Units or Single Units to pay for their own lodgings, and most had it deducted from their meager salaries. The national board stated in the *Handbook of Standards* that this requirement "places the worker in a more intelligent and responsible relationship to the unit." The national board of directors suggested that in the rare situation requiring Individual Units, the Land Army supervisor should draw up a contract with the farmer that stated in writing the terms of the type of labor, minimum and maximum hours allowable, and wages paid directly to each state WLA worker. The contracts gave the WLAA the right to inspect worker conditions at any time; established general requirements as to food, sanitation, and so forth; and forced the farmer to relinquish any right to claim compensation for damages should the hired labor be unsatisfactory.

The board also required WLAA supervisors to make every effort to inspect conditions of both Individual and Single Units "without such inspection and investigation, no individual worker may be known as a Land Army worker or wear the insignia."[29]

The typical farm work of the WLAA members, nicknamed the farmerettes, included a standard eight-hour day. The national board of directors argued that the ten-hour day was not permissible unless the work was "varied and intermittent, and the spread of time should in no instance exceed 12 hours."[30] Training in most programs consisted of a full day's activities and left little idle time. A typical day in the life of a trainee for the WLAA included "6:45 a.m. rising bell, 7:15 breakfast, 8:30 to 11:30 field work, 12:00 luncheon, 1:00 to 4:30 classes, 4:30 to 6:00 free period, 6:00 p.m. dinner, 7:30 to 9:00 individual work or classes, 10:00 p.m. quiet house."[31] Once farmerettes completed training, supervisors placed them on farms where their skills were in most demand. Helen Kennedy Stevens remembered her time serving the WLAA, "We were all city girls, and sublimely ignorant of farming. We had to be taught several things, among them the difference between a nice little tomato plant and a weed. Since we could not learn all the plants and all the weeds, our rule was 'Anything growing in rows is plant, anything growing at large is weed.' There is a tragic tale of one girl who tenderly cultivated a row of plantain weeds and pulled up the lima beans that were interfering with them."[32]

Success for the farmerettes resulted not only in the satisfaction of a crop well tended, but in personal wages. In New York the laborers in training earned 25 cents per hour picking berries as part of their training and the locals credited them with saving the berry crop in the upper part of the state.[33] Though WLAA labor standards regulated wages and workload, not every farmerette was placed or paid equally. The *Handbook of Standards* stated that trained or experienced workers should earn the same wage as male agricultural laborers while others could earn less than male wages. There was no standard for male agricultural labor across the nation, so adherence to this request was difficult to monitor. Though the wages for the "experienced" brought some level of equality among wage-earning women, the national board urged that women be placed in jobs that were more "fitted" to their limitations of "muscular ability" and urged states to restrict women from such tasks as plowing, repetitive work, or work requiring bearing more than fifty pounds.[34]

Much like the British version, the uniform of the WLAA was of great significance to both the labor standards of the organization and to the female workers. The *Handbook of Standards* stated that women should not wear skirts or clothing that "constricts the muscles" and thus should adopt the uniform designed to "meet the needs of the woman worker."[35] Uniforms varied from state to state as did the availability of fabric, but the most common WLAA uniform consisted of a smock, "knickerbockers" of navy blue or khaki, a hat, "good heavy shoes," and cotton golf socks.[36] To the women of the WLAA, these uniforms were often the material, tangible representations of their experiences. Many felt great pride the day they purchased their uniforms, and they proudly wore them around their urban neighborhoods upon each return home. Some WLAA members saw the opportunity to wear a uniform as a reason to join. Helen Kennedy Stevens recalled the first night the recruits at the Women's Agricultural Camp in New York obtained their uniforms. All thirty of the women raced upstairs to try on their overalls and get a good view in the one mirror available. Others found the uniforms amusing at first, but later stifling—both physically and socially—and altered them to suit their personalities. To some American women, like their British sisters, uniforms also represented conformity and so they found ways to express their identity through alteration of the uniform, such as cutting the pants into "too" short shorts during the hot summers.[37]

Though the WLAA recommendations on labor standards reflected the ideas of equality for all, the standards set for living quarters, though intended to protect both the worker and the food supply, met resistance by farmers and concerned urban citizens.[38] In an effort to protect the women from exploitation, the WLAA recommended standards based on the social and physical welfare of the women workers and laid out rules of boarding, payment, and working conditions in the manual distributed to farmers and WLAA workers alike. The organization and its standards frightened some, however, as a potential vacuum for socialist influence. In response to the rising demand for standards, the *Handbook of Standards* attempted to establish ground rules for politically acceptable ways women could remain working in the agricultural industry. The manual's introduction tried to calm fears of radicalism: "As we pass through the present transition period from war time to peace, our land Army program changes with the changed conditions, and we foresee, in the permanent opening of the industry of agriculture to women, the possibility of unwise precedents be quite unintentionally established unless clear-cut standards are defined and their practice urged by us at the outset."[39]

The WLAA placed approximately 15,000 women in farms and various emergency units in 1918 and sought to continue the service and increase the numbers to 1,000,000 even after the war's end.[40] As other war services disbanded and prepared for return to a peacetime economy, such a strong and large organization of women aroused concern and fear if continued. As the postwar Red Scare raised fears of the influence of socialism on labor organizations, one reader of the newspaper the *Republic* warned of the future WLAA:

> If the system is to have any chance of growing, or even of surviving, it is of the utmost importance that it should not fall into the ways of semi-social, semi-philanthropic, semi-parasitic organizations, but should be placed under expert leadership competent to work out and enforce proper standards of food, hygiene, social relations, hours and pay. Such an enterprise is peculiarly in danger of being shifted off a sound economic basis, since it appeals to so many vague ideals: the ideal of taking part in food production, the ideal of healthful labor under the sky, the ideal of group association in work and living. These are of the soundest ideals; but they must not be allowed to make easy the task of the would-be exploiter.[41]

Despite the interest of Harriot Stanton Blatch and others for the WLAA to open up the field of agricultural labor to women, neither the private sector nor the government provided funding for the WLAA after the war's end. Disagreements arose between the leadership of the WLAA and the Department of Labor over the future position of the organization as labor leaders. This further complicated things, and as a result the WLAA of America disbanded in January 1920.[42]

Societal Prejudice and Understanding

Living conditions for the American female agricultural workers were a source of contention and concern. Farmerettes in Single Units often found expectations for domestic household help in addition to tasks they were trained to do. The WLAA Board of Directors did not want the volunteer female laborers to be used as domestic servants and made a standard forbidding work inside the home by any farmerette. In violation of the standards, many farmers and their wives asked workers to perform various domestic duties. Farm women, used to the prewar focus on help and education to rural households offered by various women's organizations including the WNFGA, expressed resistance to the standard that female WLAA laborers not perform service work inside the home. This standard set the urban farmerettes apart from rural women and caused a considerable amount of tension between the farmers, their wives, and the farmerettes. In some cases farmers and their wives viewed this standard as disrespectful to farm women, and thus WLAA laborers and administrators were viewed as radicals and often mocked for their lack of agricultural experience or less-than-ladylike actions in the fields. In contrast, farmerettes enrolled in Community Units found assistance from "special house workers" to clean and prepare meals, though they had to pay for this service out of their meager salaries in addition to room and board.

American and British women found relief from the hard days of farm work in local towns or in organized dances, plays, and discussions that frequently took place in hostels and dormitories many of the volunteers resided in. Many of the recruits filled their time during tedious chores or idle time with songs and poetry about their experiences.[43] These lyrics expressed both nationalism and individualism. Many were set to the popular patriotic tunes of the day; lyrics set to the tune of "Over There" displayed the commitment of the farmerettes of the WLAA and give a sense of life on the farm front:

> Brother's got his gun, gone to france, [sic] for the fray,
> Sister's gone away, first of May, for the stay,
> Planting crops to win the war.
> Kaiser's Bill's afraid, Hindenburgh [sic] is dismayed,
> Watch that Yankee maid learn a trade, use a spade,
> Soon a farmer she will be
> Planting crops for liberty.
>
> Plow away, plow away, Giddap horse, turn the ground under there,
> Bog crops we're sowing, the plants are growing,
> The girls are farming everywhere.
> Kaiser Bill, write your will,
> Food we'll send without end to a friend
> We are working, there'll be no shirking,
> And we won't stop farming
> Until food has won the war.[44]

Other songs dealt with the prejudice and social stereotyping women faced entering into farm work. Though many women were experienced workers prior to their service in the WLAA, there were many reports of marked discrimination and prejudice on the part of the press and farmers. In response to the criticisms, some authors penned songs and poetry to show that though women may have been socialites and such before the war, once war began they meant business and were serious assets to the nation.

> Nellie was a pedagogue,
> And Sue a social light
> But when the Germans sank our boats
> They both came out to fight,

Grabbing up a rake and hoe
They joined the food armee
And now they're out upon the farms
A-fighting for the free.

It's a hard job to plant potatoes,
It's a darn sight worse to hoe,
It's a hard job to weed tomatoes
When the pesky things do grow.
Farewell to all the bright lights,
Good-bye old Broadway,
We are all out here to help our country
And you bet we'll stay.[45]

America, I raised my girl for you,
America, she's a Yankee through and through;
She can farm and she can knit,
Ever ready to do her bit.
America, she's not the only one,
Every girl to you is true.
Just place her with another, and she'll equal any brother
America, here's my girl![46]

Overall, American women responded with enthusiasm to the call of the WLAA to provide additional farm labor. Like their British sisters, American women who participated in the organization of the WLAA were primarily white, Christian, and middle class, though some working-class women volunteered weekends and holidays for short-term harvest help.[47] Women of color in both nations already held jobs at the beginning of the war, so wartime employment for them meant moving up into factory jobs that paid higher wages. Though some middle- and upper-class women saw factory labor as a man's domain, the full-time, urban middle-class women of the WLAA did not see the labor on the land as degrading or immoral, but rather used the opportunity of placing women in agriculture as a means of spreading progressive ideas. Carol Maynard wrote in 1918 about her experience as a WLAA member: "I do not know of a single girl in this camp who is at all likely to develop into a peasant type of woman. Those on Long Island truck farms would be peasants anyway. You see them in New York tenements. Women of intelligence will not degenerate mentally or physically through being farm laborers. Rather they will raise labor to their own level, will give it greater dignity."[48]

Emma L. George edited the American WLAA newsletter, the *Farmerette*. As editor, George received a wide variety of letters of viewpoints and perspectives on the WLAA and on the larger role of women in agriculture. She also collected news of training schedules and current events in the lives of WLAA workers for the *Farmerette*, as well as letters, poems, songs, and personal reflections on life and work in the WLAA. Some articles published in the *Farmerette* for distribution to WLAA members touted openly the significance of farming for Americanization—a process of enforcing white middle-class values, beliefs, and lifestyles upon America's immigrants, African Americans, and the poor. George's own personal reflections reveal quite a different story, a story of women whose experience working the land "shoulder to shoulder" with those of unequal backgrounds humbly led them to great humility and a broader sense of humanity and of position in a place where "hoeing corn is a miraculous leveler of artificial barriers. Breed, social posture, education all go into the melting pot and in their place strength, skill, quickness become the essential values."[49] Tied to and involved in various international organizations, the *Farmerette* offers interesting perspectives on the role of internationalism in civilian wartime aid.

One of the articles submitted for publication in the *Farmerette* titled "Helping to Make Americans," offered detailed arguments for participation in cultivation not only to obtain victory but to obtain and maintain a predominantly white American middle-class consensus: the tenets of Americanization. In the years after the war, Americans feared those who spoke, looked, acted, or appeared differently than the average middle-class American family. In a period of heightened xenophobia, Americans looked desperately to find ways to either force others to behave and think as they did or to force them to leave the nation entirely. Additionally, many Americans feared the growing militancy of the suffrage movement as activists picketed the White House each day, an action seen as unpatriotic when the nation urged women to focus on wartime service. One article in the *Farmerette* focused on the effort to influence the young women who left their homes and were without the influence of parents or other moral political guidance on the relationship of social standing and wartime behavior. Though this article refers to the "war garden," an urban food production program, the *Farmerette* published it to persuade the female agriculturalist about the patriotic significance of cultivation:

> The United States must be fortified against Bolshevism. The social unrest which leads to the red terror of destruction is induced by food shortages and famine, at least its flames are fanned into their fiercest height by

lack of food. Therefore, food production is the great fundamental problem which must be worked out in order that panic and pestilence many not get started. . . . This is Americanism of the best type.

It has been found that the garden furnishes a means of helping to make good Americans. . . . The immigration department of the Y.M.C.A. is using this method to teach foreigners how to help themselves, to learn the American language, and to become good citizens of the nation; and the garden is the cement which helps to hold that foundation in place. . . . The man who is happily engaged during his spare time, or part of it, in caring for a garden, is not likely to be running after red flags even if they should come his way, and listening to soapbox orators most of whom have never produced anything but who desire to divide with the rest of the world.

. . . Spread the message both by example and precept. Plant a garden yourself and get others to plant. If there is a big vacant lot in your neighborhood, organize a group of community gardeners and begin to grow some food. You will be growing Victory Bonds and good Americanism at the same time. The world must be fed before you can check social unrest. You cannot argue with an empty stomach. After a good dinner anyone is amenable to reason.[50]

The perspectives in this article, like those in many other speeches, newspaper commentaries, and personal conversations of the time, hindered in some ways the initial labor goals of the suffragists like Harriot Stanton Blatch because the words speak more to cultivation as a tool for Americanization and political gain rather than to support of women's roles in agricultural labor. In some ways perhaps these articles were printed in efforts to establish a distance from Blatch's and other leaders' militant stance on suffrage (and history of "soapbox" oration on Wall Street). In order for the WLAA to find success and acceptance, Americans needed to feel secure in allowing a uniformed army of women into the world of labor previously denied to women. In the article above, the scathing commentary on "soapbox orators" and the need to "check social unrest" was likely to warn the reader against unwanted and un-American criticism of the American status quo. Thus this article encouraged farmerettes to cultivate an American identity of democracy, but not an equal identity for themselves as laborers. In that sense and from this perspective, cultivation was a tool for identity, but one of the values espoused by white, patriarchic American society.

Despite such criticism and commentary, farmerettes forged their own identities based upon their personal memories. One farmerette, listed merely as "Mrs. David Force" wrote this poem about her experience in the WLAA,

> And so with joy their work is done
> That food may never fail,
> Their brothers brave who fight the Hun
> That freedom may prevail. . . .
>
> . . . [A]nd it's more than fields and cattle,
> More than houses, more than lands—
> For the spirit's holy battle
> Farmerette's memory stands.

Though national governments did not invent the WLA movement, they eventually attempted to lead them and organize such efforts for the greater good of the nations they were trying to protect and preserve. Through organized government efforts, such movements transformed into intensive propaganda campaigns to both effectively aid the homefront effort by increasing the national and international agricultural supply and to inspire patriotism to ensure loyalty during wartime. This does not mean that nations wholly accepted women as agricultural workers, however. It was one thing for women to volunteer to help the nation; it was quite another for a patriarchal society to admit it needed the help of women and was willing to allow them to do "men's" work and praise them for it. In the United States, the ties of suffragists to the WLAA program did not go unnoticed. While American suffragists were often negatively labeled "suffragettes" just as English women were, the attempt to discredit women who farmed resulted in labeling them "farmerettes." Though this pejorative conjunction of farmer and suffragette initially served to draw attention to the women in a negative light, the women claimed ownership of the term, just as they had suffragette and placed their own meanings upon it that brought a new identity with it of patriotism and women's service.

After the war's end British subjects, like their American allies, wanted to return to a stable, quieter, happier lifestyle. For many, this identity included the political and economic restructuring of gender roles as well. Nonetheless, agricultural labor was essential to survival on the home fronts of England and the United States and for the survival of all of the Allies; therefore, nations had to come to grips with their stereotypes of women laborers if they planned on winning what would be known as the Great War. In this way, the WLAs on two continents utilized the labor of women to cultivate political identities about national strength and endurance. Women's organizations were vital to the development of the WLAs during the First World War. International organizations facilitated the transnational exchange of ideas among British women regarding the training of women and girls in agriculture, but during the initial years of war Englishwomen's organizations did the most to promote national and regional movements that developed into the British WLA. Similarly, American women's groups shifted their foci from the transnational to the national to solve the international food crises, and in doing so cultivated identities both national and social. Women like Harriot Stanton Blatch brought to the WLA a nuanced view of the position of women in labor, linking ideas about women's place in agricultural labor to women's suffrage. In many ways her stance on suffrage both elevated and constricted the position of the WLAA. Her militant suffragist stance suggested militancy and a redistribution of labor that many Americans feared.

Correspondingly, one of the reasons for the decreasing activity of women's international organizations during the First World War was first, the immediate needs of the nations that women felt compelled to assist with, and second, the rise in nationalism that resulted from the intensity and threat of the war to destroy their homelands and cultural traditions that shaped much of their identity. British and American women's organizations wanted not only to serve their country and advance women's place in occupations, but also to take the opportunity to educate rural women on the deficiencies of the rural household. Lady Gertrude Denman's Women's Institute was significant in forming the foundation of the education of rural British women. Many women's rights activists saw the lack of modern labor-saving conveniences and devices in the rural home as a symbol of an under-evolved society that promoted the unnecessary labor of women. The mere fact that farmers requested WLA workers to assist with domestic chores as well as farm labor supported the activists' theories, and the WLA regulation forbidding workers from any labor outside that of the male farm laborers gone to war signified the cultural statements the organization intended to make about the identity of modern, educated British and American urban women.[51] In some ways the British and the American WLAs, then, were like physical manifestations of the ideas of rural education and assistance that the WIs and the WFGUs offered in the years preceding the war.

Despite the international exchanges of ideas regarding women's agricultural labor, women on different continents faced very different challenges due to the proximity of battles in their country of residence. Thus the American agricultural experience was notably different from Britain's and that difference reflected in the organization of female laborers. Where Britain faced immediate scarcity, the U.S. government sought to ensure a victory by supplying its European Allies with food—presenting a symbol and identity of American abundance. The American version of the WLA in structure and purpose resembled the British organization, with certain differences in perspective. The smaller national campaign of the WLAA reflected the difference in national need. With no apparent domestic shortages of food and without the rationing restrictions of their British sisters, American women focused more on the opportunity to gain employment in factories and other forms of labor that American men left behind to serve in the war. To American activists, getting women into the workforce in larger numbers seemed to be the avenue toward greater social awareness of the lack of gender and political equality. Nevertheless, agriculture was still an aspect of such labor, and as women watched their brothers, fathers, husbands, and friends leave to fight on the war front, some organized to join the war effort by fighting on the farm front.

Though Britain's initial agricultural struggle posed a serious threat to national security, near the end of the war it boasted the "finest harvest for 50 years," and government officials told reporters they should explore England "'as she had never been seen before'" and boasted the nation now consisted of "miles of grain" and was "a golden land."[52] Though the areas of Berks, Bucks, and Oxfordshire brought in record harvests in 1918, not all areas of the countryside prospered, for some areas such as the Horsham district suffered from both wireworm and heavy rains that softened the clay soil.[53] Some farmers' corn crops suffered from blight and did not prosper as a result of increased labor and government incentives like awards offered for the best crops.[54] Despite the losses in some areas, however, the government sought to promote England as a land of plenty.

The agricultural change wrought by women certainly changed the dynamics of gender relations in labor after the war. The increased harvests were not due solely to women, however; non-enlisted men, children, and prisoners of war participated in various cultivation campaigns as well. To many children, gardening and assisting in agricultural planning meant getting to take part in the effort to bring brothers and fathers home sooner. For many farmers still reluctant to employ women, prisoners of war seemed an economical alternative. Mr. Herbert Padwick of Britain's West Sussex War Agricultural Committee argued that prisoners of war made up a large proportion of the farm labor required in West Sussex. Among prisoners, work ethics and motivation differed though many prisoners "joked" that they were going to give their best efforts to show their enemies what kind of nation they were fighting.[55]

While America and Great Britain ushered female workers out of the factory and watched them "dispersing quietly to their homes," some women who served in and organized the WLAs went back to the urban areas claiming their personal and political spaces in the postwar society. Others stayed on in the WLAs, the only wartime organization that continued after the war's end, due to the continued need for foodstuffs for the Allies and for war-ravaged Europe.[56] For women who had served on the land, one of the benefits of war-time service was a newly found political strength. As soon as the war came to a close in November 1918, women began to once again form prewar organizations designed to promote the advancement of women and often established new organizations in their place. In Britain, the National Political League met the week after the signing of the armistice and announced publicly that the proposed schedule of events included speeches by members of the WLA.[57] Women who cultivated victory in allotment gardens or in home war gardens did not find the same public praise or political leverage at the end of the war however. Members of the WLAs of the United States and Great Britain displayed the success and importance of women's labor, whereas urban women who remained in the home during war merely showed their success and importance to maintaining the home and thus strengthened the argument made by male-dominated labor that women's place in strengthening the nation remained in the home. Thus the production of food both liberated and domesticated women during the First World War. Women achieved the limited right to vote in Britain in 1918 and in the United States in 1920; however, years of depression and another world war continued the liberation and domestication of women by bringing women into the workplace in ever increasing numbers *and yet*, at the same time, more firmly established the domestic sphere as feminine and women as symbols of national production.

For women of England and the United States, cultivation was not only part of a centuries-long process of providing for their families, but also a way of sowing the seeds of hard labor and reaping newly found national and personal identities. Although WLAs at the turn of the century comprised mostly urban, white middle-class women with education and social standing to support them, their efforts were part of a much larger wartime homefront effort of conservation and production that included working-class women in the factories and women unable to leave the home. As for the legacy of the land girls and farmerettes, such organization set a precedent not only for labor organization in the Second World War, but for reinterpreting women's place and space, in both agriculture and in society.

CHAPTER 3

Sowing the Seeds of Victory

One of the few occupations left to mother after the disruption of her sphere at the end of the eighteenth century was the preparation of food. In the minds of men, food, from its seed sowing up to its mastication, has always been associated with woman. . . . Mention food and the average man thinks of mother. That is the Adam in him.

When the world under war conditions asked to be fed, Adam, running true to his theory, pointed to mother as the source of supply, and declared . . . that the universe need want for nothing, if each woman would eliminate waste in her kitchen and become a voluntary and obedient reflector of the decisions of the state and national food authorities.

. . . In the same way, when food falls short and the victualing of the world becomes a pressing duty, the governing class adopts a thesis that a politically less-favored group can, by saving in small and painful ways, accumulate the extra food necessary to keep the world from starving. The ruling class seeks cover in primitive ideas, accuses Eve of introducing sin into the world, and calls upon her to mend her wasteful ways.

—Harriot Stanton Blatch, *Mobilizing Woman-Power,* 1918

Everyone who creates or cultivates a garden helps, and helps greatly, to solve the problem of feeding the nations; . . . every housewife who practices strict economy puts herself in the ranks of those who serve the nation. . . . This is the time for America to correct her unpardonable fault of wastefulness and extravagance. . . . Let every man and every woman assume the duty of careful, provident use and expenditure as a patriotic duty.

—Woodrow Wilson, "The President to the People," 15 April 1917

THOUGH WOMEN FOR CENTURIES cultivated gardens for both pleasure and subsistence, during the First World War cultivation took on a patriotic meaning for the women of England and the United States. Gardening in wartime transformed cultivation from an aesthetic or culinary practice to a practice symbolic of the gardener's level of patriotism and support of the nation

during a time of crisis. Though many urban women joined the homefront efforts at large-scale cultivation by joining the WLAs of England and America,
many more urban women remained at home and supported the home front
in the way they were instructed: from their kitchens and gardens. Whereas
gardening and cultivation had long been associated with personal identity,
during the First World War these actions and their products were symbols of
political identity as well. Thus the kitchen garden yielded to the implementation of the war garden. This smaller-scale cultivation from the kitchen garden
turned significant results that, upon closer examination, reveal two unique
stories of identity from cultivation: one political and one personal.

Though England and the United States developed similar administrations
and programs to deal with food issues during the war, the two nations used
food in different ways to win the war. When American president Woodrow
Wilson argued that "food will win the war" in 1917, he might have been
talking about American foreign policy to aid the Allies, but the campaign
slogan he used and the new administration it represented reflected similar
structures created by Great Britain in 1914. Both nations and their administrations urged the populace to increase the national food supply to support the
effort to decrease international food shortages and win the war. Though both
nations sought the help of women, what is most significant about their food
administrations is that they set precedents for utilizing food as a political tool
and for developing new identities for women.

Though Wilson's slogan was not gendered, the supporting idea behind
it was. In wartime food was the "fruit of the land" that nations claimed, and
in gendered ways the nation looked to women to continue that reproductive
metaphor and represented them as mothers of the nation. This image and
symbolism of women as mothers of the nation varied and often complicated
policy as nations simultaneously depicted women in conflicting ways. Nations visually depicted women as the mothers of the nation, and yet the wartime programs treated them as if they were "sinners" that needed instruction
on how to do the same work others glorified them for. The food agencies of
both the United States and England encouraged women to make changes in
the home to promote an Allied victory, and by nations doing so set precedents
about gender, political roles, and identities for decades to come. Whereas the
British government encouraged and eventually required the participation of
women in wartime service by means of an official registry of women workers
to address the national food supply and labor crises, their American counterparts encouraged solutions based more on conservation and waste management to ensure national and international stability. From this perspective, the
British solution to national food shortage was increased rural production,

whereas the American solution to international food shortage was decreased consumption and increased efficiency of the urban areas.

Perhaps the most common way women confined to the home aided the international agricultural shortage was to focus on the cultivation of a home garden and the preservation of its produce. Either by increasing the efficiency of an existing garden or creating one for the first time, women on two continents grew as much produce as they could for their family in community lot gardens, their own yards, or window boxes to conserve the available produce for the rest of the nation. When rationing of meats, sugars, and fats in Britain began in early 1918, gardening proved vital to ensuring families had enough of the kinds of vegetables they desired to provide interesting and satisfying dishes. Though no official national campaign for a British war garden began, the Ministry of Agriculture and the Ministry of Information encouraged individuals and families to grow their own vegetables and preserve them through canning as one of the ways subjects could protect their families and preserve the future of the empire.

Just as the British eagerly utilized every inch of available land for cultivation, Americans actively promoted the creation or expansion of urban and suburban community gardens as well as household kitchen gardens for a variety of reasons. These gardens, first known as "war gardens" then after the war as "victory gardens," were not promoted in ways to scare citizens about food shortages. Rather, the government encouraged citizens to consume less produce from commercial agriculturalists while noting citizens should take the time to enjoy the mental and physical benefits of gardening as well. Americans did not promote war gardens as a means of survival, but rather as a display of the bounty of America; a citizen's physical act of gardening was an expression of the strength of the nation. In fact, the American government encouraged citizens to use their bounty of natural land resources to further contribute to "sowing the seeds of victory" (see figs. 3.1 and 3.2).[1] In this way, cultivation was more about patriotism and an expression of political ideas than about direct need. American war gardens comprised vegetable, fruit, and herb gardens that shaped the nation in profound ways. More than producing surplus food to benefit the war efforts, they produced cultural and social benefits that reflected both the desired outcomes of the national campaigns and unexpected social changes that altered the dynamics of domestic life in varied ways.

The United States turned to gardening and cultivation as a tool for victory like no other nation during the First World War. During the three years prior to the American entry into the war, when the U.S. government officially remained neutral, farmers supported Britain and her agricultural needs

FIGURE 3.1. Frank V. DuMond, *Liberty Sowing the Seeds of Victory*, 1917. Library of Congress, POS-US.D84, no. 1.

FIGURE 3.2. James Montgomery Flagg, *Sow the Seeds of Victory!*, 1918. Library of Congress, POS-US.F63, no. 13.

by selling and shipping supplies. Herbert Hoover, an independent global mining consultant, shifted his efforts to feeding the starving people ravaged by war. Before America joined the war, he recruited volunteers to distribute food, transportation, and money to people in need. As chairman for the Relief of Belgium, Hoover worked with Belgian leaders to feed the entire nation during the war, depending upon private contributions and government grants for support. Hoover continued his efforts at food distribution from an office in London, where he oversaw the distribution of two million tons of food to nearly nine million people of both the Entente and the Central alliances. Though Hoover was an international businessman before the war, his efforts at relieving global hunger established an identity for America as a leader in the distribution of food.

The United States examined the world food shortage caused by years of war and estimated that, in order to continue to supply the dairy, livestock, sugar, and wheat products necessary, it needed to step in and take charge of distribution, purchasing, and sales. Part of that government intervention included reducing public consumption of these food products from large farms. Though famed suffragist and WLA leader Harriot Stanton Blatch traveled the country speaking out against the chastisement of women's wastefulness and encouraged instead increases in large-scale agricultural production with female labor, Hoover's philosophy rested on the idea of efficiency; he believed that increased production was not as significant as reducing wastefulness and understanding proper cooking methods. He believed that whatever the public lacked in packaged goods, largely in demand by the government, they could make up for in fresh vegetables grown in their own plots. To do this, the U.S. government turned to agricultural colleges and the Department of Agriculture for advice on how best to educate the American people about this situation. In large urban areas, the Food Administration encouraged citizens to cultivate for victory through demonstrations and training lectures. Through state and local community support, educational meetings, and home demonstrations, volunteers educated and encouraged citizens to plant every available plot of land in hopes of lightening the public demand and need of such products. To incorporate more vegetables in their diets—in order to consume less of the food needed for soldiers and Allies—the USDA encouraged Americans to sign a pledge of food conservation and to practice "Meatless Mondays" and "Wheatless Wednesdays" (see fig. 3.3). In addition to conservation and waste management, American citizens filled their plates and stomachs with fresh vegetables they planted on rooftops, vacant lots, and even in city parks to provide the "ammunition" needed to win the war.[2] To combat suggestions that women should take the place of farmers in the fields, Hoover's Food Ad-

FIGURE 3.3. Paul Stahr, *Be Patriotic: Sign Your Country's Pledge to Save the Food*, United States Food Administration, 1918. Library of Congress, POS-US.S72, no. 1.

FIGURE 3.4. *Heroic Women of France Toiling to Produce Food.* Wynkoop Hallenbeck Crawford Co., between 1914 and 1918. Library of Congress, POS-WWI-US, no. 145.

ministration produced propaganda displaying Frenchwomen "toiling to produce food" in what appeared to be backbreaking labor in the fields of France (see fig. 3.4). The message to women was simple: repent wasteful habits in the kitchen and conserve food to avoid the hard labor like that of Allied women.

DORA's Gardens

England's food crisis brought many people to see agricultural production as challenge met only by hard work and dedication. To others, however, complete self-reliance in agriculture seemed nearly impossible and at times, comical:

> Hard's the fight with Nature in our uncongenial climate,
> Cuddling plants and coaxing 'em, and oh, the weary time it
> Takes to get a slender crop—we toil the Summer through;
> England, needing quick returns, is looking now to you!
> Food that comes from tropic lands, needing heat upon it,
> You could grow without a thought, if you'd doff your bonnet;
> Thousands of you, growing food on your daily trips,
> Helping to economise the tonnage of our ships.[3]

England's "fight with Nature" rested not only on an uncongenial climate but also on a long history of food importation. Britain relied on American agricultural exports for survival for a number of reasons. First, American farmers provided agricultural exports at significantly lower prices on the international market than the British market price, so it made economic sense for Britain to turn to the importation of its agricultural needs. Second, Britain produced only one-fifth of its own agricultural needs and relied on imports from other nations such as France, Spain, and the United States for such goods. Thus a threat to the supply of agricultural labor was one thing, but when combined with a threat to imports England most desperately needed, it promised defeat if not checked in some way. Importation created an economic interdependence between the United States and Great Britain: When American farmers produced an increase of cheap grain in the 1870s, changes in British agriculture resulted, as cheaper imported grain made more economic sense than the more expensive, homegrown grain. As a result, many British farmers could not make a living from agriculture and moved to urban areas to seek employment. Britons estimated that in 1882, their nation reached its maximum acreage under plow, at 13,839,000. By 1914, however, that amount fell to 10,306,000 acres and reflected the growing public interest in buying cheaper, imported goods. For example, in 1919 the per capita wheat consumption of both the United States and Britain was approximately 360 pounds. In 1861–1865 the amount of wheat the British imported equaled about 135 pounds per capita; in 1886–1890, that rose to 236 pounds; and in 1911–1913, to 294 pounds of the average 360 pounds consumed per person.[4]

From the moment Britain entered the war, the price of food increased moderately until the fall of 1916 when a world food shortage became suddenly clear.[5] The rising prices sparked fears among the population about nutritional minimums and equity in distribution.[6] In an effort to stabilize the national economy the British government passed a series of acts, known collectively as the Defense of the Realm Act (DORA), from August 1914 to March 1915. DORA was a series of regulations and restrictions granting the government greater power over labor and censorship and the takeover of private factories, shipyards, and vacant land deemed significant for increased production, whether industrial or agricultural. The act was, among other things, publicity for mobilizing England in support of the empire. Encouraging urban allotment gardens on all available vacant land was just one way the government utilized DORA to reduce dependence upon imported food and to defray rising food prices.[7]

The garden was not new during the First World War, as it served as a symbol of everyday life—an extension of the domestic sphere and of general English identity for centuries. The English division of labor during the decades leading up to the war provided a female sphere of the cultivation through kitchen gardens for the working classes and through ornamental gardens of flowers and some vegetables for the upper classes. Though many people cultivated these gardens for the food they provided, most regarded the act of cultivation and what they cultivated as expressions of class identity. Thus, when the government asked women of the higher classes to stop growing flowers and to start growing vegetables instead, tensions arose about what was considered peasant labor and what was considered recreation for ladies of higher social status.[8] For the working class, however, the cultivation of food was not a class issue, but an issue of the challenges of increased production with limited resources in the cool English climate. Humor regarding those challenges manifested in the popular culture of the day:

> Motor engines, motor engines, do not wear a bonnet!
> You have artificial heat—grow something on it!
> Precious artificial heat, costly to install;
> Turn it into a hot-bed, growing food for all!
>
> *Must* you have a superstructure? Let it be a hot-house
> Forcing (say) some early peas—the only decent pot-house;

Oh, if I could only see in walking down the street
No unpatriotic waste of all that lovely heat![9]

Thus, convincing British people to take up gardening was not the issue at hand as DORA and the new Minister of Food Control stressed the importance of maximizing the existing garden to ensure stability of the household. In 1916, the Board of Trade, invested with powers to do what it felt necessary "in the interest of the public and for maintaining the supply of any article or commerce," set forth a program to control production, consumption, and price levels of all foodstuffs.[10] Leading the program, Lord Devonport took the position as England's first food controller in December 1916. Although he had the power to regulate the production and manufacture of food from the farm and factory to the distribution of it, he delegated the home production encouragement to the Board of Agriculture and Fisheries, an agency given the power to "enter on land and cultivate it if, in their opinion, it was not being cultivated in the best interests of the country."[11]

British wartime gardens had characteristics similar to their American counterparts in that they derived primarily from urban movements to use the natural resources of the nation to promote security on the home front during the war. They differed somewhat in that the British government did not release the same kind of full-scale national campaign for war gardens as the Americans did. Instead, the nation focused more on the larger task of conservation and efficiency in all areas of the home, from rationing of market items to proper trash disposal to the recycling of products that could be repurposed for use around the home or could aid the war effort in some way. Gardens continued to serve as a symbol of national identity; however Britain focused on the larger task of farm work as crucial to meeting the wartime agricultural needs of the empire.[12]

The British government's appeal to the public for rural and urban agricultural help in 1917 came too late to prevent food shortages across England in 1918. While the British WLA started its first season in 1917, in 1918 then British Food Controller Lord Rhondda requested seventy-five million bushels of American wheat and five thousand copies of the American National War Garden Commission's handbook on gardening, *War Gardening: Victory Edition*, to distribute to local community homefront leaders.[13] This exchange of ideas did not create an entirely new garden population, but rather inspired the efficient use of the existing gardens in wartime and tied the cultivation of land to patriotism and national identity.[14]

Although British women volunteered to take the place of male farm workers, urban agricultural areas needed additional service as well; however, measures to encourage urban cultivation did not necessarily aim toward women alone. Britain registered about 225,000 women for wartime work; however, many women did not have the opportunity to take on additional work outside of the home or the ability to relocate to rural areas for agricultural work.[15] For these women, wartime work meant changes in lifestyle and modes of housekeeping. Thus in British urban areas, much like in the urban areas of America, domestic movements organized to promote rationing, recycling, and the production of small amounts of produce. In many instances the British Ministry of Information placed its focus on school gardens so that children also had a chance to contribute to the war effort. Even in this scenario, however, women served in vital roles, teaching the children how to cultivate and thus representing themselves as "mother" of the nation and showing the way to the cultivation of victory.

The British Parliament eventually mandated allotments of land for communal opportunities to garden. Any vacant lots of land not used or taxed were released to take over by the government for use and allotment to urban populations for cultivation. The *Weekly Dispatch* estimated that the British people cultivated over five hundred thousand allotments in 1917.[16] Any land not in commercial or residential use could be subject to the definition of "slacker land." It is worth noting that the American National War Garden Commission considered vacant lots of land "slacker land" if not put to good use, and the propaganda used by the commission reflected the sentiment.[17] Though it is not clear which nation first pushed the pejorative definition of slacker land for communal cultivation, certainly an exchange of ideas occurred between the agricultural organizations of each.[18] The allotment garden in England, built on a long tradition of tensions surrounding the loss of open lands and the movement toward leased land for cultivation, brought both opportunities for increased production and generalized anxiety in the government about how to manage it and bring slacker land under its program of production.

The Agricultural Organization Society (AOS), built on the premise of volunteer farmers and urbanites providing guidance and assistance to cooperatives and allotment societies seeking to establish land leases, faced a rocky growth period from 1893 to 1912. As wartime grew near, however, the interest in allotment gardening and food conservation grew. In 1917, the AOS received funding from the British Board of Agriculture and Fisheries and established a board of directors that included Conservative member of Parliament and agricultural specialist Lord Bledisloe. Another notable member of the association was Lady Gertrude Denman, wife of a former governor-general of Australia. Denman worked with the organization in the beginning war years to produce women's groups that focused on a food campaign encouraging both rural and urban housewives to conserve food, can vegetables and fruits, and sell surplus produce from their kitchen gardens. These small women's groups evolved into the Women's Institutes (WI) that Denman went on to lead in 1917. Through this work she also came into contact with Meriel Talbot and joined the leadership of the WLA. For English women, Denman was a primary political figure for both urban and rural women involved in the production and conservation of food.

The wartime food campaigns took to the presses of England. Newspapers such as the *Weekly Dispatch* published articles reminding women of the importance of conservative consumption and domestic agricultural production. "Questions Every Woman Is Asking" on August 19, 1917, explained to women the importance of using flour and butter in recipes, of conserving fabric in clothing, and of making effective use of allotment gardens. Wartime propaganda encouraged women to think of time spent in wartime planning as a patriotic way to use their time and argued, "women who have taken up gardening will not go back to the old do-nothing fashion of wasting leisure time. Every scrap of land is verdant and fair: it is literally bursting with the fruit of the earth, as if the very gods had set themselves to provide some compensation for the sorrow of the world."[19] Nonetheless, the economy needed to continue and remain stable, meaning some advertisers had to find ways to be patriotic *while* consuming. Even the entertainment industry needed special advertisement to survive the economic strain of war. When director Gilbert Miller presented a new play at the Globe Theatre in October 1917, the newspaper made a special note about Miller to assure its readers and potential patrons of Miller's patriotism and wartime efforts: the author of "Theatreland Gossip" said of Gilbert Miller, "Everyone who knows him likes him and respects him. Before[,] the war gardening . . . interested him almost as much as play producing. Now he never leaves London."[20]

Though British urban agricultural activities mirrored American efforts, Britain continued to depend on imports of American foodstuffs to sustain the nation. In reaction to this precarious dependency upon Americans, the British press took steps to assure its readers of the sincerity of American aid and participation in the war. In October 1918, journalist P. W. Wilson told the British people that Americans' "voracious" appetite for propaganda and political speakers made them one of the most patriotic nations in the war. He noted the rationing, gardening, and industrial changes that American women and children undertook in order to aid the Allies. Mr. Wilson also boasted of the 5,250,000 war gardens planted in America in 1918, a 51 percent increase above gardens planted the previous year. The number seemed impressive and inspiring to Mr. Wilson who wanted to motivate Britain to keep hope alive

FIGURE 3.5. "Our Win-the-War Garden Suburb Enthusiast (as the storm bursts). 'Madam! Madam! Will you kindly put down your umbrella? It's keeping the rain off my allotment.'" *Punch, or the London Charivari* 152 (30 May 1917): 355.

FIGURE 3.6. "Intensive Culture for Flat Dwellers: Sowing Early Mustard and Cress on Winter Underclothing." *Punch, or the London Charivari* 152 (30 May 1917): 352.

during the war.[21] The British press responded to these requests to motivate urbanites in a variety of ways, though most were positive toward production. The weekly satirical magazine *Punch, or the London Charivari* poked fun at the requests to cultivate urban areas beyond what people were accustomed to. *Punch* cartoons depicted scenes ranging from overeager allotment gardeners to urbanites unsuccessfully attempting to grow food inside their homes (see figs. 3.5 and 3.6).

The British minister of agriculture, R. E. Protheroe, considered the "land campaign," the program that promoted both urban allotment gardens and the rural WLA, as "one of the greatest achievements of the war." He noted in May 1918 that British allotment gardens numbered eight hundred thousand, producing an estimated eight hundred thousand additional tons of food for the nation.[22] A widespread "Feed the Guns" campaign urged both urban and rural production of food in order to shift the wartime national budget toward the purchase of munitions instead of imported food. A large-scale pageant to promote this campaign took place in November 1918 and included parades of female war workers, boy scouts, bands playing patriotic tunes, and displays of munitions from around the world as well as aircraft flying overhead.[23] The pageantry included specimens of German, French, Greek, Italian, Serbian, and South African munitions and tanks. Though the press noted that French and Greek detachments could not participate in the pageant "on account of influenza," the *Daily News* did note the appearance of "Jackie," a baboon dressed in a khaki uniform "perched on one of the field guns taken by the South Africans." Met with "roars of laughter," this baboon depicted the racial stereotypes and biases of the British Empire—though the nation was enmeshed in an economic crisis that threatened its survival, food symbolized many things to the empire, including ideas of racial superiority.[24]

The Food Administration and the National War Garden Commission of America

American President Woodrow Wilson acknowledged the importance of consuming less and producing more when he announced to the public that "Food will win the war." Wilson pledged to fight the food shortages in Europe by increasing imports and looked for efficient ways to increase Americans' productivity. He provided $4.3 million to the state and county extension agencies as part of the Emergency Food Act to promote increased production. In a letter to the American people published in a 1917 issue of *Garden Magazine* he asserted, "everyone that creates or cultivates a garden helps, and helps greatly, to solve the problem of feeding the nations."[25] He established the Food Administration in 1917 and named Herbert Hoover the food administrator. In Hoover's effort to improve the American ability to aid Europe, he initiated homefront campaigns toward preparedness, which included increased efficiency in local farmer's markets and other means of locally supplied food. The goals of the administration were to oversee all the production, transportation, sale, and consumption of food and to maximize efficiency while preventing abuses and greed. The Food Administration developed programs to target such demographic groups as children, African Americans, and women.[26] Included in such programs were lecture series headed by Harriot Stanton Blatch, director of the WLA. In this role as head of the Food Administration Speaker's Bureau, Blatch brought examples from successful agricultural schemes abroad to the U.S. Food Administration and traveled across the country lecturing about the importance of food in winning the war.

To win the war, American and British people needed to consume less and produce more (see fig. 3.7). The methods of food consumption and conservation varied according to the agricultural needs of the nation and region; but the need to ration certain food items, whether officially or socially, inspired many people to find alternative recipes and ways of feeding their families. Nations placed the heavy burden on women to prepare satisfying nutritious meals that either required very little scarce meat, produce, and other foodstuffs, or none at all. Officials urged Americans to follow such rules as:

Each day one wheatless meal—the evening meal.
Each week two wheatless days—Monday and Wednesday.
Each day one meatless meal—the morning meal.
Each week one meatless day—Tuesday.
Each week two porkless days—Tuesday and Saturday.
Every day a fat saving day.
Every day a sugar-saving day.
Use fruits, vegetables, and potatoes abundantly.
Use milk wisely.[27]

Nationalistic attitudes in part shaped the American war garden movement. Though the Food Administration's campaign urged Americans to grow as much as possible to increase the availability of commercially grown food to ship overseas, many Americans argued that a nation with so many resources and such an abundance of land was wasteful if citizens did not use what they had more effectively first. For these people, consuming less was more important than producing more. Still, for American gardeners the act of cultivation calmed personal anxieties about the opportunity to protect their families and communities and in turn their nation if their food supplies suddenly dimin-

FIGURE 3.7. A. Hendee, *This Is What God Gives Us,* 1917, Library of Congress, POS-US. H45, no. 1.

ished just as Britain had so profoundly experienced. In this way, individual and community gardens were intensely personal and national, though they were serving a greater international purpose.

After Americans recognized the international need for food, many wanted to help, but few took on the task of fortifying the nation with "Men, Munitions and Money" like Charles Lathrop Pack did. He claimed that he single-handedly created a national war garden campaign and created the national War Garden Commission "weeks before" America's entry into the war.[28] As president of the organization, Pack set about organizing a national and international propaganda campaign to promote gardening as the primary tool for victory over the Central Powers. What were his reasons for selecting gardening as his wartime cause? He argued,

> When the drums sounded the call to colors in the summer of 1914, three million Frenchmen shouldered their rifles and marched away from a large proportion of the five million farms of France; and mostly these were one-man farms. Russia, a nation almost wholly agricultural, mobilized perhaps eight millions of men. All the men of fighting age in Belgium were summoned to the army. England, possessing only a "contemptible little army," straightway began a recruiting campaign which within a few years swelled the ranks of her forces to five millions. Austria, Bulgaria, and Turkey likewise mobilized their full fighting forces. Altogether, twenty or thirty million men were called away from their usual pursuits. The vocation of the majority of them was farming. Thus, at one stroke, practically all the farms in the embattled nations were swept clear of male workers.[29]

Pack acknowledged that Europe relied on the importation of goods to fill its food needs. He argued that transportation of such imports was not only costly in times of war, but also increasingly more difficult due to German submarines. England produced only one-fifth of its own food supply before the war and direly needed agricultural imports. Noting that many of the European nations such as France and Italy faced similar agricultural situations, he argued it was imperative that the United States step up its exports to help out nations in need and prevent the collapse and defeat of the Allied nations. He likened the situation to a biblical one: "The children of Israel could not make bricks for Pharaoh without straw; and when we attempted to create food for famishing Europe we experienced similar difficulty, though our shortage was of manpower."[30] What he failed to mention, however, was that the United States simply mimicked a plan set forth by Britain three years prior to create a minister of Food Control in charge of both international food exchanges *and* domestic food production. Though Pack downplayed the governmental role in the war garden movement, he symbolizes the intensity of patriotism and desire to aid Europe during wartime that some 3,500,000 American people shared in 1917 as they dug up their land to plant the seeds of victory.

Referring to decreases in farms and agricultural workers over the last decade, Pack thought it nearly impossible to repair the agricultural system of America to aid the international struggle, which was the reason why he felt the American solution must focus on urban cultivation. In the decade prior to the war, Pennsylvania's farm laborers went from 160,000 to 80,000 and New York State lost 45,000 farm laborers (including women) in just one year from 1917 to 1918. These laborers left for better pay and living conditions in the urban areas, and so it seemed America was in the midst of a growing agricultural crisis. With shrinking farming systems, the nation would need to rely on urbanites and their communities to do their share to consume less and produce more. Thus the campaign program for urban cultivation and conservation of resources began.[31] American cities took on the call for cultivation with great pride and showmanship; in fact, many held parades and marked campaign kickoff days as "War Garden Days." In San Francisco, for example, their parade was so elaborate that it contained over eleven hundred marching students, soldiers, city officials, and veterans as well as floats with vegetables and even girls dancing "the dance of war gardens and victory" in front of San Francisco's city hall. Other cities produced their own local campaigns to promote local cultivation in order to free up commercially raised food for war needs. The Marion, Indiana, War Garden Association expressed to its citizens that they should "Earn the Right to Stay at Home—Plant a Garden."[32]

It was not just municipalities and local communities that organized war gardens, however; many churches, schools, and businesses used every available plot of land to cultivate what they could to help in the war effort. Alice K. Parsons and Jeanne W. Dennen, principals of the Girls' Collegiate School of Los Angeles, California, claimed their school garden design promoted preparedness and patriotism among young girls and referred to their students as "minute women."[33] Other preparedness programs the school provided included "practical work—cooking, sewing, stenography, typewriting and bookkeeping. . . . All this prepares a girl for life in her future home." No less patriotic or gendered was Mrs. Cooper Hartman's School for Young Ladies in New York City where students converted the backyard of the townhouse where the school was held into a war garden. Lindenwood College in St. Cloud, Missouri, aimed to "fit young ladies for lives of usefulness," and responded to the war with the development of courses in "gardening, typewriting, first aid to the injured, sewing, knitting, etc."[34]

Although some Americans found obtaining important materials such as seeds difficult, the National War Garden Commission urged the nation to grow war gardens through posters, literature, and local media.[35] Americans responded favorably to such propaganda and produced an additional $350 million worth of produce and canned 500 million quarts of fruits and vegetables as the result of some 3.5 million war gardens planted in 1917. The movement grew with 5.2 million gardens planted in 1918, producing some $525 million worth of food and canning 1.45 billion quarts of fruits and vegetables as a result. For Americans, the Jeffersonian ideal of every man a farmer and every farm (or garden in this case) a symbol of independence and democracy was now real and tangible; everyone from the farmer to the urbanite with only a window box in which to plant a few herbs or perhaps one vegetable could assert their independence and assure an American victory over the Axis.[36]

Pack, in an article titled "Making a Nation of Garden Cities," said of the men, women, and children who took up the noble act of gardening, "Both as individuals and as members of various organizations they have gone about this as true soldiers of the soil, in the same spirit with which their husbands, fathers, brothers, and friends went into the army and the navy."[37] Pack acknowledged that in addition to proving gender equality in the war effort, patriotic acts such as gardening also boosted morale. Pack argued that as a result of such effective propaganda campaigns, societal attitudes about gardening changed, and suddenly "gardening came to be *the* thing."[38] Pack was not the only person to argue the importance of cultivation; many people, organizations, and businesses participated in the booster campaigns for decreased consumption and increased production.[39] In a newsletter for the Women's Land Army of America (WLAA), the National War Garden Commission stressed the importance of cultivation for the morale of the nation:

> What is the most useful thing I can do to help my country at the present time? That is a question which hundreds of thousands of women throughout the land have asked themselves time and time again during the past few months.
>
> Here is the answer of the National War Garden Commission of Washington: "Plant a Victory Bond in your Victory Garden!" Here is the way the Commission argues the matter.
>
> . . . One of the greatest educational forces of the war was the war garden. It taught millions of people the values of thrift. It has been said that "a nation which saves is a nation saved." No more patriotic act can be performed this year than to plant a garden to help pay for the Victory Bonds which you are going to buy.

... The National War Garden Commission, then, says to the women of America: "You can do nothing better than to encourage and inspire home food production." Spread the message both by example and precept. Plant a garden yourself and get others to plant. If there is a big vacant lot in your neighborhood, organize a group of community gardeners and begin to grow some food. You will be growing Victory Bonds and good Americanism at the same time.[40]

Though the concept of cultivating victory appeared new to the nation, the concept of community gardening was not.[41] Many local community ordinances mandated that owners use every inch of available land in some productive way to support the war effort. In large urban areas, citizens made vacant lots into allotment gardens where individual families cultivated a particular allotment of land to produce enough supplemental food for their family and to help others less fortunate. In contrast to English allotment gardens, American communities that divided property did not always lease the land; communities and land owners negotiated terms under which the land could be used. Communities also promoted gardening for its mental and physical benefits and promoted gardening to immigrants as an activity important to participate in. In this way, community gardening was not only an act of patriotism but also of Americanism—it was an attempt to create political consensus among those members of society that the American middle class feared.[42]

Pack saw the American effort as a unique experience, characterized by ingenuity and imagination, "[Americans] with that vision without which people perish, possessed imagination. They saw little mountains of foodstuffs springing up everywhere, and the products of these fountains, like rain-drops on a watershed, uniting to form rushing streams which would fill the great reservoirs built for their compounding. The tiny fountains were innumerable back-yard gardens and vacant-lot gardens."[43]

The American war garden campaign was effective in portraying food as a weapon. Through propaganda, citizens acquired visual representations of their gardens as their own personal ammunition in fighting the war. Poster artwork created by Maginel Wright Enright depicted a woman with her hoe peering over a hill with vegetables militantly fighting the front line with her (see fig. 3.8). The poster used the familiar phrase "Over the top" to describe the efforts of women in gardening and illustrated a woman peering over a small row of vegetables as a soldier might peer over a trench. With her vegetables animated and looking stern, the poster suggested they are fighting the front line and protecting the woman. With the woman in back, behind the trenchlike garden row, peering over, her vegetables are fighting in front with-

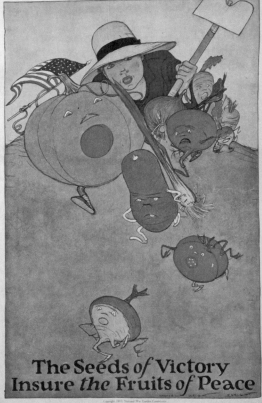

FIGURE 3.8. Maginel Wright Enright, *War Gardens over the Top*, 1919, Library of Congress, POS-US.B383, no. 3.

FIGURE 3.9. Maginel Wright Enright, *War Gardens Victorious*, 1919. Library of Congress, POS-US.B383, no. 5.

out hesitation and are symbolic weapons to win the war. In contrast, after the war another poster by the same artist expressed that every war garden should be "a Peace Plant" and depicted the same woman marching happily alongside her vegetables, no longer needing their protection but now leading them on to peacetime (see fig. 3.9). Thus the artist displays in the two posters the dichotomy of the woman war gardener's identity: simultaneously protected by the national bounty yet responsible for leading the nation to the bounty.

War Garden demonstrations and publicity spread quickly across America. Although the National War Garden Commission did not begin a local campaign in New York City until February 1918, members of the National League for Women's Service organized a massive citywide garden party in May 1917 to publicize the international war garden movement.[44] Party organizers flew Allied flags above white party tents and set up booths representing each of the Allied nations. Each booth of the Allied nations represented a different industry vital to the war effort; America's was agriculture. Here the activists of New York City made it known to residents that if America joined the war to create peace among nations as President Wilson claimed, then America was going to use agriculture as its strength and cultivate its way to victory.

Gendered nationalism was on display as well: women worked to display the positive industrial and economic contributions of each of the Allied nations.[45] The *New York Times* noted the booths in New York City, representing the Allied nations "all of which were presided over by pretty young women," were a great success among the crowd and that later "girls in the costume of the ally they represented made sales [of vegetables] throughout the crowd."[46] As the costumed women walked through the crowds of consumers at various produce stands, the uniformed American Juvenile Naval and Marine Scouts made their way through the crowd as well, selling war recipes and sheet music of patriotic tunes. The reporter for the *New York Times* claimed "there was everything at the market," including "The Seventh Regiment Band" and a dance pavilion where the mayor's wife opened the festivities. With the "hot dog man" doing business in Washington Square as well, the patriotic festivities lasted into the evening. All in all, the league raised over $1,000 and set a major precedent for establishing food as a weapon to win the war and as the pathway to peace as other cities began similar fairs or demonstrations of their region's abundance.[47]

The U.S. Army also took on the role of demonstrating how to raise war gardens. Though military camps across the United States possessed unused land suitable for gardening, it took the initiative of the National War Garden Commission and Camp Dix soldiers including Lt. Col. Edmond Tompkins, camp quartermaster, and Col. J. S. Fair to pursue approval to utilize the land for such a laborious agricultural task in advertising the war effort. The U.S. Army also organized gardens as a way for convalescing soldiers to regain their strength and return to the battlefield. It was later reported by Pack that the inspector of the southern command of the British Army, upon reviewing the American camp in New Jersey, acknowledged American soldiers' ability to cultivate land as therapeutic and noted the potential benefits for many injured British soldiers. In this respect, the "agrarian myth" of cultivation as a character-building activity presented a patriotic opportunity for making good soldiers as well good citizens and subjects of the United States and Britain.[48]

The Food Administration encouraged women to teach children the values of gardening and cultivation.[49] The U.S. School Garden Army, uniquely designed for school-age children, recruited female teachers to lead the cultivation process so that children could contribute to the war effort as well. Propaganda inspired and motivated the children, but the propaganda directed toward them focused more on songs and poems about the bravery and significance of their labor rather than on posters and radio scripts, which were more adult in focus. As children sang songs to tunes such as "Over There," they showed their support for the American women "sowing ev'rywhere" until "it's over, over there!"[50]

After the war the National War Garden Commission reported that though Americans planted an impressive 3,000,000 war gardens in 1917, over 5,285,000 war gardens existed in 1918. Therefore, in a nation of 100 million people and 20 million households in 1918, over 25 percent of households had war gardens. Put another way, this equaled one war garden for every 20 people in America. The products of these gardens multiplied the available food supplies. Americans canned more than 500,000,000 quarts of food in 1917 and an estimated 1,450,000,000 quarts of food in 1918. Not only did the gardeners obtain nutritious food at little to no monetary expense, but demand for the transport of foodstuffs declined, which freed up labor, expense, and fuel for the war effort. This also made the sending of food to a starving Europe possible, which supports the argument that the war was won as much with food as with bullets. Though the National War Garden Commission estimated in 1919 that the monetary value of the war gardens of 1918 was only $525,000, it may never be possible to accurately determine the value the gardens brought the nations that cultivated them.[51]

The effort to sustain the Allies was truly an international event. As a result of the successful food campaigns of the United States and England, Canadians, Australians, and New Zealanders all sought to assist their nations' war efforts and contributions to the British Empire by creating their own victory gardens. In the urban areas of these nations, women turned toward the United States and its war garden programs for examples. Moreover, Cuba, India, China, Japan, the Philippines, Alaska, Hawaii, South Africa, and many "South and Central American countries" looked to the United States for advice and materials on war gardening to promote urban agricultural production in their own land.[52] This interest equated an identity of abundance with American political strength and marked the United States a leader in food production.

Comparison of the food campaigns of Great Britain and the United States during the First World War shows that though the national efforts and campaigns got off to a slow start, women eagerly volunteered to help in less formal ways. Local urban groups and national and international nongovernmental organizations stepped in to help when the governments of both nations hesitated to admit any problems existed or that they needed the support of women. This laissez-faire attitude toward development of agricultural programs to assist the war effort was dangerous—had it not been for the last-minute efforts of governments brought about by the constant offers for agricultural assistance, increased and more severe food shortages appeared certain.[53]

What the women who participated in such efforts sought and gained often differed somewhat from the government-sponsored ideas. While many American and British women joined the WLAs for a sense of adventure and a chance at living a single girl's life outside the home and family, other women sought opportunity to express national and personal identity through the challenges of urban domesticity during the restraints of wartime. While some American women joined in the cultivation and promotion of war gardens as an extension of Progressive Era Americanization, many cultivated war gardens for enjoyment, and others gardened for the chance to avoid long lines and shortages due to limited food supplies of certain products by exchanging fresh foods for canned or processed foods in their daily diets.

There was a definite dichotomy between the rural and urban efforts at cultivating victory. Whereas the WLAs supplied women to rural areas to replace male labor lost to war duties, the victory gardeners were primarily urbanites confined by domestication to help the war effort in a limited geographical area. This confinement thus motivated urbanites to help win the war by consuming less and creating spaces of abundance in hopes of harvesting both a surplus of food and victory for all. For Americans, a growing urban population meant propaganda campaigns were needed that focused on the abilities and concerns of urban dwellers. Whereas the WLA of both Great Britain and the United States attracted young females of mostly middle- and upper-class

FIGURE 3.10. J. Paul Verrees, *Can Vegetables, Fruit, and the Kaiser Too*, 1918. National War Garden Commission, Library of Congress, POS-US.V48, no. 2.

backgrounds who looked to escape the clutches of the household, war gardening attracted more varied participants—men, children, and married and older women of all classes. While the WLA liberated women from gendered labor roles and rules, the war garden and food conservation movements entrenched the stereotype of women's sphere in the home.

The movement from floral to vegetable gardening during the war stemmed from transnational ideas, as did the association of women with cultivation. Newspapers, magazines, and gardening manuals stopped touting gardens as aesthetic assets of the home and started promoting them as practical, patriotic, and essential to a nonwasteful society. After the war was over, however, the exuberance with which the gardeners created their gardens waned and prospering nations such as the United States entered the Roaring Twenties, a time of marked extravagance and waste. English gardeners retained their gardens because they remained part of their identity; however, vegetables soon gave way to a return of flowers. Other nations such as Germany suffered economically as a result of the war and the Treaty of Versailles, and as a result, entered a period of shortages and want after the Allied home fronts decided to "Can Vegetables, Fruit, and the Kaiser Too" (see fig. 3.10). Food would, from this point on, be used as a diplomatic tool to "starve out" less desirable groups and ideologies. Food may have won the war, but it would also lead to the start of another in less than two decades.

Part II.

THE SECOND WORLD WAR

*Motherhood has not yet been classed as a nonessential industry!
There is small chance that it will ever be. The mother of small
children does not need to put on overalls to prove her patriotism.
She already has her war job. Her patriotism consists in not letting
quite understandable desires to escape for a few months from a
household routine or to let a little money of her own tempt her to
quit it.* There must be no absenteeism among mothers.

—J. Edgar Hoover, *Woman's Home Companion,* January 1944

CHAPTER 4

The Aftermath of War
GENDER AND AGRICULTURE IN
THE INTERWAR YEARS

*If many of the seeds of reform planted before the war are not left unwatered [sic]
to die, that is the most weary humanity can hope for.*

—Harriot Stanton Blatch, *A Woman's Point of View: Some Roads to Peace,* 1920

T HE "SEEDS OF REFORM" planted by international women's leaders sprouted
in the years after the First World War. Though the outcomes varied from
the expectations of the reformers, a harvest of new perspectives on women's
roles proceeded in the years following the Treaty of Versailles. In the initial
years following the war, women in Great Britain and the United States gained
considerable ground in political and social rights as a result of the recognition
for wartime service. After both peaceful and aggressive attempts at political
and social change, it was the wartime defense work of women, so willingly
provided, that elicited change. Women in England found increased appreciation for their work efforts in the form of media attention and the opportunity to engage in politics by means of the limited vote bestowed upon them
in 1918 through the Representation of the People Act. This act gave the vote
to women who either met certain property qualifications or were married to
men who held those property qualifications or by means of a university con-
stituency. In this way, Parliament approved female suffrage for the middle and
upper classes only and denied the vote to women of lesser means. Women also
gained the opportunity to serve in British Parliament with the Eligibility of
Women Act in 1918, and wider representation in suffrage came to the women

of Great Britain in 1928 with the Representation of the People Act, which granted women over the age of twenty-one the same enfranchisement as men.

In the United States, the suffrage parades, soap box orations, and daily picketing of the White House initiated by Harriot Stanton Blatch kept the spirit of the movement alive for women and visibly present for male politicians who might otherwise have ignored it in the years leading to war. Despite public criticism of the work of the Women's Land Army of America (WLAA) and labeling the female laborers as "farmerettes," in many ways Blatch's direction of the WLAA changed the dynamic of the suffrage movement from one of speeches and dissent to one of patriotic action. In recognition of the tenacity and commitment of women in peacetime as well as war, Congress passed the Nineteenth Amendment to the Constitution granting the right to vote to all women in 1920, which was then ratified by the necessary number of states (thirty-six). The enfranchisement brought more than just the vote for women; for many it brought the opportunity to serve as elected representatives in state and federal government. In 1920, Blatch commented on the international success of women's suffrage as a result of their leadership in wartime service: "The spread of self-government for women was not checked by the war. In fact, the vote was the prize won by women for unquestioning service. Their ideals as giver and protector of life were sacrificed and defeated, but they achieved a political revolution."[1] For many women, the fight for an equal political voice ended as they gained victory over unequal representation. For others, however, the fight had just begun as the new position of women in labor and politics, presented by years of wartime service, elicited political and social concerns.

Though the movement for female suffrage in America began in the mid-nineteenth century, few women of the initial fight lived to see the fruits of their labor. American women of the 1920s faced varied and competing roles, ranging from those based upon nineteenth-century traditions to those presented in film and media as the "New Woman." The New Woman was a woman of independent thought and a representation of women's political and social liberation. Style of dress, changes in norms for education and courtship, and the lifting of social restrictions such as gendered bans on smoking all contributed to a new sense of liberation for many women. Combined with the era of affluence espoused by many Americans in the 1920s, this new social and political freedom for women provided the opportunity to express themselves through their social behaviors. This new freedom encouraged women to find opportunities in education and in labor, a declining agricultural economy often discouraged women from pursuing lifelong careers in agriculture. Though women participated in wartime agricultural labor in 1917–1918, the two decades that followed brought increased challenges for women gaining successful careers in agriculture. In addition to economic difficulties, societal changes promoted the modern female as urban and regarded rural living as something to be reformed. It appeared that the New Woman was an urban woman, and with her emergence, the idealism of a rural life for women laboring on the land waned.

Women in England experienced similar social change in the 1920s when restrictions on fabric and a shift from a wartime to a consumer economy led to progressive changes in fashion and female style. Socially, single English women pushed boundaries as "Bright Young People" frequented nightclubs, consumed cocktails, and experimented with drugs, much to the chagrin of the older generations. In general, some English elite women pressed harder against the social boundaries that restricted women's roles than did the working class. This new position for women was not for elite women only however; working-class women experienced new social and political freedoms both as a result of wartime service and of the trickledown effect of the boundaries pressed by the elite. Famed suffragist leader and reformer Millicent Fawcett proclaimed that "the war revolutionised the industrial position for women—it found them serfs and left them free." Thus the postwar era for Englishwomen brought not only political equality in the vote and a newfound place in labor, but also freedom from the constraints of the Victorian era.

Ironically, many of the upper-class reformers that fought for female suffrage and space in labor in the years leading up to and throughout the war, altered their perspectives on roles for women and attempted in the interwar years to merge the newly won political rights with a movement to view the role of women as mothers in a new light. For them, the glamour of the society women and the boldness of the New Woman and the Bright Young People were signs of an obtuse society with a misplaced sense of priorities. Viewing the devastation of the war on children's health, many women turned away from the fight for political and economic equality for women and instead turned toward promoting a better appreciation for women as mothers and producers of the nation. To them, mothering and feeding were the real actions of nation building, and they called for a greater respect and recognition of both as tools for world peace. To them, the younger generation of women flaunting glamorous lives while others went hungry was distasteful and a waste of women's potential.

During the interwar years, suffrage and labor leaders like Blatch and Lady Gertrude Denman continued their journeys as social reformers in both national and international realms. For Blatch, her passionate career promoting suffrage took a turn when America engaged in war with Germany in 1917.

Energetic about supporting the war and reeling from the division already existing within the suffrage movement, Blatch turned her focus away from oration on suffrage and toward women's wartime service as proof of women's worth and ability to keep their nation strong. During the war, Blatch and other suffrage and reform leaders such as Jane Addams set out to recruit women's service to the nation by means of food production. At the end of the war, however, the YWCA Women's Press asked Blatch to write an international account of the constructive effects of the war work women completed. Gravely disappointed with the hunger and physical and economic devastation she found in Europe, Blatch's outlook on the war changed. Instead of the positive look at women's war work that the press consigned her to write, Blatch wrote a scathing analysis of the destruction of war, caused and committed by men, and called for more attention to world hunger and support for mothers with children. In a surprising analysis of the effects of the war, Blatch's stance on women's position in the home seemed to change, as now the role of the nurturing mother seemed more significant to her than that of the woman seeking equality in the labor force. She likened the destruction of the earth by means of war to a destruction of femininity and motherhood and argued, "more vivid than the picture of the villages crumbled to dust, more keen than the sorrow of Rheims destroyed, is the appeal to me of the outrage on the fields and forests, on the hedgerows and orchards—of the indignity to nature herself. . . . The bosom of mother earth lay gashed by her sons."[2]

Blatch continued by suggesting that women knew best how to nurture humanity and therefore they should be treated with more respect in the postwar years because they were vitally needed in the reconstruction process. She claimed that it was a masculine destructive force that led too many children into positions of hunger and abandonment. "War has brought its harvest of hate in the hearts of men" she urged, and suggested new paths for peace based upon the mothering instinct of women.[3] She suggested that the world's postwar reconstruction efforts did not focus on what Europe really needed for survival and criticized the priorities of national leaders:

Europe under its masculine regime is not meeting this situation with single-eyed purpose. . . . Perhaps the day will come when the mothers of the world will regard the money cost of giving their babies fine bodies and brains with an abandon equal to that adopted by men in pursuing the sport of riding to hounds, racing horses, or bull fighting. . . . War is a method of argument purely male and adult. Men protect their own children in peace time but in a state of war the interest of the child is not permitted to stand in the way of victory.[4]

Blatch asserted that an appreciation of this nuanced republican mother-hood was tied to women's liberation: "If women as women have a special contribution to make in the upbuilding of a nation, and I presume there is none so cynical as to assert the contrary, obviously they must first have full opportunity to be themselves." In her visits to Europe to gather interviews and observations to write the book, Blatch spoke with many leaders of women's groups, including the former director of the British Women's Land Army, Merial Talbot. Talbot, then working with the National Federation of Women's Institutes (NFWI) alongside Denman, provided the perspective of British women's roles in society that helped Blatch to gain international perspective on the situation of childhood hunger and solutions to it. Just as the local Women's Institutes (WI) of Great Britain shifted their postwar work to supporting the role of women as mothers and household managers, so too it seemed Blatch changed her perspective on what place women should hold in society. For Blatch, however, promoting women was not so much asking them to return home after wartime work as placing that role in a new light of respect in the political realm. She claimed, "Leaders of the women workers . . . see the full value of the protective instinct of women in the home, but apparently they are unaware of the role the same instinct should play on the world stage. The woman is diverted by her very leaders from exercise of her most impelling motives."[5] Thus Blatch, the woman of leisure class who stood on a soapbox on Wall Street not two decades earlier proclaiming to all men who would listen the importance of women to have equality, changed the direction of her attention as a result of witnessing the profound destruction of the war.

Also in contrast was the movement and transition of power and leadership of women's spheres to the working classes. Blatch urged that future progress for women needed to turn from leadership of the leisure class to activism of the working class. Blatch now believed "it is not one whit less dangerous for women of leisure to assume to speak for and lead self-supporting women, than it would be for workingmen to have as spokesmen and leaders men of the capitalistic class. The woman of leisure draws the workers where she herself can go, and that is away from unionism and towards legislatures. If such leadership continues, the self-supporting woman will discover that she has escaped from the political domination of men only to find herself under their complete economic domination."[6] In an effort to address the needs of the working class and mirror the work already under way in England, she called for "central kitchens" to supply mothers and children, national child-care, and better public education for women who worked outside the home. Motherhood pensions became a topic Blatch focused on as the postwar years progressed. Gaining support from politicians such as former U.S. president

Theodore Roosevelt, Blatch believed that the United States was on a path to improved respect for women by means of economic freedom. Centered on a peculiar involvement of the production of food, Blatch moved from suggesting the cultivation of place and space in labor to promoting the cultivation of national and gendered identities of women as mothers of the nation.

In England, postwar work for reconstruction and women's roles in society centered on women's social and political organizations, and the foremost organizations in that movement were the local WIs. The National Federation of Women's Institutes (NFWI) formed in 1916 as the umbrella organization for the local chapters and worked to establish policy and public relations for the group as a whole. Denman, with a history of social reform and interest in the recruitment of women for war service, accepted the position as chairman of the organization (see fig. 4.1). Despite her many other leadership commitments in wartime as well as peacetime, Denman held this position until 1946. Though the Food Department of the Board of Agriculture initially funded the NFWI, Denman wanted the organization to be self-supporting and not affiliated with politics; the organization reached that goal by the 1920s. Though Denman wanted to keep the organization separate from political affiliation, this did not mean that members of the WI stayed away from politics. Under the leadership of Denman, women of all classes exchanged ideas, strategies, and hopes for better lives. In 1919, WI member Madge Watt formed a local WI at Sandringham—the country estate of Her Majesty the Queen—of which the Queen became president. In 1921, WI member Margaret Winteringham was elected as a member of Parliament for Louth, making her the second woman ever to be elected to Parliament.

The NFWI took on the role of strategic planning for women's organizations in the 1920s and 1930s. Bringing together women from all classes of society, from the lady of the manor to her scullery maid to the farmwife, the organization provided an opportunity for women to work together in ways that perhaps had never been possible. The NFWI did have a social aspect in the organizing and planning of local parties and theatrical festivals, though education about women's and children's health, sanitation, and food production were primary goals of the group. In this way the local WIs served much like the county extension agents and home demonstration agents of the U.S. Department of Agriculture, though for Englishwomen a newly found social connection, removed from the ties of the government, brought unity between rural and urban women. At the head of this British movement was Denman, bringing the leadership of both women's place in agricultural labor and efforts to improve home management for housewives into one complete educational organization. At first glance it may seem as if the two motives were in

FIGURE 4.1. *Lady Gertrude Denman*. Unknown photographer. Frontispiece from Gervas Huxley, *Lady Denman, G. B. E.*

contrast to each other, as efforts to improve home management hardly sound liberating or progressive. In reality, however, members of the WIs were some of the most radical of their time. Many of the first officers were suffragists, and some were quite notorious for their tactics to gain political attention. For example, Edith Rigby, known for sabotaging sports fields and throwing black puddings and bombs at Winston Churchill in 1913, found the idea of the WIs inspirational, proclaiming it "a pillar supporting the temple of national enlightenment."[7] Thus English reformers, much like their American counterparts, perceived control over the education and progress of home life a highly desired outcome in the wake of a war so destructive to human life and progress.

Others such as American social reformer Jane Addams were influenced by the International Council of Women toward her national efforts at conceiving a progressive future for the working classes. In her postwar work *Peace and Bread in Time of War*, Addams suggested that peace and bread were "inseparably connected" as hunger only perpetuated strife and conflict. She further argued that as producers and managers of food, women of the world had a duty to focus on finding both local and global solutions to the situation. Thus the leadership for women in both England and the United States took an interesting turn in the postwar years, as the leaders, heavily influenced by international events and need, shifted their reform focus from both food production and education to childhood health. Consequently, while the reformers saw this shift as a progressive move for the world's populations, many political leaders saw this as an opportunity to exhale: the movement of women to achieve political and economic equality seemed diverted. It was through this transition that the Progressive Era focus on women's role in labor as a path to equality yielded to the dire economic, nutritional, and health needs in the postwar world.

Women's role in labor did change in the postwar years as new opportunities for women in labor presented new challenges. In both England and the United States, a marked wartime decrease in the number of women employed as domestic servants meant that women sought new occupations, and often those new occupations provided skills that women used after the war's end. Skills however, did not necessarily mean better pay. As the years progressed after the war, women in England saw their pay revert back to prewar levels, which equated about one-half that of men. In England, hostility toward married women "taking" the jobs of men after the war prompted a social stigma against hiring married women. In America, the years immediately after the war brought prosperity and an abundance of labor opportunities for workers. Even though some Americans did not favor the idea of women as equally paid laborers, there was work to be found for women in America. Just as new opportunities in clerical labor emerged in America, women in areas such as farming or industry started to face wage discrimination as fears over male wages and employment levels increased. The government and several women's unions took on the task of directing that desire to work, however. The Department of Labor organized a Women's Bureau, which investigated and reported about the conditions of labor opportunities for women, often reporting about the influence of work upon a woman's relationship with her family. While women of both nations gained some ground in agricultural labor after the First World War, the years of economic depression brought increasing stress on the unemployed in both England and the United States.

From Depression to War: An Agricultural Struggle

In the years after the war, Herbert Hoover headed the American Relief Administration, providing relief to the millions of people starving in Europe, including Germany and Bolshevik Russia. He worked to blend the efforts of many local and private groups and institutions to aid the world's economic devastation and access to food. Despite national criticism for this global focus, his work earned him the title of one of the "Ten Most Important Living Americans" by the *New York Times*. His interwar efforts established a precedent in both American and international politics. The economic, environmental, and social devastation of the global depressions brought new levels of bureaucracy into British and American culture when society called for assistance and national intervention. Economic devastation brought with it a birth of two unique political cultures built upon the creation of agencies to cure future ailments of the nations. Both the United States and England experienced significant shifts in rural and urban demographics in the interwar years; however the shifts represented divergent demographic representations. Whereas more than 60 percent of all Americans lived in rural areas in 1900, by the end of the First World War that number decreased to nearly 48 percent. In addition, with the growing economic struggles and the devastation of the Dust Bowl, many people in rural areas gave up hope for a future in agriculture and moved to urban areas. By 1940, the number of people in the United States living in rural areas decreased to 43.5 percent and continued to decline year after year. For the British, however, though the percent of rural dwellers remained smaller than urban dwellers, in the postwar years the "rural idyll" began to grow as overcrowding in the cities led to a growing movement toward deurbanization among the middle and upper classes. Though farm populations dwindled, life in the country prospered. In the year to come, second homes of the elite built in the countryside turned England's country life into a wealthier lifestyle than that of the American rural farm families with declining economies. It is no wonder, then, that the WIs of England continued to draw greater social connections between the elite and the farm women as there was less geographic separation between the classes. For the United States, however, the divide between the urban and the rural populations shifted more toward the haves and the have-nots as America faced the agricultural struggle of the 1930s that sent many farmers migrating to the urban areas for economic survival.

In correspondence with the decreasing farm populations, the governments of the United States and Great Britain sought strength in the management of the dwindling employment of farming. For the people of Great Britain, agricultural training for women rested in the expertise of the many private agricultural and horticultural training schools developed to train women in the wake of the First World War. The Women's Farm and Garden Union (WFGU) in conjunction with the local WIs also coordinated training for women. American women seeking training in agriculture found it in the many college programs designed for women during the First World War. By providing agricultural training as a form of study for women, these colleges legitimized agricultural labor for women, albeit minutely. As the need and desire for female labor waned in the postwar years, so did the programs aimed directly at women. Study in agriculture or horticulture for women rested in local gardening clubs or the Women's National Farm and Garden Association (WNFGA). Not having an umbrella organization like the WI to coordinate such training in America, training was ad hoc and sporadic at best, providing more education in heavily populated urban areas where membership numbers proved larger. As a result, small communities and rural women turned to the extension agents and home demonstration agents of the Department of Agriculture to provide training and information on innovation and modernity in agricultural practices.

The mechanization of agricultural labor became the international symbol of modernity in both the interwar and postwar years. Joseph Stalin argued that the Soviet Union should climb out of its fifty-year deficit in industrial development and develop the largest agricultural production in the world with the use of new technology and the tractor. Stalin's "harvesting campaign" in 1931 sought to increase agricultural production to twenty million hectares through the use of tractors.[8] Not only limited to the Soviet Union, the international image and association of tractors as progress and symbols of a modern nation fueled economic recovery campaigns across the globe. Whereas the tractor was a machine of destruction, to many it was the savior of a solid economy as a cultivator of wealth. Propaganda posters and popular culture images portrayed women atop tractors as powerful political symbols of victory for many nations. This connection of political ideology and the mechanization of labor spread into the war and postwar period, manifesting itself into many diplomatic quandaries for the Western World.[9] During the Second World War, however, the symbol and image of women and tractors blended two things the Western world still found uncertain: the power of machinery on the farm and the power of women as farm workers.

How the image of women as symbols of victory played out in the years of global depression, however, is less obvious. What is clear is the stress upon agricultural labor and the use and abuses of technology on farms. The American Great Depression affected land use in a myriad of ways. During the decade of the 1930s, Americans suffered not only severe economic losses but environmental and agricultural losses as well. Overuse of the soil without rotation, combined with environmental changes, led to a disastrous effect on the farm populations. During the severe drought across the Great Plains region that came to be known as the Dust Bowl, people in that region lost crops, homes, and lives as a result of the thick dust storms that blew away their understanding and pride with relentless antagonism. It is not unreasonable to say that Americans suffered economically, environmentally, and psychologically. Thus for the rural populations who lived in the Southern Plains, the environmental challenges of the Dust Bowl compounded the national economic and psychological challenges of the Great Depression that were brought about after decades of overproduction and underconsumption, a series of economic recessions, and the culmination of these events—the stock market crash on October 29, 1929.

The effects and devastation of the Dust Bowl stretched far beyond its geographical borders, however, as the loss of crops in this region greatly affected the food availability in other areas of America and abroad. Many European nations increasingly relied on American agricultural exports and thus the shortages affected those who sought America's export. On the other hand, European nations lagged in recovery from their own postwar economic depression, and the American economic instability brought about by the stock market crash did not help matters. Thus for these nations, their ability to consume American exports was diminished simply by their own economic woes. Either way you look at it, that agricultural shortages in the United States negatively impacted exportation to Europe or that European economic depression increased the need for importation, it was a bleak time and agriculture was a primary factor in the creation of such bleakness. The American "New Deal" and Depression era agricultural organizations of the 1930s responded to the dire need of suffering Americans. Under the leadership of American president Franklin Delano Roosevelt, the Civilian Conservation Corps (CCC) and the Tennessee Valley Authority (TVA), among other initiatives, brought the environment under tighter governmental management and consideration. Through the CCC, the USDA, and the Soil Conservation Service, training for men, by men, served as the new standard for modern agricultural production. From this point forward, such organizations viewed the land, from the farm to the forest, as a resource to stabilize and preserve the economy of the nation. This added a level of bureaucracy to the management and use of lands, a bureaucracy that provided a structure for organization of the American domestic war effort a decade later.

The global economic depression after the First World War affected not only the British economy, but also British agricultural production. Just weeks after the armistice of the First World War, the British government mandated a cease and desist order on the destruction of all materials not potentially edible and ordered they be used in the making of oils and fertilizers.[10] The growing European demand for wheat at the turn of the century inspired farmers in America and Canada to produce as much as possible for export. This dependence proved profitable up until the reconstruction efforts of the First World War when many nations suffered economically and North American droughts and drops in agricultural production limited food exports. Though nations such as Italy and France held substantial land resources for agriculture, in the 1930s they both relied heavily on importation of certain basic foodstuffs.[11] This growing demand on North American agriculture placed European nations, and especially England, in a dangerous dependency that threatened economic stability. As a result, Lady Denman worked with other NFWI leaders to continue to recruit and train additional agricultural labor and to promote increased production in urban areas.

Globally, nations suffered to varying degrees due to the economic instability brought about by overindustrialization and world war. To deny people consumer goods due to a poor economy was one thing, but to deny or deprive people of food was a threat to survival, a threat that no one forgot when increasing international hostilities intonated war. Adolf Hitler preyed on such social threats by using hunger as a topic for discussion and blame. Playing to the fears of the German population, he addressed the issue of hunger to gain support of the German people who suffered greatly at the hands of grudging European policy after the First World War. For Germans, paying reparations for the First World War, combined with decreased ability to import foodstuffs due to environmental damage caused by war, left little ability to support the increasing agriculture need. This need, combined with skyrocketing inflation, left millions starving and looking for solutions. Food meant survival and a hope for the future and for many of the poorer classes, who sought political change, the Second World War was fought over such means of survival. Though other nations did not suffer from hunger quite to the extent Germany did, the collective memories of the depression years certainly center on "doing without" and more often than not that meant food.[12] Reviewed from that perspective, the cultivation of national lands was first and foremost as significant as fighting on the front lines. Thus, in the simplest of terms, cultivating victory meant ensuring survival (see fig. 4.2).

The interwar years altered the international power dynamics of food and politics. While Great Britain faced reconstruction costs and social transitions, the United States moved forward as a leader in reconstruction with food as the tool for success. Through its efforts at reconstruction after the war for the millions of hungry people in Europe, America gained the reputation as the provider of abundance. When suffrage leaders of Great Britain and the United States focused their attention on international child health and hunger relief efforts, governments treated leaders' suggestions to commemorate and support the role of motherhood as a cure for the disruption of society caused by female activism and as an opportunity to remove women from their small place in agricultural labor and place them back into traditional spheres of home management.

If the First World War did anything to promote the acceptance of women as legitimate and effective agricultural workers, it convinced farmers that

FIGURE 4.2. Lee Russell, *Do Your Part*, 1940. Farm Security Administration, Library of Congress, LC-USF345-007869-ZA.

many women farm laborers worked as hard and as well as men. The Second World War was markedly different from the First World War, however. Convincing both governments and a new generation of farmers to accept women laborers a second time brought varied challenges to both nations. These dynamics changed in part from national and international trends and ideas about food relief, and in part from the changing stances on women's roles in the home as expressed by suffrage leaders after the war. Women used agricultural labor and management as a springboard for increased social activism by means of public service. In recalling work of various women's organizations during the interwar period to bring relief to the hungry and needy of the world, many women expressed intense satisfaction in the work they pursued in the 1920s and 1930s. More than acceptance from men and government agencies, women found increased appreciation for their work among themselves; many found, as Blatch proclaimed, "the Anglo-Saxon woman has not so much lack of faith in her men folk as unbound faith in herself."[13]

❦ CHAPTER 5

"A Call to Farms"

I am peeling carrots at the kitchen sink. Nothing unusual about that, but for the past sixty years, every time I do this job, my mind goes back to my first day as a farm labourer. It was in April 1941 and there were an awful lot of carrots, at least five acres of them. Because this was fiddling work, the local gang of women casual workers had been called in. We had to pick up the carrots as they were ploughed out, rub off any soil and put them into net sacks.

There were also the six Land Army girls who were already employed on the farm before I arrived. The carrots were all shapes and sizes and some looked rather rude, as carrots do sometimes. This was the delight of the village women, who roared with laughter and made suggestive remarks and waved the carrots around, looking at us girls to see how we were taking it, especially at me, the newest recruit and a bit shy. Laughter is infectious and it was all good humored and when the long back-breaking day's work finally ended, I pedaled my bike wearily eight miles home.

—Joan Snelling, *A Land Girl's War*, 1920

F OR JOAN SNELLING, life as a British "land girl" during the Second World War brought adventure, romance, and farming experiences she never forgot. Born in London in 1922, Joan learned of the outbreak of war while on holiday with her family in Norfolk. Fearing the air raids expected upon the urban areas of the country, her family split up after hearing the news. While her father returned to London to go back to work, Joan, her mother, her sister-in-law, and a niece stayed in a rented bungalow to wait the war out. Her family expected the war to be over by Christmas. It of course did not end that quickly, and at seventeen years of age Joan made herself useful to the household by gardening and acting as the household "handyman." In 1941 however, England issued a Register for Employment Order for all women between the ages of eighteen and forty-five. At eighteen Joan decided to try out her new-found gardening skills and joined the British Women's Land Army (WLA) in

Norfolk where she remained an additional thirty years after her Land Army service.[1]

Though not all female agriculturalists during the Second World War claimed similar backgrounds or experiences, Joan Snelling's story exemplifies many basic themes in the lives of those who worked in the fields of both England and the United States. Conflicting public attitudes, varied demographics, and hard labor are just some of the challenges shared by the female laborers. While WLA and national leaders espoused the sometimes conflicting rhetoric of women's wartime roles and nationalism, women laborers faced competing opinions about how best to produce food for the nation and the world. Responding to the "call to farms," these women of mostly urban backgrounds struggled successfully and occasionally unsuccessfully to increase the food supply of the Allies in the face of adversity. With the direction of new government leaders and old reformers alike, women forged new paths in agricultural labor. While political goals influenced women's service in the WLAs less than it did during the First World War, government agencies of both nations used the political significance of the cultivation of food to brand national identity ironically for both creation and destruction. As the image of the female agricultural laborer emerged in the popular culture, American and British women faced food shortages with hard labor and a sense of adventure amid a world of political strife.

The British Need

The threat of a new war affected the British in distinctly different ways than the First World War did. Remembering the loss of nearly one million British lives and sacrifices made during the First World War and observing the geographic and economic destruction in the decade that followed, the British people feared the potential devastation of another global war.[2] Whereas the air raid precautions of the First World War seemed like adventures and novelties to some Britons initially, the seriousness of the destruction of the first war prompted a markedly more somber attitude toward preparation for a second war. By importing nearly two-thirds of its food supply before the war, the threat of food shortage once again plagued England.[3] As soon as the threat of war loomed heavily enough over Europe in the 1930s to warrant a concern for national security, the British began preparations to fortify England against civilian casualties and hunger. One preparation was the organization of a renewed WLA in June 1939, three months *before* Britain made declarations of war on Germany. Despite some hesitancy by rural farmers, the British government had no other choice than to encourage the employment of all available able-bodied adults to continue the work of the nation during the war crisis.

Women's clubs and organizations urged the government to respond quickly to the threat of war and supply the fields of England with female laborers trained in agricultural trades. Lady Gertrude Denman was one of the many female public figures eager to assist in the recruitment of female labor. Lady Denman previously served as the assistant director of the British WLA in the First World War; therefore she was a logical choice to assume the role of honorary director of the WLA during the Second World War. Denman's interest in contributing to the war effort stemmed from her previous international philanthropic adventures. Her past political activism as a reformer for suffrage led her to serve in many political and social organizations before her work with the WLA. She married Lord Denman, the fifth governor-general of Australia, and served the British Empire as chairman of the National Federation of Women's Institutes (NFWI), a women's educational and social organization, from 1917 until 1946.[4] In 1917 during her service as assistant director of the British WLA in the First World War, she continued to aid in the promotion and structure of women's groups as the head the NFWI.[5] Gertrude, known as "Trudie" by her friends, spent the larger part of her life organizing education and support for women in the production of food and in the general management of the home and care for children—roles she felt were immensely valuable.

Shortly after the British entry into war in September 1939, government publication of propaganda and instructional pamphlets emerged and some recruited women to service in the WLA. Denman publicly announced that the WLA already recruited over ten thousand women, and the trainees grew in numbers by the day. The announcement came with a warning, however, that the war demanded the immediate attention of every woman able to help, and argued,

> Germany is trying to starve the British People into submission. To win the war, our country must defeat the blockade. This is the joint task of the British Navy and of Britain's great field force of agricultural workers. . . . The calling up of men from the land has been slow and the growth of the Land Army correspondingly gradual. Farmers' memories are short, and in spite of good work done on the land by women during the last war, the Land Army has had to encounter much prejudice against the employment of women's labour. This prejudice has now almost everywhere been overcome through the really magnificent service given by the first few thousand employed volunteers who worked through the bitter winter of 1939 under conditions of great difficulty and loneliness and have stuck to their jobs ever since. . . . Men are beginning to go from the land into the fighting services; huge new

tracts of land are being ploughed up to produce food for the people of this country and feeding-stuffs for stock. Every acre of pasture that goes under the plough means a demand for additional labour.[6]

She urged women desiring to spend their wartime service in a country environment rather than in a factory environment to consider the WLA as their own form of military service, for "it is in the fields of Britain that the most critical battle of the present war may well be fought and won."[7]

In addition to the leadership of Denman, British women found encouragement from other female public figures during the Second World War as well. Britain's Queen Elizabeth extended words of encouragement and gratitude toward the thousands of English women who worked to achieve victory through agricultural labor. In a speech to the WLA at the Mansion House on December 7, 1945, she proclaimed: "During the years of war, my thoughts have very often been with the Land Army. You came, in those distant days six years ago, with your great gifts of youth and strength and with high purpose, to serve your Country in her hour of need, and never have British women and girls shown more capacity or more pluck. On the farms and in the fields, forests and gardens, you took your place in the Battle of Freedom, and through your endurance and your toil you supplied the needs of the Island and sustained the life of the nation."[8] Such praise of the land girls and their achievements was widely popular during the era, but the praise itself held multiple purposes. The praise unified a nation of women left alone to sustain and then perhaps prepare to rebuild the empire after the mass destruction of two world wars within a mere three decades. Queen Elizabeth reaffirmed this notion at the end of the war: "The Land Army has been fortunate that even in the darkest war years its task has been mainly one of creation, not of destruction. Now ahead of us lies the greatest creative task of all—the building of a peaceful and peace-loving world. Some of you—many of you, I hope—will share in this task by continuing in your present work where you are still so greatly needed. And because the service of the land girl is honoured and appreciated, she can contribute richly and usefully, to the life of the community in which she lives and works."[9]

The British women who joined the WLA volunteered to aid their country in its great time of need, but many found unexpected personal rewards. Many land girls made friendships that lasted the rest of their lives and some found romance and marriage a potential benefit of working on a bachelor's or widower's farm.[10] English girls who joined the WLA came from a variety of occupations and families. From former textile mill managers and factory workers to daughters of soldiers and local businessmen, these young women sought not only to aid the war effort, but also to find some kind of war work that appeared to provide a sense of healthy diversion when the talk of death and destruction loomed around every corner. Just as in the First World War, the WLA again offered women the opportunity for adventure outside of their parents' homes and neighborhoods.[11] In a time when the threat of air raids made the heavily populated urban areas of England unsafe for children, English families supported young women of the WLA, who were too old to be relocated to the English countryside with their younger siblings and neighbors, to instead engage in rural agricultural work and activity that better protected them from the dangers of urban living during wartime. The numbers of WLA recruits reflected this increased support, as nearly twice as many women enlisted in the first few months of the Second World War as enlisted during the initial months of the WLA in 1917.[12] The government soon spread news of the work and encouraged international attention on how young English women were poised and ready to "swing into action" (see fig. 5.1).

Not all recruits were young single women, however. Some were in their twenties and thirties and held other reasons for enlistment. Some women were relatives or fiancées of soldiers fighting the war and felt the need to be useful and speed their loved ones' return, whereas other young women simply sought a life in the country outside of the urban threat of air raids. Irene Gibbs, Anne Hall, Irene Grimwood, Joan Snelling, and Pat Kemp are just a few of the many English land girls who recall vividly the struggles and benefits of working as a land girl. Irene Gibbs, a single woman just twenty years old, decided to leave the factory work of cigarette making to join the WLA in 1942. Gibbs made the decision to leave Churchman's cigarette factory to have the chance to aid the war effort in a cleaner environment "in the open air," and thus found the work of the WLA the right fit for her. The county office where she signed up and interviewed displayed enough visual propaganda in pictures and posters adorning the walls to inspire women to imagine themselves as one of the land girls leading horses and driving tractors among other farm work. Irene fixed her eye upon an image of a baby calf when WLA county secretary Mrs. Sunderland-Taylor approached her and warned, "It won't be all baby calves and sunshine, you know" (see figs. 5.2 and 5.3).[13]

Anne Hall, a twenty-year-old hospital clerk from London, and her sister Cara joined the British WLA in June 1940, much to the dismay of their father. He called their enlistment "impetuous" and warned them about the hard labor and life of a farm worker. Despite such discouragement, Irene and her sister Cara found the training provided by the WLA quite enjoyable and encouraging, though Irene admitted their inexperience at many basic tasks surely provided their trainers and hosts "many a laugh," such as when a trainer sud-

FIGURE 5.1. *Food in England*, 1940. "The British Women's Land Army swings into action. Shown here at haymaking, these typists, clerks, and sales-girls are helping during the crop season to supply England with much-needed food." Office of War Information, Library of Congress Prints and Photographs Division, LC-USE6-D-010011.

FIGURE 5.2. *Food in England*, 1943. "A woman in Britain's Land Army clears out a pig-house. Along with many other British women she works on a farm to supply her country with essential food." Office of War Information, Library of Congress Prints and Photographs Division, LC-USE6-D-010009.

FIGURE 5.3. *Food in England*, 1943. "Smiling with health, this former London dressmaker who joined the Women's Land Army in Britain claims she won't go back to dressmaking. More than 100,000 women this year will be enlisted in the Women's Land Army." Office of War Information, Library of Congress Prints and Photographs Division, LC-USE6-D-010005.

denly asked her sister Cara to stop a cow from leaving the shed, whereby immediately she flung her arms around the cow's neck, only to be thrown to the ground. After completing the four weeks of hands-on training followed by a week of rest, the two girls arrived at their first assignment ready for duty and unaware of how different life on a training farm was from life on a small family-owned farm. Against British WLA policy, the farmers provided only one bed for the girls to share instead of the required individual beds specified by the WLA and requested that the girls assist in the housekeeping in addition to their farming duties. Upon the girls' protest of the conditions provided at the farm, the farming couple gave the girls additional outdoor chores such as chopping wood or bringing in coal and found additional field duties to keep the girls occupied in between regular farm chores.[14] As a result of the farmers' dismay toward urban women taking on farm work previously performed by men, it was not uncommon for farmers of both Britain and the United States to assign duties beyond the WLA guidelines, much to the dismay of the workers and WLA leaders attempting to keep the duties focused on future career skills rather than on the tasks of domestic servitude.

English farmers signed formal agreements with the WLA to pay each worker for her services, although the WLA allowed them to pay a worker less if the farm provided room and board to the worker. This payment was the only form of compensation the women of the WLA received for their services, outside of occasional travel passes. Anne and Cara found difficulty with this arrangement as, after a month of work at their first assignment, the farm did not provide any payment for their work even after their inquiry. After they wrote to their local representative expressing concern for the conditions at the farm, the local WLA transferred the girls to temporary positions picking potatoes at Sparsholt Farm Institute near Winchester, and the family they left replaced them with a combination of family members and friends that were "Austrian Jewish immigrants" who, Anne and Cara agreed, seemed to be a better fit for the mix of domestic and farm work that the family needed and wanted.[15]

Transferring to Sparsholt Farm Institute, a larger professional farm, Anne bid farewell to her sister, who left the WLA to attend college. Anne found herself in a considerably more comfortable atmosphere in a dormitory for land girls that included accommodations such as running hot water and a personal cubicle with walls around her bed as well as a dresser and wardrobe for her personal use. "How I wished Cara could have enjoyed this luxury accommodation with me," she recalled. Anne's comfort in her new position increased as she obtained a more permanent position at Sparsholt Farm Institute that paid thirty-five shillings a week, considerably high wages for a land girl in 1940 and 1941.[16]

British land girls during the Second World War typically earned anywhere from 28 to 32 shillings a week, depending upon the training and experience of the worker, the type of employment, and accommodations provided, though some earned more. Toward the end of the war, some workers earned as much as 48 shillings to £1 a week, and for some land girls who continued to live at home while traveling back and forth to farm, this wage made them feel relatively wealthy in wartime.[17] Regardless, average wartime agricultural wages for men rose from £1 to £3 per week by the end of the war, and the average weekly wage in 1940 was £4.6; and though women did not earn at the same rates as men, opportunity to take on their factory and other skilled jobs during the war did bring increases in women's income levels. Thus women worked on farms not for financial gain but for other more ideological reasons.

Anne and her sister Cara found farm life to be every bit as hard as their father warned them it would be, but found satisfaction in it as well. Anne recalls fond memories of milking both by hand and by machine, harvesting corn, and caring for horses. Land girls who stayed in hostels found their social lives altered because of service in the WLA but never boring. The alteration of English life did not mean that individuals shunned all forms of entertainment; the girls found various forms of diversion and entertainment on the occasional Sunday afternoon off or in the evening after the completion of all the farm work. Anne, Cara, and many other land girls like them found comfort in making friends out of strangers they met in local pubs, cafes, and theaters while away for a few hours each week from the farms they enlisted to serve. Many hostels held dances, and most gave the girls some autonomy to travel to the local entertainment venues without chaperons, provided they met the curfew established. At these venues, many land girls had the opportunity to mingle both with men ineligible for military duty or with English or American soldiers stationed in or returned to England for some reason. Many women developed relationships with American soldiers filtering into the war effort through England and such relationships affected the social perception of young American soldiers in and around England.[18]

The WLA often only provided brief training of the women who enlisted, and for the most part the training was unregulated. Although some successful training facilities developed, due to the immediate need most new WLA workers simply trained on farms with more experienced land girls. Many land girls with an interest in a career in agriculture went on to obtain certificates from university programs that offered certification for women and in general proficiency in agriculture near the war's end. Through agricultural training programs, the British WLA sought more than the mere protection of foodstuff levels during wartime, however. By promoting many young women into agricultural positions, the empire relieved reformers in cities of the burden of removing women from employment considered "less desirable." The monthly newsletter of the British WLA, *The Land Girl*, often made note of the changes in lifestyle many women made to serve their country. In many ways, this type of reporting served to illustrate how such an organization reformed and improved the lives of many young women. Many of the articles presented for the laborers implied that the WLA was a vehicle to transition women from bad to good through labor on the land. For example, *The Land Girl* detailed the success of a winner of the WLA quarterly prize for "outstanding long and good service." A contributor to *The Land Girl* noted that the winner, Mrs. A. E. (Hodder) Price of Gloucestershire, formerly worked as a barmaid during her single life, and according to the contributor, the experience with the WLA aided her in obtaining an apparently more socially acceptable career as well as a husband, for Miss Hodder married a farmer's son. In describing Hodder's newfound career in agriculture, begun as a member of the WLA, the editor claimed, "it must have been quite a change to move into the dairy . . . but evidently Mrs. Price enjoyed the change. . . . To come on the land straight from the bar and do 'milking and G. F.' for over six years bears splendid witness to this volunteer's character as well as to her industry and skill. Gloucestershire must have been very proud of Mrs. Price when she was presented with her prize."[19]

The British WLA served the political interest and represented the national image in other ways as well. It requested and promoted several active members to represent the WLA and the empire in international affairs. A delegation committee of the WLA chose Pauline Spaulding to represent the WLA and in a larger sense the British Empire and Western ideas of progress as part of a "delegation of young people" known as the Anglo-Soviet Anti-Fascist Youth Organisation. An issue of *The Land Girl* noted that Miss Spaulding served the WLA for three and a half years, held a proficiency badge as a milker, and was "particularly interested in progressive and intensive farming," implying the strength of Western ideals of production though training and employment programs associated with the British WLA. By spreading the image of the WLA through members such as Pauline, the Anglo-Soviet Anti-Fascist Youth Organisation displayed women and agriculture simultaneously as symbols of the strength of the empire.[20]

Britain rewarded the women who served in the WLA in very different ways than it did men in the armed services: land girls did not receive wages, gratuities (payment upon the end of service to ease the transition back into civilian life), or employment placement assistance upon the end of their service.

What little reward the women received came in the form of encouragement and occasional public acclaim. Queen Elizabeth and Princesses Elizabeth and Margaret Rose encouraged the women of the British WLA on July 3, 1943, by hosting a party at Buckingham Palace for three hundred land girls to celebrate the fourth anniversary of the British WLA. At the party each girl was presented to and shook hands with the queen and princesses.[21] As the years progressed, the British WLA also rewarded land girls for their terms of service with badges to be sewn onto their armbands. Members sewed the red "half diamond" onto the green armband for each six months of service to the organization; after four years of service the green armband could be exchanged for a red armband and then exchanged for a coveted yellow armband after eight years of service. At the end of the war, however, some WLA members had completed only six years of service, yet in a public display of acknowledgment, Queen Elizabeth herself awarded "golden armlets" to 235 members.[22] One ex-land girl claims Britain awarded her a "golden badge" for ten years of service, but unfortunately no official service records found confirm that as of yet.

The American Need

As in Britain, the American campaign for the WLA in the Second World War was more governmentally structured than in the First World War. Unlike its British counterpart, however, the Women's Land Army of America (WLAA), so active during the First World War, did not reorganize at the outbreak of war in Europe or even at the initial American entry. In fact, the Department of Agriculture (USDA) officially rejected the idea of the organization of a WLAA at the beginning of the war. The USDA claimed a "national organized uniformed group of women [was] less promising than other potential farm labor reserves, particularly that of rural citizenry and school youth."[23] As a result, Eleanor Roosevelt and other leaders of women's groups encouraged small local groups of female laborers like the Connecticut Land Army to test the viability of a second land army. With varied amounts of training and support until a unified support system was established, these initial groups provided the foundation for the second land army. After touring England's homefront efforts during the fall of 1942, Eleanor Roosevelt promoted American involvement in a WLA, though she noted the "physical differences" between England and the United States, that is, the differences in the amount of land available for use warranted differences in structures and needs of such an organization.[24] After the visit, Eleanor Roosevelt sent a telegram to Lady Denman offering her congratulations for the work of the WLA and continued her world tour, including a stop in New Zealand to see the skilled work of the WLA there. She then returned to the United States with a determination to see an organized WLA bring paid war work for the American women already organized in unpaid farm service.

In March 1943, President Roosevelt signed an executive order consolidating the Food Production Administration, the Commodity Credit Corporation, and the Extension Service all under a division of the USDA and delegating great wartime powers to Chester C. Davis, the new Food Administrator. In a press conference, President Roosevelt promised to provide more machinery and labor for farmers in need and announced the possible deferment from the draft of some 3,550,000 servicemen by the end of the year because of their vital roles on the land. While admitting that these deferrals excused many young men from service, he suggested that plans to organize a "land army" were inevitable because many young men would leave the farms to join the service or move to urban areas seeking higher wages anyway.[25] His idea of a land army included high school students, foreign laborers, women, and others who could volunteer for full- or part-time work on local farms.

Despite awareness of the dire shortage of farm labor in the face of allied food shortages, many in the American government like Secretary of Agriculture Wickard opposed the official call for women to farms. Congress did not approve a budget for the funding of the WLA as a small part of a mobile farm relief bill until 1943. After much evidence of successful university training already under way for women to work on farms, as well as the prodding by President Roosevelt and his wife, Eleanor, Wickard acquiesced. In April of that year, Congress attempted to pass a bill allotting $40 million for agricultural labor relief that included importing farm workers from Mexico and the Bahamas, employing workers over 65 years of age, and employing women to fill the remaining gap; the Senate ultimately approved $26.1 million of that amount for the creation of such a diverse "mobile land army." For America, the image of sending white middle-class urban women to the fields to work was not as prevalent or as accepted as it was in England. The USDA initially supported importing immigrants and temporary foreign labor rather than sending in female agriculturalists. This is reflected in the propaganda of the food campaigns of the USDA, which blamed food crises on the waste of middle-class households and promoted white middle-class women to fight on the home front from their kitchens.[26] To be fair, influence from former WLAA director Harriot Stanton Blatch encouraged attention on women as mothers of the nation. Nonetheless, as the war progressed and the agricultural labor shortages increased, and as the number of volunteers for a female land army increased, acceptance of white female farm workers increased as well. Finally

FIGURE 5.4. *Florence Hall,* 1943. National Archives and Records Administration, Washington, D.C., 16-G-24-A-N-4736.

in 1943 the USDA formally adopted a revised WLA (leaders dropped the second "A" from WLAA) to work in cooperation with the U.S. Crop Corps, a USDA-sponsored organization already recruiting urban men and boys to farm work.

In April 1943 the American WLA organized under the leadership of Florence Louise Hall, former senior home economist of the USDA Extension Service (see fig. 5.4). Hall's experience in agriculture also included living on her family's farm as a child and receiving an honorary degree in home economics from Michigan Agricultural College in 1933.[27] Just as Harriot Stanton Blatch and Jane Addams, Hall's experience with the Food Administration stemmed from food production and conservation in the First World War, when she worked in 1917 as one of Hoover's home demonstration agents, training both rural and urban women. Though much less publicly lauded than her British counterpart, Lady Gertrude Denman, Hall attempted to make herself and the WLA visible to the American public and posed for many publicity photos alongside workers to promote the organization and to assert the strength of its leadership. In many ways the dichotomy of women's equality in labor through the WLA and the promotion of women's sphere in the home mirrored that of Denman. Though historian Stephanie Carpenter claims Hall's mixture of a rural background with an urban education, former career in the USDA, and extension service made her the ideal representative for the female farm laborer, the irony of those positions as promoting both food conservation labor in the home yet increased production through advancement in women's space in labor conflicted and reflected the changing ideas about women's identity expressed decades earlier by Blatch and Addams.[28]

In a public announcement about the details of the new organization, Hall stated that the WLAA aimed to recruit approximately sixty thousand members, and offer training, placement, housing, and transportation. Of those sixty thousand, ten thousand would serve as year-round workers.[29] Hall hoped to recruit the others from urban housewives, college students on break, or industrial workers in second or alternating shifts. Thanks to the attention by the media to the recruitment of women farm workers, however, more than three hundred thousand "non-farm women" worked on farms from September 1942 to September 1943; for the entire year of 1943, that number rose to about six hundred thousand when counting part-time workers assisting in the harvest during their vacations, college holiday breaks, and so forth.[30] Part of the success of the recruitment of urban women to farms rested in the organizational efforts of people outside of the WLA. Both the U.S. Employment Service and the American Women's Voluntary Service recruited and placed farm personnel in the WLA.[31] Alice Acheson, wife of Assistant Secretary of State Dean Acheson, for example, worked through the American Women's Voluntary Service to recruit women farm workers. Dean Acheson's work implementing the Lend-Lease program to aid Great Britain with supplies surely influenced her own work in relieving food shortages. In September 1943 her success in labor recruitment earned her the position of chair of the Women's Advisory Committee to the WLA.[32] In that same year, M. C. Wilson, chief of the USDA Department of Field Statistics and Training, encouraged women to participate in agricultural production: "The United Nations must have food and it is the farmers of America who must grow this food. The patriotism of city women as well as farm women will bring them to the farms so that the United States may fulfill this obligation to its allies."[33] In 1944 the WLA recruitment goal increased to four hundred thousand women even though the USDA estimated that the nation needed nearly eight hundred thousand women to fill the agricultural jobs left by men, thirty thousand in New York State alone.[34]

The initial plan called for organizing women into three laboring classes: the first class of laboring women to work year-round, live on-site at participating farms, and receive the going wage of other farm laborers in that particular region; a second class of seasonal workers such as teachers who "either could not or did not want to spend all their time at farm work"; and a third class of emergency laborers for short-term assignments such as harvesting crops for single day or weekend or for weeklong projects.[35] Unlike the First World War, however, the American WLA looked for some of the enlisted women to perform duties that might include relieving "farm women of household cares to free them for more laborious agricultural service."[36]

This difference in attitudes toward women's acceptable place in work and in the home is reflected in the identity of the female home worker in America during the time as the USDA and the popular media placed more attention on returning labor to the home than on promoting the technological advancements that might free women from extra labor in the home.[37] These differences profoundly shaped the identity of the nation, homebound women and female agriculturalists alike. For America, women and women's labor in the domestic sphere (especially in the kitchen) symbolized the abundance of the nation. For women managing a household, programs the USDA offered in food conservation referred to her wasteful past and called for her to repent, thus creating an implied identity attached to the domestic sphere where women must prove their worth in efficiency and labor.

Like their British sisters, American women found resistance to their employment as serious agricultural laborers. "Here, as in England, farmers are not ordinarily enthusiastic about getting city women as helpers," claimed M. C. Wilson, chief of the Division of Field Studies and Training of the USDA.[38] A 1944 recruitment manual distributed by the WLA of the U.S. Crop Corps illustrated the success of female worker placement on farms, and the role that the WLA played in it. The recruitment manual also suggested women take on jobs that suited their nature, such as dairy work. It claimed, "In year-round jobs, women excel at dairy work, where gentleness and high standards of cleanliness are important."[39] The USDA also urged that farmers consider women for jobs such as feeding chickens, hens, cows, and other animals as well as for jobs operating machinery in which dexterity and speed were important. Targeting the hesitation of some farmers to employ urban women, Wilson further argued: "many a seasonal farmer is skeptical about the whole thing. But as the labor pinch is felt more and more on the farm this attitude tends to moderate. War necessity has caused this normal reaction largely to disappear in Great Britain, where farmers report very satisfactory results from their Land Army girls. A recent national poll indicates that about 41 percent of American farmers are now willing to try the girls."[40] Nonetheless, farmers often preferred to employ boys too young to enlist or migrant workers instead of white urban women deemed not suited to heavy farm work.[41]

During the war, some Americans worked in factories, some took clerical jobs, and some participated in wartime service programs that offered compensation for the work involved. It is in this capacity that many American women joined the WLA. What made the WLA farm worker different from the industrial icon of Rosie the Riveter? Both were women and both put in long hours of hard manual labor. Both groups earned money for their families and helped the nation at the same time. Did they have similar backgrounds with similar goals? How did these women visualize their roles? Historian Katherine Jellison argues, "Like Rockwell's Rosie, the smiling woman on a tractor symbolized women's competence in using heavy equipment to perform 'men's work'."[42] Quite often images of women on tractors found their way into newspapers or onto the cover of magazines such as *Click* (see fig. 5.5). This was not a practice unique to the United States, however, but rather an international practice to show people the strength of young urban women utilizing heavy farm equipment (see fig. 5.6). When First Lady Eleanor Roosevelt went to England to observe the work of the British WLA in 1942 she symbolically rode on a tractor to see the work of the women. Representation of women on tractors served not only to symbolize the strength of female farm labor—many of the glamour shots of well-groomed tractor-driving women also served to attract young urban women looking for alternatives to urban wartime service.

Images used for publicity and recruitment inspired women to join for a variety of reasons. Women who participated in the WLA were typically white, middle-class, single, urban, and young, though some African American women were members as well (see fig. 5.7).[43] Some joined for a sense of adventure inferred by the publicity stories and photos, and some joined to gain better health while working outdoors. Those that joined did not do so for wealth but for a myriad of personal or political reasons. Reporter Lucy Greenbaum of the *New York Times* interviewed New York WLA workers about their motivations for enlistment. Greenbaum asked, "Why were they devoting their vacations or entire summer to working on a farm? Were they out for pay or patriotism?"[44] Her interview indicated:

> A desire to frequent the farm instead of the beauty shop has been shown in the Empire State by 400 women.
>   . . . There was not one who said she wanted to make money. They all asked to make expenses and a little over to buy an extra dress. They felt that farming as war work held compensations other than weekly wage.
>   . . . College girls on vacation particularly did not care about the pennies. An art major at Sarah Lawrence does something different every summer. Last year it was camping, this year she overruled her mother, who wanted her to take her oils and hike to the mountains for inspiration. She hiked to them, but for agriculture, not art. Several other students considered the trip in nature an outing, a chance to enjoy the scenery and swimming as well as to work.
>   The girl expressed the desire of many men who dwell in the duskiness

FIGURE 5.5. *(left)* Cover of *Click* magazine, September 1943. Photograph by Elliot Clarke. Triangle Publications, Inc.

FIGURE 5.6. (below) *Members of the British Women's Land Army Harvesting Beets.* "A woman is driving the Fordson tractor in the foreground, while three others with pitchforks are loading the beets on the truck behind the tractor," 1943. Library of Congress, LC-USW34-000622-ZB.

of cities to identify themselves with a clod of earth, feeling that if they only had a chance to commune with nature, life's problems would be solved.

. . . Several confessed their main object was to lose weight, even though farm life is popularly supposed to build people up. "I want to be built down," protested a plump sophomore. Others admitted they were out after a deep tan.[45]

Life on the farms of America was not what many of those girls dreamed it would be, however, as many found the laborious work challenging to both their stamina and appearance. As Greenbaum further noted, "The Women went through initiation with Spartan coolness. Hair that started in trim curls soon turned into Medusa's locks. Shapely red nails dried and split. Peaches-and-cream complexions took on a leather texture. Life had much in common with that of the army."[46] Pay or patriotism, the article asked. Though desire born from patriotism was not obvious in the interview, the small pay—compared with that of urban wartime work—made farm work an option only for those who did not have financial need.

Public figures and celebrities joined in the patriotic recruitment effort and helped promote the enlistment of many women of leisure to farm labor. Mary Esther Edge, the daughter of Governor Walter E. Edge of New Jersey, made headlines when she volunteered with the WLA to pick peaches on a farm near Glassboro, New Jersey, during her summer break from Radcliffe College. Miss Edge earned $10 a week to reside in dormitories provided for WLA women at Glassboro State Teachers' College and worked on the farm of Henry Reuder, earning between $2 and $3 a day picking and packing peaches.[47] For many women of middle or upper class, signing up for the WLA was both a symbol of a desire for an adventure in rural life and a trend for society girls to show their patriotic support during the war. As the WLA became more popular among the leisured classes, the glamour shots of women in uniform graced the covers of *Harper's Bazaar, Click,* and other publications concerned with ladies' social and physical appearance.

Training the urban American woman for rural life varied across the nation. Typical training for the WLA involved brief instruction on-site at the farm of employment.[48] Workers who obtained training at colleges and university programs, such as those at the University of Connecticut, Maryland University, or the University of California, gained not only considerably more knowledge of agricultural processes, but also opportunities for the best placements, living conditions, and pay. Though the leader of the University of California training program, Mel Werner, claimed the students in his program "will be subject to Waac-like discipline. There will be 'officers' and

FIGURE 5.7. *Mrs. Sam Crawford*, 1943. National Archives and Record Administration, Washington, D.C. Though African American women did participate in the Women's Land Army, they represented a very small percentage of the membership, as many African American women, like other working-class American women, either continued on in their prewar occupations or took higher-paying jobs in the factories.

'privates,'" most programs took a less rigid approach and simply provided basic knowledge and training of agricultural skills needed when working on a farm.[49] The University of Maryland developed an agricultural training program designed to return "the 'farmerette' of the First World War days 'to a degree heretofore believed impossible.'"[50] The course ran four weeks, with classes in horticulture, raising poultry, and dairying; pupils also ran the college's cannery where they learned the skills needed to properly can and store vegetables. Dr. T. B. Symons, dean of the university's farm extension service, claimed the reluctance of farmers to hire urban women was unnecessary and predicted the university-trained worker would be more efficient and willing than the average city dweller to labor on the land.[51]

The workers received "regular unskilled labor wages" for their services, paid directly by the farmers or other employers. Congress supplied money only for the WLA to conduct recruitment as well as some training, housing, and transportation.[52] Wages depended on the type and quantity of work— some farmers paid women by the piece such as in picking and packing strawberry quarts at five cents a piece, whereas other jobs such as husking corn or thinning lettuce earned thirty-five cents an hour. With the cost of room and board at approximately $10 a week, that left somewhere in the neighborhood of $8 a week "in reserve for a rainy day" or to send home to families in need. In some locations, dormitory camps for the women organized in former Civilian Conservation Corps camps of the Great Depression and New Deal years.[53] Most farmerettes earned less than the newly established minimum wage, a wage designed to provide basic security for food and shelter. In all, the American women of the WLA earned roughly the same amount per week as their British counterparts—rates nearly half that of factory labor and barely enough for room and board.

The *New York Times* reported that women "leaving thoughts of long red nails and lacy dresses behind" enlisted in the WLA after Eleanor Roosevelt's press conference during which she and Florence Hall described the program in detail and a home economics specialist from the USDA modeled a WLA uniform.[54] Though many women sought to join the WLA to get the chance to wear an official uniform, the American WLA required the women who participated to purchase their own uniforms: dark blue cotton denim overalls, a powder-blue tailored cotton shirt, a denim "butcher boy" jacket, and an adjustable cap with visor to shield them from the sun.[55] When the nation's denim supplies decreased due to the conversion of looms to make fabric for tents, WLA staff worried about the availability of some fifty thousand uniforms for the summer of 1943. The national presses featured Hall's opinions on, and her dealing with, this problem as a headline in many newspapers. Would these women prioritize fabric and labor over the war needs of male soldiers to meet the cosmetic demands of a uniform? Alternatively, would trained farm workers have the attire necessary to complete the jobs properly? The workers felt the acquisition of these uniforms vital to successfully carrying out their duties, as many had gone without civilian allotments of the fabric over the previous year; government supply of the uniforms seemed their only hope of sturdy clothing for the tough agricultural labor ahead of them. The fabric districts of New York suggested that the women take "pot luck" with whatever fabric they could find and create their own work clothes; but Hall denied the fabric districts' claims of shortages and noted the organization had the denim needed to provide for uniforms for the women who enlisted and that the uniform production would not take fabric away from male soldiers' needs.[56]

As the war progressed, the need for female agricultural workers increased and neither farmers nor the government wished to return to periods of scarcity witnessed during the Depression years. In February 1945, C. Chester DuMond, New York State commissioner of agriculture and markets, asserted that regardless of how quickly the war ended, changes to the farm labor requirements for 1945 were not possible. Quick to make clarifications about the government and the USDA's interest in hiring women, however, DuMond encouraged young women to continue service if previously employed in farm labor and outlined "mutual advantages" of farm labor in that "the knowledge of food gained by young women on farms would be an asset in later life when they were housekeeping."[57]

Not every state accepted the WLA service with open minds about female farm labor. Some states such as Texas and Colorado refused to allow the WLA to form due to preconceived notions about women's place and space in agriculture and chose instead to hire Mexican migrant labor. In November 1944, the Texas State Extension Service estimated that in that year, between 250,000 and 300,000 fewer people worked on Texas farms than in 1940. Despite national efforts at recruitment during wartime, the farm labor shortages in Texas remained throughout the war. Though the federal government asked Texas to increase its agricultural production by 37 percent over its 1940 production outcome, it was a struggle for Texas.[58] The choice of who to employ and not to employ was part and parcel of a racialized and gendered culture that left Texas agriculturalists struggling to meet production goals.

Though there was an abundance of women willing to travel to farms in need of labor, some states in the southern and western parts of the United States, including Texas, resisted on grounds that farm labor was not deemed appropriate "women's work" and instead relied on cultural stereotypes that defined farm labor in terms of race. Farmers formally resisted the formation of a WLA on the grounds that it was the first step in a socialized labor force and as such denied "free market" labor. Regardless of personal and political reasons, by resisting the WLA they resisted the thousands of trained and eager workers ready to help relieve the agricultural burden. Texas men and women expressed their dislike for the official employment of women as farm labor in the local newspapers. Texas newspapers did not discourage women from farm work per se; they simply made derogatory references to urban women trying to take farm jobs. Whereas many Texan newspapers revered the strength of the farm woman, they were less likely to show respect toward urban women desiring to help out on farms. News articles criticized the leader of the WLA, both her appearance and her level of experience living on a farm, inferring that she was not qualified to lead a group of female farm workers.

Women in Texas faced pressure to conform to the accepted behavior of a "southern lady": laboring in the fields was not part of that. This idea stemmed from the antebellum era when the sharp division of white and black society excluded white women from all labor performed by slaves. Though white farmers sent black slave women to work in the fields, southern culture did not deem it "proper" for white women to do the work of slaves. After the Civil War, these cultural definitions of labor and whiteness remained as white growers continued to employ men and women of color for farm work but shunned the idea of formally employing white women. For a poor white farm woman to help out on her family's farm when needed was one situation; the formal employment of white women as farm workers was a completely different situation and often not entered into willingly.

In the years leading up to the Second World War, the definition of an American southern lady was more about what she *was* rather than what she *did*; thus farm women were more likely to perform laborious field tasks when needed but felt themselves in a class apart from black or Hispanic women. Farm women maintained the household and though that included food production in the terms of raising small animals for meat, daily dairy chores, and perhaps maintaining a kitchen garden, field labor was the primary exclusion from a woman's "sphere" in farm labor. Though many white farm women performed fieldwork at least once a year due to necessity, they were less likely to admit to it publicly. In a letter to the *Semi-Weekly News* of Farmersville, Collin County, Texas, in 1910, Mrs. Vina Cochran stated simply, "I believe God made man to till the soil and women to care for the house."[59] White landowning families held fast to the cult of true womanhood and the stigma of field labor, thus maintaining the image of their wives and daughters as "southern ladies." This upper- and middle-class construct meant that women of landowning families were less likely to admit to their labor in the fields and more likely to separate themselves from the work still deemed beneath them as white southern ladies. Cultivating vegetables in a kitchen garden was acceptable behavior, and as such cultivating foodstuffs could be seen as an extension of it when in need. Many still considered picking cotton work to be performed by hired laborers, reminiscent from slavery, and thus not a suitable form of work for white women. Forty years after the Second World War when asked about her experience picking cotton, one woman of a landowning family "drew herself up to her full height, glared, and vehemently declared 'I *never* picked cotton!'"[60] This does not mean that white farm women considered labor too difficult or beneath them. Farm women tended to see themselves as supervisors of the labor of the farm, secondary to their husbands but more capable in many tasks than the people of color they hired for assistance. When necessity arose, poor white farm women worked in the fields alongside the field hands. The majority of them worked full-time in the fields during the picking seasons and many of them took the lead of the field labor when husbands or sons were ill or left to find additional paid labor in the surrounding towns. Despite the abundance of American women willing to perform wartime labor in agriculture, in August 1942 the governments of the United States and Mexico founded the Bracero migrant labor program to alleviate agricultural shortages nationwide. The benefits were twofold: the farms of America got the much needed labor to ensure the requested production levels and thousands of impoverished Mexicans found employment in the fields of America.

International Spread of WLA

Australian, Canadian, and New Zealand wartime food campaigns centered on both strengthening the domestic agricultural production and on assisting the national efforts and campaigns of England in support of the British Empire. Close ties of Australia's women's organizations and government to British WLA leader Lady Gertrude Denman led to the prompt creation of an Australian WLA. Much like the WLAs of Britain and the United States, the Australian WLA recruited both part-time seasonal and year-round farm workers to engage in harvesting, fruit packing, pruning, and so forth. Uniforms were of less significance to identity for the workers of the Australian WLA; the organizations supplied full-time year-round recruits with unique uniforms for work and supplied part-time seasonal help with only badges to identify themselves as members.[61]

Marion Kelsey was a married Canadian woman who sought refuge and hope in the British WLA when her husband was at war. For Kelsey, joining the British WLA meant staying closer to her husband on the European Continent. During leave times, she and her husband arranged to meet and spend what few precious moments they had together. A tragic accident left her husband paralyzed and for Kelsey, those memories of their European wartime adventure were most precious.[62]

In addition to Canada, Britain also urged New Zealanders to assist the war efforts as well by creating their own version of a WLA. After much prodding by citizens concerned about the nation's current agricultural production and after much debate and contesting of a New Zealand WLA by the Minister of Agriculture, New Zealand organized a Women's Land Army, later to be renamed the Women's Land Service (WLS) in 1942. After public discussion and governmental doubt about the viability of such an organization, women's groups of New Zealand established their own regional chapters of a larger national service.

Women of New Zealand showed their patriotism and eagerness to join other women in the war effort in ways similar to their American and British sisters. Though New Zealand men fought on the front lines in foreign lands, New Zealand women fought on the domestic front to ensure the nation's survival. Diane Bardsley argues in *The Land Girls: In a Man's World, 1939–1946* that a common complaint of the 210 former members of the New Zealand WLS she interviewed was of the formal lack of recognition for their service. Men who fought in foreign lands returned home seeking a return to their former lives and society and encouraged women to return to their prewar traditional roles. When women inquired about their service records after the war was over, they learned that the government destroyed their service records because it did not consider them "official army combatants."[63]

Of the war organizations for New Zealand women, the New Zealand WLS was the largest, officially registering 4,290 women, though many more served in unofficial capacity on farms.[64] While WLAs in Britain and the United States focused primarily on the production of agriculture, in New Zealand the WLS was more varied. Women service workers in New Zealand served more frequently on dairy and sheep farms. Most female farm laborers had experiences similar to those of their American and British sisters: struggling for acceptance by the rural communities, future careers in agriculture, and lack of postwar recognition. Many New Zealand women resented the national rejection of their identity as laborers and contributors to the war effort. Joyce Young, a New Zealand land girl who worked in South Taranaki, was among many who wrote poems to support the WLS. One such poem, titled "The Call of the Land," reveals such sentiments:

> Come lend an ear, you maidens fair
> And hear our country's call,
> While there is still one woman left
> This land shall never fall.
>
> We'll pit our strength behind our boys
> Who fight on a foreign shore
> And keep this land of theirs for them
> For now and evermore.

So rouse yourselves from tears and grief
Then listen to this plea
New Zealand needs some help right now
The help of you and me.

The men within the land they call
For lassies strong and brave
So wear a smile, don overalls,
We're treasures here to save.

And when some day the lads return
Triumphant back to you
They'll say "Thank God for a place to rest
'Ere starting life anew."[65]

Women of the Allied nations, just as in other areas of the globe, represented the literal and figurative mothers of the nations they served. When the thought of women performing work traditionally performed by men reached the masses, some viewed it with hostility or fear for the future of society. One member of the New Zealand Farmers' Union exclaimed in response to the call of New Zealand women to farms: "Women who can cut the throats of sheep and carry heavy loads will not make healthy future mothers of the race."[66] Obviously this gentleman's definition of "healthy" underestimated the physical requirements and demands of childbirth and caring for small children. And for women who worked outside of the home, many factory jobs could be just as demanding and physically straining. Women of the Allied nations carried not only the heavy loads of agriculture, but also the heavy cultural loads of women's "sphere."

In all, the land girls of the Allied nations achieved their goal of sustaining agricultural needs. Whereas Britain imported nearly two-thirds of its food supply before the war, with the help of the WLA that percentage dropped to approximately one-third by 1942.[67] The WLA organizations of Britain and the United States differed, however, in that the British land girls typically worked full-time year-round at their posts; the majority of the American land girls typically assisted in seasonal work on holidays and vacations. This explains the variances in the numbers of recruits. Though the initial recruitment goals of the American WLA in 1943 totaled 60,000, the enlistment reached over 600,000 in 1943 alone.[68] The total number of British women that joined the WLA is tough to measure because of the lack of official records, though newspaper and archive records indicate that at its peak in 1945 the WLA claimed as many as 77,000 women enlisted at one time.[69]

Like urban women with their plans of rationing, recycling, and victory gardening, the rural agricultural laborers of the Allied nations used the cultivation of land as a weapon to win the war for their nations and allies and to forge identities for themselves as well. Through transnational comparison of the similarities and differences in the WLAs and their members, important details emerge about the collective and individual identities women forged from their experiences, such as differentiating themselves from rural women as they brought their college educations about farming to the farmhouse, removing themselves from parental supervision and control, acquiring an equal wage for equal labor, and gaining public acceptance of women as farm laborers. Due to the lack of many official service records, recently published personal memoirs and old diaries contain much of what is now available to learn about the individual lives of the land girls.[70] By comparing these private recollections, however enmeshed with nostalgia, a clearer understanding of the interconnections of identity to cultivation is possible.

Overall, women who served in the WLAs of Britain and the United States held different perspectives on women's sense of place in wartime work than did their urban neighbors who could not leave their homes to volunteer such efforts. Connected to those personal histories were the perspectives of those who tried to either encourage or discourage women from finding a place and space in agricultural labor. However different those perspectives, public or domestic, they were influenced by perceptions of the role of food and the cultivation of it for the survival of the nation. Those personal ties of women to the land and the battles they fought, both socially and politically, left lasting memories similar to those of Joan Snelling musingly recalled in kitchens around the world.

CHAPTER 6

Freedom from Want
THE ROLE OF THE VICTORY GARDEN
IN THE SECOND WORLD WAR

The proposal that want be abolished from this world would be pretentious, or even ridiculous, were it not for two important recent discoveries.

One is the discovery that, beyond any doubt, men now possess the technical ability to produce in great abundance the necessities of daily life—enough for everyone. . . .

Another is the discovery (or rather the realization) that the earth is one planet indivisible, that one man's hunger is every other man's hunger. . . .

. . . Freedom from want, everywhere in the world, is within the grasp of men. . . . Prosperous times have been enjoyed in certain regions of the world at certain periods in history, but local prosperity was usually achieved at the expense of some other region, which was being impoverished, and the specter of impending war hung over all. Now the industrial changes of the last 150 years and the new prospect implicit in the words "United Nations" have given meaning to the phrase "freedom from want" and rendered it not only possible but necessary.

—Franklin D. Roosevelt, Message to Congress, 6 January 1941

"FREEDOM FROM WANT" was not only a powerful political message by President Franklin D. Roosevelt, it was also an ideology that the people of both England and the United States strove to adopt during the Second World War. After decades of hunger and economic depression, the nations looked to increased and improved food production as an answer to strife and conflict. "Want" and strife drove policy, and after female political activists shifted focus away from political equality and toward collective action to combat hunger and disease, nations turned to women's roles as nurturers and producers to aid in the crisis.

Just as in the First World War, a transnational exchange of ideas regarding solutions to food shortages during the Second World War resulted in the development of varied community and national homefront campaigns to increase food production. Whereas women's organizations and clubs of England and the United States pushed to reinstate the Women's Land Army (WLA) in both nations, political leaders sought both urban and rural solutions to Allied food shortages. The urban programs of each nation differed, however, because their agricultural situations and political goals varied. Shortages demanded that English political leaders encourage the reinstatement of the WLA months before the declaration of war, and both rural and urban women in England focused on food production for national survival. Urban efforts demanded that all available land in urban areas provide space for cultivation and urban people turned their attention away from ornamental gardening and toward food production. Thus during the war English identity tied directly to the production and distribution of food. American political leaders focused less on the WLA and more on the importance of individual citizens producing more food as a representation of American abundance. This political focus also marked a shift in the focus of many women on the role of home management as part of nation building. The United States recognized the mounting global food shortages and used the agricultural abundance of urban and rural cultivators as a political tool. As a result, Americans forged new identities symbolized by the abundance of the garden connected to the white middle-class kitchen. Regardless of agricultural opportunity or the homefront programs promoted, the cultivation of urban lands altered perspectives on the meaning of abundance in an uncertain world and shaped both political and personal identity.

For U.S. president Franklin D. Roosevelt and British prime minister Winston Churchill, the reasons for fighting the Second World War rested on certain freedoms the world should expect and fight to preserve for themselves and others. Meeting in August 1941, over three months before the Japanese bombed Pearl Harbor, the two leaders drew up a list of reasons for victory and a plan for a postwar democratic world, known as the Atlantic Charter. Though part of a bigger plan in shaping their future postwar economies and political allies, the leaders addressed the freedom from want as essential to framing a stable postwar society. This small political statement affected not only the wartime homefront campaigns of Great Britain and the United States, but also diplomacy in creating a postwar society. For the people, "freedom from want" served as both personal and political goals to consume less and to produce more foodstuffs for the war effort and as an international symbol of postwar democratic values.[1]

Though the language of the Atlantic Charter reflected the political ideologies of both leaders, the inclusion of freedom from both want and fear stemmed from Roosevelt's earlier speeches and from his ideas of New Deal reform of the 1930s. President Roosevelt's State of the Union address to the U.S. Congress in January 1941 urged Americans to unite in support of their neighbors by giving them four essential global freedoms to fight for. This famous speech, the "Four Freedoms" speech, inspired artist Norman Rockwell to offer his talents to bring Roosevelt's words to life through his painting of a white middle-class family gathered around a dinner table abundant with food. This speech served as a backdrop to the congressional approval of the Lend-Lease Act in March 1941, an act that put into action the campaigns that argued food fought for victory. The food campaign of the Second World War differed from those of the First World War when nations focused on conservation and agricultural labor as necessities for survival. In the Second World War, Roosevelt's ideology of food as an essential freedom to fight for not only influenced the way both nations promoted wartime agricultural production, but also metaphorically put food on the front lines as both ammunition and as a symbol of postwar democracy and abundance. This metaphor identified agricultural laborers, whether rural or urban, as "soldiers of the soil."

The American Victory Garden Campaign

The demand for food to sustain the soldiers and people of the Allied Powers provided incentive for revitalizing old agricultural programs and inspiration for Americans to place those programs at the center of the homefront effort. Ladies' magazines addressed the importance of the production of food and told readers "to see that all of our children have the right food and enough of it is about the biggest job we can do for America. . . . Study nutrition at a Red Cross class and keep your family well, or study canteen work for larger-scale feeding. If you are qualified, teach instead of learn. And when spring comes plant a vegetable garden."[2]

The demands for food during the Second World War prompted Americans to establish the War Food Administration (WFA) within the U.S. Department of Agriculture (USDA), a program designed to educate citizens on the vital role of food as a fighting element of victory. The WFA estimated wartime food needs to include not just ensuring citizens had enough to eat, but also feeding soldiers, Allies, and liberated countries to aid in the reconstruction process. To achieve these goals, America needed to both increase production and make the most effective use of the food and materials on hand. Therefore the WFA in cooperation with the Office of Price Administration (OPA), the Office of Civilian Defense (OCD), and the Office of War Information (OWI) developed programs to educate the American population about the seriousness of production, consumption, and conservation during wartime. The program revived the victory garden concept used in the First World War to maximize American food production and to increase the government's purchasing power through distribution of foodstuffs from the nation's farms. The victory garden became the symbol of both production and conservation on the home front in a time of destruction on the war front abroad.[3]

As the war progressed, propaganda reflected the increased supply of food abroad, noting that though 75 percent of food during wartime stayed in America for American citizens, 13 percent went to American soldiers abroad, 10 percent went to American Allies, and 2 percent went to "others."[4] Many Americans concerned about what a food shortage might do to both national security and the preservation of the nation argued that Americans needed to grow more food for Americans, and by doing so, use food as a weapon to assure a victory over the Axis and thus bring about the resumption of the American way of life. From this perspective, the propaganda needed to promote production also needed to de-emphasize the Great Depression and emphasize the positive growth the nation made just before the war. The USDA estimated that food production in the latter half of the 1930s increased year by year, yet despite such a significant increase, the USDA urged American farmers to plant 380 million acres of land by the end of 1944 and estimated such a figure to be the highest cultivated acreage in American history.[5] One 1943 wartime pamphlet stated that Uncle Sam met the needs of the world by calling for increased production of both foodstuffs and livestock. In all, Uncle Sam's acreage goal in his call to farms and ranches for production totaled a billion acres. The USDA estimated that such increases in farm and ranch production would only increase the nation's supplies by 5 percent, because increased efficiency on the farm over the previous decade brought about little room for improvement by education alone.[6] Thus the USDA sought to develop civilian programs to maximize production and minimize waste. The amount of land under cultivation was of significant value for propaganda purposes; the USDA, together with the OWI, used such figures as evidence of the growing number of people doing their patriotic duty to aid the war effort. Though rural agriculture provided the bulk of food production, it neared its threshold; thus to see any significant gains, urban Americans needed to supplement that production. Once again the Victory Garden program provided the means for average citizens to cultivate victory.

The international popularity and acknowledgment of wartime gardens as vital to national aid and security grew over the decades after the First World War and was reflected in the growing number of gardens and gardeners. For example, in America the number of victory gardens increased from 15 million in 1942 to over 20 million in 1943 according to the USDA records.[7] The USDA also estimated that in 1943 alone, approximately 20 million of those gardens produced 10 billion pounds of food.[8] By 1944, officials reported that the 20 million gardens harvested in 1944 yielded some 40 percent of the nation's vegetable supply. Such production complemented the larger agricultural needs of America, both to aid troops fighting overseas and as part of the diplomacy of the Lend-Lease program. The OWI provided radio scripts and urged announcers to reassure Americans that only 2 percent of all American agricultural production went to such programs.[9]

The national homefront propaganda campaigns encouraged women to do everything they could to help fight the war from their kitchens and cellars. Prepared with immense detail, the USDA national food campaign organized a schedule of when, where, how, and which topics of propaganda should be presented. The OPA assumed responsibility for constructing programs on price control and rationing; the WFA constructed programs of food production and use; and both organizations claimed the OWI and OCD were there to "assist" the various programs constructed.[10] A carefully orchestrated campaign detailed for consumers month by month and week by week every food- or salvage-related action they should take to ensure that their consumption and waste did not threaten the safe return of their husbands, brothers, sons, and fathers—for, after all, food was the "arsenal of democracy."[11]

Though the USDA and OWI designed the campaigns to promote increased production of food and decreased consumption of unnecessary items, both campaigns formed part of a national image of women as mothers of the nation who were responsible for its morality and survival. For example, despite national need for female labor, some American officials discouraged women from working outside the home and from participating in wasteful or ignorant household routines that hurt the progress of victory.[12] J. Edgar Hoover urged female readers of *Woman's Home Companion* to realize the significance of the "mother" to the well-being of the nation and of her children, thus reinforcing the national image of the woman's responsibilities in the domestic sphere. He argued:

> In the first place, unless family finances absolutely demand it, the mother of young children should not be a war-worker mother, when to do so requires the hiring of another woman to come in and take care of her children.
>
> Hard pressed as our manpower authorities have been, they have adhered steadfastly to the principle that patriotism does not consist in one person or a group of persons giving up duties which only they can per-

form to assume different duties which others can perform just as well or perhaps better.

Motherhood has not yet been classed as a nonessential industry! There is small chance that it will ever be. The mother of small children does not need to put on overalls to prove her patriotism. She already has her war job. Her patriotism consists in not letting quite understandable desires to escape for a few months from a household routine or to get a little money of her own tempt her to quit it. *There must be no absenteeism among mothers.*

That last sentence should, I believe, be taken literally. It is the essence of the whole program. The happy home—the one in which there is no delinquency, no matter which adjective you want to place in front of it—is the home where the child rushes in and calls, "Mother!" and gets a welcoming answer.

To back it up there should be a hot meal ready to serve and a mother fully dressed and ready to receive not only her own children but their friends. . . . The mother who does not provide that decent place is definitely falling down on her war job. Whatever rearrangement of her own eating, sleeping and working hours is entailed, she must be ready to give her children and their friends . . . hospitality and decency.[13]

In the spirit of J. Edgar Hoover's analysis of women's place and space in the nation, women looked to the USDA food programs as guidelines to change their "wasteful" ways and provide the decent and hospitable home their nation deemed necessary to be patriotic and successful as a wife and mother. American women then cultivated identity as the mother of national decency by focusing much of their attention on food production and the "hospitable" consumption of it and by providing soldiers a mental image of something to fight for. Suburban housing advertisers contributed to placing women in this position by encouraging them to dream of a decent and hospitable postwar home where the children had "better" rooms, the husband his own den, and women their own gardens in which to continue the domestic responsibilities the nation implied were necessary for the safety and decency of the nation. Even when some mothers resisted these societal ideals and still felt inclined to step up and take a war job, the press scolded them for neglecting their gendered national duties.[14]

If women needed more of a supportive example of how they should behave in wartime, Eleanor Roosevelt provided it through the countless trips she made to view and support female war workers, whether in the factory or on the farm. Perhaps the most personal example she set in demonstrating wartime behavior was the planting of a victory garden on the White House lawn in 1943. To the struggling middle and working classes fighting inflation and worrying about rationing, her attempt to grow beans and carrots on the White House lawn during wartime provided a humble and sincere appeal. Growing vegetables was not new to the White House, for many of the presidents and their wives had been avid gardeners while living there. John Adams planted a garden at the White House in 1800, Thomas Jefferson improved upon it and planted an orchard, and Andrew Jackson constructed an orangery there in 1835. In fact, Woodrow Wilson decided to graze sheep on the South Lawn during the First World War to prevent the need to mow. Though previous residents of the White House planted and used the lawn for personal pleasure, Eleanor Roosevelt's garden held a strong political purpose. This garden was a statement to the nation that it was the patriotic duty of every person, from the First Lady to the lady next door, to plant and cultivate for victory.

The USDA chose April of each year of the war to promote the victory garden, as April was the time deemed most effective for planting summer and fall vegetables to ease the nation's agricultural burdens. The widely publicized campaigns promoted cultivating victory through the production of food, no matter how small or large in scale. In April 1943 the USDA promoted the planting of Eleanor Roosevelt's garden and encouraged Americans to follow the lead of the First Lady in sacrificing for the war effort. In contrast to the public image of the First Lady's garden as a symbol of national sacrifice, the First Lady and her staff actually performed little work in the garden. Instead, a young girl, daughter of one of the White House staff, tended to the long-term success of the garden. April 1944 was designated as the month to increase current production of both personal and community gardens. The WFA designated April 2 through April 8 as "Grow More in '44" week to praise the farmers of America for their past and present efforts of "success on the farm front" and to educate them about ways to improve production.[15] The WFA reserved the July campaigns for "Home Food Preservation"; and in August the specific campaign drive promoted the Crop Corps—local calls to action for men, women, and children to volunteer to help in local harvests. Though November's campaign was officially "Food Fights for Freedom," the WFA deemed October, November, and December as a time of lessened agricultural effort on the homefront, so national campaign managers took full advantage of this time to highlight the virtues of decreased consumption in the home. The WFA worked together with the OPA to encourage women to keep the "Home Front Pledge," a pledge, much like those of Hoover's Food Administration in 1918, to verbalize and to literally sign that they would buy no more than their allotted share and would refuse to buy from black markets.

The USDA deemed the effective cooperation of the WFA and OPA essential to homefront success; as a result the latter organizations carefully structured campaigns to be free of conflict with the goals of one another. For example, the Food Campaign organizers of the WFA stated very plainly that "OPA rationing programs will be 'angled' toward the program of the month insofar as that is possible."[16]

The WPA, in cooperation with the OPA, the OWI, and the OCD, published training materials for wartime block leaders and county agricultural extension agents to train home demonstrators to inspire "full acceptance of individual responsibility in every home" and to educate them on how to do so. Though home demonstrators prepared a variety of educational programs for communities, the basic goals of each demonstrator included discussion and distribution of the folder "You Can Shorten the War with Food"—a selection of materials designed to promote homemakers to take an official pledge to obey rules of rationing, to limit consumption, and to do their part in production by means of gardening and of work on local farms. Other demonstration goals were to encourage participation in community food projects, supply homes with print materials outlining the programs each community had to offer, discuss the importance of food and nutrition during wartime, distribute the "National Wartime Nutrition Guide," and, finally, to ask each homemaker to complete a food quiz at the end of the meeting.[17]

The USDA distributed training information to state agricultural extension agencies to pass on to community leaders, to help organize training efforts at the local and neighborhood level. Community leaders often relied on garden clubs and women's voter leagues to distribute information and train households in compliance. Organizations, interested community leaders, and businesses distributed pamphlets and articles about food as a weapon to win the war and to ensure an adequate food supply at home. The USDA and members of the agribusiness community such as Beech Nut Seeds and International Harvester, among numerous others, distributed such material to the public. In addition, such popular magazines as *Ladies' Home Journal*, *Click*, and *Time* quickly joined in the campaign in both official and unofficial ways by supporting advertisers who promoted homefront campaigns and by publishing articles on homefront activities. On occasion, USDA pamphlets closely resembled modern-day women's magazines as a way to attract the attention of American women. Some pamphlets included articles like how to "Eat Your Way to Beauty," which encouraged consuming fruits and vegetables and forgoing excessive consumption of rationed foods such as sugar, oil, meat, and butter.[18] The article urged women to consume more nonrationed foods, get involved in activities that provided fresh air and exercise, and can foods properly so they contained the largest amounts of vitamins that promoted beauty. Though the article made good health sense, the underlying message was clear and straightforward and mirrored similar articles in other women's magazines: if women eat fewer rationed foods, participate in such outdoor activities as victory gardening, and follow the campaigns on how to can foods and produce a hospitable home for their husband and children, they will not only speed the war effort, but also will look good. This glamorized and occasionally seductive image of the well-groomed woman tending to the homeland appeared in many women's magazines and contributed to the image of women as symbols of the land the soldiers fought for.[19]

Community volunteers provided home demonstrations on how best to obey the rules of rationing and to decrease consumption. WLA leader Florence Hall, with two decades of experience in home demonstrations and USDA representation, served as a unique leader by bridging the urban and rural campaigns. With Hall at the lead, the lines between urban home management and rural agricultural labor blurred from one of domesticity to one of public employment. Those spheres brought contrasting roles of food conservation to food production, and of mending "wasteful ways" to producing abundance. A home demonstrator might train an urban woman in proper canning and home management techniques on a weekday, yet on the weekend serve a part-time shift on a local farm as part of the WLA. The OWI and the WFA aided in the home education process by supplying the demonstrator, typically a woman, with training materials and literature to distribute to individual neighborhood homemakers or at community lectures on topics of homefront efforts. When demonstrators went door to door requesting time to educate housewives about the "proper" way to recycle, cultivate, prepare, and can food, they also promoted and spread middle-class ideas about how a woman should maintain a home, raise children, and maintain proper gender roles in the home. In this way, the promotion of the home demonstration was, at its core, Americanization. Community leaders gave public lectures with aids provided by the WFA food campaign: charts, graphs, films, fact sheets, pamphlets, food quizzes, and even scripts. Other methods of distributing information about the food campaign and encouraging patriotism included art classes, cooking schools, school cafeteria programs, and restaurant menu items. Other methods included community events and contests to inspire a sort of competitive patriotism. Essay contests for children on topics such as "How My Family Is Making Food Fight for Freedom" suggest a certain implied encouragement to families to set the best patriotic example so that the essays portrayed their family efforts in the best possible light to friends and neighbors.[20]

The food campaign of the USDA used children as a tool for spreading its message to adults. For example, of the many things the WFA encouraged children to do, most centered on spreading fear: "Boy Scouts, Camp Fire Girls, etc. might make stencils of the faces of Hitler and Hirohito, then get permission from housewives, restaurant operators, dieticians of institutional kitchens, etc., to paint the likenesses of the dictators on garbage cans, along with some such caption as 'Feed me well and prolong the war.'" The WFA encouraged high-school home economics teachers to alter their lesson plans to mirror the themes of the food campaign and to teach topics such as "nutrition-in-wartime" and "Play Square" in coordination with fine arts and mechanical arts departments that "can whip up nice looking exhibits by coordinating their efforts."[21] Female schoolteachers and county extension agents teaching these examples of wartime service to the youth of America presented American food as one of the most valuable assets of America, and they recalled the return of abundance as a motivator for victory.

Images of wartime production and consumption and their connection to the "garden" reflected gendered ideas about the role of women and nature (see fig. 6.1). Due to the nature of a predominantly male military, some genderization of homefront programs comes as no surprise. Acknowledgment of gender is important, however, when examining the government perspective in the food campaigns. One gender—male—was treated with reverence as having assumed knowledge, and one—female—as naïve, innocent, and at times too inquisitive for her own good. Though women's community organizations sponsored educational pamphlets and women's magazines promoted victory gardening, in many gardening education images, men often served as instructors of females in proper gardening methods.

A photo from the personal collection in the FDR Library labeled "Secretary Plowing Boston Commons, 4/11/44, Victory Garden Program" (see fig. 6.2) provides an example of gendered roles in victory gardening. This photo leads the observer to think the men plowing the Boston Commons are authoritative: they are dressed in suits and look serious about what they are doing and appear to be measuring the progress of society in some way by measuring the amount of land tilled in the Boston Commons. In most other photographs and graphic images, men are positioned as instructors or are measuring the progress of the gardens; women are poised to either pick the vegetables dutifully or assume pin-up-type poses complete with baskets of produce—never in a position of instruction or authority (see figs. 6.3, 6.4, and 6.5).

Race figured in propaganda and social attitudes toward the production of food. Though much of the OWI focused on the image of the white single

FIGURE 6.1. *War Gardens for Victory. Grow Vitamins at Your Kitchen Door*, Lithographed by the Stecher-Traung Lithograph Corporation, Rochester, New York. Library of Congress, LC-USZC4-4436.

FIGURE 6.2. *(opposite, top)*
Secretary Plowing Boston Commons, 1943.
Franklin D. Roosevelt Library Digital
Archives, library ID 7769(161).

FIGURE 6.3. *(opposite, bottom)*
Office of War Information, *Professor
Harry Nelson of San Francisco gives his
daughter and her Girl Scout friends some
pointers in transplanting young vegetables*,
1943. President Franklin D. Roosevelt
Library Digital Archives, library ID
66298(8).

FIGURE 6.4. *(right)*
Cover of *Harper's Bazaar*, May 1943.

FIGURE 6.5. *(below)*
Ann Rosener, *Frequent watering of the
Victory Garden is necessary during the early
stages of growth*, 1943. President Franklin
D. Roosevelt Library Digital Archives,
library ID 66298(1).

woman worker taking the jobs men left behind and the white married homemaker taking responsibility for the morality of the nation, it rarely included
African American women in print and radio campaigns. When they were
included the women depicted played supporting, subservient roles to white
women or were depicted as mammy figures. Historian Barbara Dianne Savage
argues in *Broadcasting Freedom: Radio, War, and the Politics of Race, 1938–1948*
that this attitude of implied superiority of the white woman worker reflected
growing anxieties about segregation, and this campaign attempted to reassure
whites that African Americans accepted segregation as their "patriotic duty."[22]
Historian Laura Lawson claims African Americans subjected to Progressive
Era instructions in cultivating their plots did contribute to the cultural abundance of the nation by their participation.[23] However, growing white middle-class anxieties about segregation led to increased efforts to promote a
radicalized idea of "American-ness" in the kitchen and garden. When African
American women came "out of the kitchen" to take higher-paying jobs in the
factories, some white women were suddenly forced to look at the responsibility of managing a household and food preparation themselves. As one white
homemaker noted, "It might have been true in Grandmother's day that two
black hands were the greatest labor saving device for doing housework, but
the same does not hold true now when there is so much electrical and mechanical equipment on the market."[24]

Thus even though the motives of the OWI, the USDA, and the consumer
industries are fairly clear through campaign documentation and advertising,
the individual perceptions of the personal roles gardeners played in cultivating victory are less apparent and varied.[25] Ruth McCord Dewar grew up in
East Orange, New Jersey, and was only fifteen years old when the United
States went to war in 1941. In a time when bread was ten cents a loaf, Dewar's family prospered financially on her father's salary of $25,000 a year as
vice president of National City Bank in New York. Despite the affluence the
Dewar family grew accustomed to, wartime homefront campaign and situations brought changes in lifestyle. Dewar recalled that her family grew vegetables in their backyard "for the first time in our lives." With food deliveries
from local grocers no longer dependable due to rationed gasoline, families of
all economic classes had to learn to produce more food. For the Dewars, victory gardening was not just patriotic duty, but also part of a community-wide
effort to survive in case of foreign attack. "It sounds funny now, but we were
petrified that the war would come to the East Coast," she recalled in 2002.[26]
Citizens darkened windowshades, extinguished or blacked out parts of street-
lights and car headlamps, and practiced air raid drills in the community to
prepare for attacks similar to those their London allies experienced.

Many young people in America probably did not fear global war or feel "uneasy" after hearing news of British prime minister Neville Chamberlain's declaration of his negotiations with Adolf Hitler as "peace for our time;" however, Californian Anona Stoetzl Kuehne recalled she did. So when the United States joined the war, homefront wartime activities and campaigns to Anona were not only means of survival but also of patriotism and pride. As a rural family, the Kuehnes suffered fewer shortages than their urban neighbors did. Years later Anona Kuehne recalled, "We were a lot better off in the country towns than the folks in the cities. In Madera, we grew most of our vegetables and had chickens and eggs. The city folk dug up their lawns and planted Victory Gardens." So instead of focusing on creating a new victory garden like her city neighbors did, Anona assisted local farmers on a temporary basis during the war at harvest time picking tomatoes, cotton, and olives.[27]

"I would rather have joined the WAC [Women's Army Corps] but, with three children under fourteen, I was not eligible," claimed Virginia Raymond Ott.[28] Like many urban women, Ott found the duties of raising children and keeping house during wartime to be challenges that prohibited her from serving in any of the many women's wartime services such as the WAC or the WLA. As the child of an Army family and wife of a colonel in the U.S. Army Corps of Engineers, Ott found wartime absences much like the ones normally experienced during military service except with the potential of danger. After her husband transferred to England, Ott moved herself and the children to her parents' home in upstate New York, where they gardened for victory and collected fallen apples from the grounds of the local hospital and a cousin's orchard for her family's consumption.

Acting individually or in small groups, many urban women of the WLA participated in both urban victory gardening and rural farm labor if able. For Mary L. Appling, growing up "untraveled" in California and having no relatives or loved ones away at war meant a life of "insulation and safety" as far as she was concerned when America went to war. As a twenty-two-year-old graduate student at UCLA, Appling felt ready to start a career as a librarian, but saw changes and challenges in everyday life due to homefront campaigns of rationing and agricultural production. Appling assisted her parents by working their victory garden, a garden "carved out of pasture land, a patch possibly 40 x 50 feet in area." As a single urban woman, Appling also had the opportunity to aid local farms when they required additional labor. A novice to farming, she and other faculty from Oakdale Joint Union High School volunteered time to assist in harvesting tomatoes on several occasions, though noting, "My first sight ever of a huge, juicy green tomato worm was rather jolting."[29]

Some young urban women needed only to observe the examples of their mothers to find ways to contribute to the homefront effort. Sara Mae Wiedmaier recalled many of the community efforts of her mother, Lillian Crawford Addis. In addition to volunteering during the war as part of the Aircraft Warning Service of Oregon, Addis used what her daughter termed "excellent gardening" skills to provide "food for whoever sat at her table or came to her door." During the Depression, Addis "brought home strays to feed"; she continued to provide food for those "stray" people, her family, and community through her own victory garden during the Second World War and through her activity in a community Victory Garden project that "covered many blocks." Many people wondered how urban housewives with families found time to volunteer in addition to the duties of keeping house, feeding and caring for children, and so forth. In a Portland newspaper, the *Oregonian*, Addis among others answered some of the questions about how they were able to budget time so that they could contribute anywhere from six to thirty hours each week to do volunteer work: "I wash on Saturdays these days instead of Mondays; I iron on Mondays instead of Tuesdays; I clean on Fridays." Lillian casually states that she has three children, ages fourteen, seventeen, and nineteen; she does all the work in the four-bedroom house and the sewing for her two daughters; and she sews one day each week for her church's war relief work. "Certainly it has meant readjusting my household schedule," she says, "but I can't go out to work—this is my way of helping." To Wiedmaier, Addis's daughter, these efforts left lasting impressions about women's efforts during wartime: "I always thought my mother was next to God. She was one of thousands of women who dealt with their personal anxiety over their loved ones in the military by answering the call to volunteer their services in the many projects necessary to carry on the war effort. I, too have been a professional volunteer. . . . Lillian Crawford Addis set a clear example for me to live by."[30]

If women did not have close family members or others to mentor them in women's patriotic roles, the media offered that mentorship through news programs and advertising. Radio, film, and "dramatic skits" offered other ways to spread the word about agricultural programs and campaigns through the popular culture of the day. The USDA urged community leaders to encourage the development and presentation of patriotic dramas in schools, churches, clubs, or community centers.[31] Posters, films, and radio dramas that these volunteers and organizations used played on the fears of women to urge them to participate in the food campaigns (see fig. 6.6). In the film *Food Fights for Freedom*, the OWI and WFA played on the fears of civilian families losing their loved ones at war, telling viewers if they did not do what was necessary to win the war, their loved ones might not return home safely.

FIGURE 6.6. Alfred Parker, *"We'll Have Lots to Eat This Winter, Won't We Mother?" Grow Your Own, Can Your Own,* 1943. University of North Texas Library, b2850376.

Food! Food has been our secret weapon of this war. Just because anyone can see it everywhere, every day. A weapon that you have in your kitchen, on your plate, three times a day, but a weapon that fights for freedom. Food won battles in North Africa. Food saves lives wherever our men fight.

Every pound of food we ship to our Allies helps to keep English armament factories humming, helps to keep British and Russian soldiers keen with fighting edge, helps to bring victory nearer. Ten percent of our 1943 food supply is ear-marked for our Lend-Lease Allies. In return, many of our men are fed by reverse Lend-Lease from Australia and New Zealand in the South Pacific, for instance.

Every pound of food we send to the peoples we liberate helps rebuild their strength and their will to fight beside us, and hastens the day when the fighting will end. The whisper runs through the underground. "The Nazis steal our food, starve our children. The Allies bring food, help us start to feed ourselves again." Food is a secret weapon.

A soldier's life depends on how well he knows his weapon. That same soldier's life may depend upon how well you understand the weapon of food, and how well you use it.

Not *all* of it can be saved, but between the plow and the plate, 20 to 30 percent of America's food supply is lost or wasted each year. Saving half of that would be like adding enough to our food supply to feed our armed forces, or more than enough to feed our Allies, in 1943. The weapons of victory, thrown into the garbage can.

The way we use our ration stamps and watch the price ceilings on both sides of the counter, can be a measure of patriotism.

Produce, conserve, share, play square—four simple every-day things to do with and about food. No *one* by itself is enough; not one can be left out, if we want to use the weapon of food against the Axis with the most deadly effect.[32]

A popular feature on the NBC Blue Network *National Farm and Home Hour* was the song "Get Out and Dig, Dig, Dig" performed by the Cadets. Its lyrics illustrate the transference of political ideas into popular culture via a news radio station:

> Get out and dig, dig, dig in the sunshine—You can make one
>   garden grow;
> Ev'ry seed you buy will gladly multiply—'Till we've overcome our
>   foe.
> Get out and work, work, work for the nation—We can keep our
>   country free;

Help the rain above feed the ones we love—Dig our way to
victory.
Plantin' beans come what may;
Turn the sod—trust in God—And the earth will show the way.
Get out and dig, dig, dig in the sunshine—Ev'ry heart will feel
a-glow;
As we turn the tide, we'll be glad we tried—To make ten million
gardens grow.[33]

Other such compositions include "Mistress Mary Quite Contrary Has A Victory Garden Now," by W. R. Williams and Howard Peterson, sent to the USDA by Chicago publisher Will Rossiter. Sung on NBC Red Network radio stations by Jack Becker and Marion Mann on the *Breakfast Club* programs, this song illuminated the connections of women and the Victory Garden program.

Oh! Mistress Mary, quite contrary, How does your garden grow?
With cockle shells and silver bells, and fair maids all in a row.
Well! Mistress Mary's changed her plans—She's even learned to
plow,
And tells the crowd she's very proud of her Victory Garden now.
There's rows and rows of potatoes; As sure as you are born,
She's raising squash! Yes Sir! By Gosh! And a flock of canning corn.
There'll be lots of ripe tomatoes
That she will can and "How!"
For Mistress Mary's up-to-date, She's a Vict'ry Gard'ner now!
There're carrots, peas and radishes, And beans in double file;
I've heard it said of her onion bed "You can smell it for a mile."
. . .
Why she's even raising flowers
Of Red and White and Blue, That form a border 'round her plot
In a patriotic hue!
When all her work is fin'lly done, And all her crops are in;
You'll find her storeroom a-heaping full
With a million vitamins.
. . .
Her cauliflow'r's just like a rose;
Her garden is a "wow!"
And Mary's helping win the war,
She's a Vict'ry Gardener now.
. . .

Oh Mistress Mary's chang'd a lot
Since she took to the plow
She's not contrary any more,
She's a Vict'ry Gardener now.

. . .

If food will help to win the war
And that we know is true
Then you should follow Mary's plan,
Be a Vict'ry Gardener too![34]

The English "Dig, Dig, Dig" for Victory

During the war the British people also practiced the dual economies of conservation and increased production of food and supplies. The WIs and the WFGA worked in conjunction with the Ministry of Agriculture, the War Agricultural Committees, and the Royal Horticultural Society to provide publications and training on how to efficiently maintain life in England while providing surpluses for the growing needs. With air raids hitting the city of London, people never knew how long their supplies would last or how long their plans for agricultural production would continue to sustain. Winston Churchill used his famous words to illustrate the gravity of many areas of British sacrifice and in 1940 tied them to cultivation: "Never in the field of human conflict was so much owed by so many to so few. Here is one way in which millions can show they appreciate that debt. Let them make a personal contribution to the Dig for Victory campaign. They will be helping to ensure that our people have that last week's supply of food that may well be one of the decisive factors in our victory."[35]

Women, men, and children recycled and reused tin, rubber, and cooking fat among other things and made efforts to reduce the amount of consumption within their households. Salvage campaign leaders of both Britain and the United States argued that every natural resource saved meant the increased chance that a husband, brother, or son would return home safe and sound. Both American and British gardeners cultivated for victory during the war, but an important difference was in the British action of making the land "useful" despite the growing fear of the possibilities of impending air raids and "Germans at the end of the garden."[36] In 1939, British Minister of Agriculture Reginald Dorman-Smith announced the launch of a radical new program to increase food supplies for England. The "Grow More Food" program, extending from the vacant lots and allotments of London to the small villages of Hyderabad, proposed to provide surplus food and to feed traveling soldiers.

FIGURE 6.7. Le Bon, *Dig for Plenty*, 1944. British National Archives, INF/398.

The program, given the clever label "Dig for Victory," urged British people to cultivate current allotment gardens more efficiently, to bring unused land into cultivation, and to promote new and innovative ways to grow vegetables in urban places like window boxes and planters on porches or patios.

The creation of war or "victory" gardens was not new in many British households, however, as their existing prewar gardens only needed modifications and renaming (see fig. 6.7). Gardens had for centuries been a staple of British home life. What people grew in them, however, changed dramatically over the course of two world wars. Those who grew flower and ornamental gardens converted them to fruit and vegetable gardens, and those without the available land planted in vacant land allotments provided by the government. For England, then, the focus of the Ministry of Agriculture was not so much the production of enough food to sustain the population, but the production of enough to supplement the grants of food provided by the Lend-Lease program of the United States.

The Ministry and the War Agricultural Committees promoted the campaign through civilian lecturers. Many traveled the urban and rural areas distributing information and advice on gardening. One male leader, Lawrence Greggain, recalled traveling in a van to local villages and dispensing advice and encouragement to the housewives and other people of the community. Advice on pest management and variety in the diet encouraged new allotment gardeners to begin victory cultivation. Some seasoned gardeners had their greatest successes in produce returns. Though the Ministry of Food intended each section of an allotment garden to provide enough land for one family to produce fresh fruits and vegetables to supplement the rationed meat, dairy, and processed foods bought commercially, many gardeners were so successful that they provided enough for their families and their neighbors, or used the excess produce to trade for other items unavailable due to rationing but freely available upon the black market.[37] The WIs attempted to curb this underground trade by providing roadside markets for vegetable surpluses.

Though the British government requested information on the American war garden campaign during the First World War, it needed no urging or assistance in developing food- and supply-rationing campaigns when war broke out, as it knew all too well the severity of the situation.[38] England had long imported large quantities of its foodstuffs, as much as 70 percent of it, and the blockade of naval ports threatened the survival of the nation. Unlike the American campaigns that urged homemakers to "Grow more in '44" and free up foodstuffs that would aid both Allies and troops overseas, or to simply do without many durable and luxury goods, the British were in dire need of additional sources of food for survival of the population. British propaganda machines took the advice and experience of the United States when it came to selling the ideas of the war, however. Since Great Britain and the United States collaborated in the international Allied Expeditionary Force and produced propaganda that resulted from a large international effort, then it should come as no surprise that Britain's Allied nation's homefront propaganda reflected the same messages and goals as America's. As America waged a psychological campaign against the Axis Forces through printed leaflets

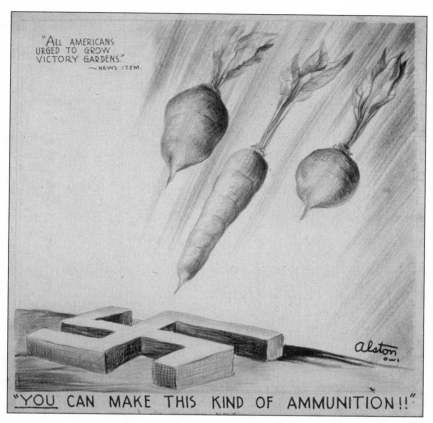

FIGURE 6.8. Charles Henry Alston, You *Can Make This Kind of Ammunition!!*, 1943. National Archives and Records Administration, Records of the Office of War Information, 1926–1951, ARC ID 535632.

dropped onto the European and Mediterranean landscapes, American and British women both found wartime employment in England in the Psychological Warfare Division of the Supreme Headquarters, Allied Expeditionary Force. These women compiled reports, news digests, and articles for newsmagazines to be distributed at the end of the war.[39] British posters and radio and film scripts also mirrored their American ally's portrayal of food as a weapon to win the war, even though the British did have a different perspective because they required resources of the colonies (see figs. 6.8 and 6.9).

While Americans promoted propaganda posters that illustrated the abundance of the American way of life, the British focused on the survival of the

FIGURE 6.9. *Tomato Heads*, 1939–1945. British National Archives, INF 3/1202.

British identity and character. Over one million leaflets and nearly two hundred thousand posters distributed across England and the colonies encouraged people to fight for the survival of the empire. The propaganda did not associate cultivation with gender as much as it did with the creation of life as patriotic symbols. The British Ministry of Information circulated a popular photo of a British victory garden, intending to use gardening as an example of the differences in British and German character. The caption read, "Where the Nazi's Sowed Death, a Londoner and His Wife Have Sown Life-Giving Vegetables in a London Bomb Crater" (see fig. 6.10).[40] One patriotic British woman replied about the hard work of cultivation, "After all, the British race sprang from the soil. The love of nature is latent in us."[41]

Under the Lend-Lease Act passed by Congress in March 1941, President Roosevelt obtained the ability to supply almost limitless aid to Britain not only in the form of war supplies but also in food. The American shipments of food included dried eggs, bacon, beans, and tinned meats, among other things. Private women's groups from around the world sent clothing and supplies to fill England's need. The Women's Voluntary Service (WVS) of England noted that when it called for clothing and blanket assistance from its international sisters, not only Americans but also Canadians, Australians, and New Zealanders and their women's clubs and organizations donated such

FIGURE 6.10. *Where the Nazi's Sowed Death, a Londoner and His Wife Have Sown Life-Giving Vegetables in a London Bomb Crater,* 1943. President Franklin D. Roosevelt Library Digital Archives, library ID 66298(14).

great amounts of clothing and sleeping supplies to England that the WVS sent surpluses to "liberated countries" to fill their needs as well.[42] With so much international communication and cooperation of women's clubs and organizations in sending supplies, it is no surprise that they shared information and goals for cultivation on the homefront.

Women's organizations initially played a vital role in organizing women's wartime service, but promoted homefront food campaigns in limited ways. The Women's National Farm and Garden Association (WNFGA) together with the Women's Institute (WI) sought to reinstate the WLA months before Great Britain declared war; however an ideological rift about the division of labor and recruitment strategies between future WLA director Lady Denman and the WNFGA left the latter out of planning for the WLA of the Second World War. As a result, membership in the WNFGA dwindled due to economic strain and its lack of labor-related agricultural programs. The organization did not offer the same kinds of home demonstration courses for victory gardening as did the American WNFGA, perhaps because of limited funds due to decreased membership. The WNFGA did assist in the training and promotion of the Dig for Victory campaign, however—encouraging urban people to support the system of allotments and providing details on how people could transform their ornamental gardens into vegetable gardens while maintaining aesthetic value.

Women alone did not fight the agricultural battle for Britain. Children as well as men not eligible to serve in the military aided in the homefront effort. Just as their American counterparts, England looked to the male population to conduct the managerial aspects of allotment gardening, and to the female and younger populations for harvesting and maintaining home food supplies altered by rationing and canning and storing. The British government sent Italian and German prisoners of war to farms and allotment gardens to help with harvests and general farm duties. Though some Britons discouraged this practice, many people recall the POWs fondly and remember that they often worked very hard to show that their nation knew best how to farm; often competitions between the POWs and the hired farm labor emerged.[43] Surviving pilots shot down over England were often sent to cultivate the same local lands they set out to destroy. David Trenbirth, a child during the Second World War, recalls the friendly relationships children often developed with the POWs: "Our parents, as far as I know, didn't object to this fraternization with the 'enemy.' . . . Perhaps it is human nature to see a surrendered (and harmless) enemy in a better light than when an anonymous and mostly invisible aircraft high above is dropping destruction, pain and death on your home."[44]

Marguerite Patten, food adviser for the Ministry of Food, recalled in 2005 the war garden she cultivated with her mother during the Second World War. When her husband, a member of the Royal Air Force (RAF) left for service, she traveled while pregnant to live with her mother. She recalled:

> Fortunately I shared her love of gardening, so we worked happily together. Both of us were busy women—my mother was still teaching and I was one of the Food Advisors in the Ministry of Food. In winter we worked weekends, but in summer we were out in the garden during the light evenings to weed and harvest fruits and the vegetables that were mature. . . . The cos lettuce and tomatoes were so plentiful we could present some to friends. When it got dark we retired to the kitchen to bottle fruits—including tomatoes—and make jam and chutney when we had saved sufficient sugar from our rations. War-time gardening was hard work but very satisfying and productive.[45]

Other women found war gardening satisfying yet challenging and at times unnerving work. With the constant threat of air attack, the garden became a mysterious place that seemed to some like a homefront battlefield. Airmen, both British and German, as well as pre-detonated bombs fell from the sky and into the gardens of victory.[46] Many a homefront war story is retold in the same fashion: while working in the garden, the sudden appearance of a plane or soldier startled and frightened the gardener to the point of terror and flight.[47] It comes as no surprise that many British built air-raid shelters either adjacent to their gardens or dug up their gardens to make room to install such a necessity. Alice Freeman, a young English woman recalls a memorable experience of leaving the garden shelter during an air raid:

> It had been going on for about an hour, when the all clear sounded. From the shelter we could hear the dog barking. I went out to shut him up, and to pop to the toilet which was also outside. I got into the garden and came face to face with a German. He had obviously bailed out during the raid, and his parachute had got caught in the apple tree. I can still see him there holding his parachute straps. I don't know who was more frightened! In minutes, about a dozen soldiers appeared with fixed bayonets. One of them climbed up the tree and cut him down. He was then taken away. I went straight off to do my gate duty, where I was armed with a wooden gun. Quite what I would have done if faced by the enemy I don't know; I would probably have had to hit him.[48]

Despite the threats air raids presented, the British population found clever ways to support both the war effort and themselves. The soft soil of Gladys Stevens's garden proved useful when a German bomber fully loaded with ammunition landed in it: the soft soil allowed the craft to glide in and land "in perfect condition." After the crew abandoned the ship, the Army intervened to inspect the plane and its contents, as it was the only German plane found completely intact. Stevens's ingenuity turned the situation into an added wartime campaign when she opened up the garden for the public to view the plane. She charged for both admission and a cup of tea to enjoy while observing the ship and donated the proceeds to the Red Cross.[49]

The British propaganda relating to agriculture and increased production reached intended audiences through print, radio, film, and stylized images.[50] Much of the wartime propaganda had international aspects as well, and though the Ministry of Information produced the majority of it, some propaganda was produced by patriotic presses and individuals. Some people felt inspired by these messages to produce their own patriotic printings. In 1941, Wedgwood employees, for example, took to including patriotic poetry with products sent to the United States. The following is an example of such communication:

Our factory's in a garden
On our pots we paint the flowers
We concentrate on export
Til victory won is ours.[51]

Americans responded by sending messages back to the company along with parcels of food, facilitated through the Wedgwood New York office. The Ministry of Information commended this unofficial international communication and suggested this kind of interaction, through shared enthusiasm, could connect the people of the United States and Great Britain over a common goal.[52]

A 1940 American film titled *London Can Take It* urged Americans not to fear for mother England, for her people were strong and united and would do everything possible, from rationing to recycling to growing food in every inch of soil available, all in the name of saving the nation from occupation. This film is just one of many films that also served to reassure the people of America that the aid the U.S. government gave to Britain for wartime economic and material assistance was not a failed investment. It served to prove to Americans that despite any fears caused by news stories of nightly air raids on London, despite fears of a city of people looting, hoarding, and fighting as a result of the war, there was one thing to be certain: "London Can Take It."[53]

During the Second World War, Americans found success in cultivating victory through the production of food. Gardeners who sought to prevent Allies from starvation found inspiration in President Franklin D. Roosevelt's words, "For food—American food—can be the deadliest weapon of all. It may save thousands of American lives. The course and length of the war may depend on how successfully we produce it—how willingly and widely we share it—how carefully we save it—how wisely we use it."[54]

Before the United States entered the war, before the Atlantic Charter and the informal alliances and symbolism that evolved from it, there was the Lend-Lease Act of the United States. With it the United States and Britain formed official and unofficial ties and alliances that centered on food and the diplomacy of food production. More than just an ally, the United States as a former colony continued to serve the mother country through the distribution of food much like the colonies of India, Barbados, and Jamaica. Though the geographical, agricultural, and food importation situations of England and the United States differed greatly, food production and conservation efforts of citizens on the homefront shared similarities that were gendered, nationalistic, and symbolic of the diplomatic role food would play in the postwar era.

Building on the success of the British and American food campaigns of the First World War, this time around nations utilized the popular media and large-scale print campaigns to urge community leaders to localize their organizations and to develop popular and efficient methods of cultivating victory. This kind of advertisement suggested women's place in politics, labor, and the home. While glamorous women in wartime roles graced the covers of fashion magazines, women gained a sense of place in labor, home management, and in the preservation of life. Women responded to national calls for increased domestic agricultural production in various ways, but the overall active participation, whether as promoters of the organization or as gardeners or farmers, reflected the newfound freedoms women in the postsuffrage society desired: such participation was more active and political and served to continue the process of liberation. On the other hand, the dual roles for women espoused by the governments caused women to experience that liberation while maintaining ties to their domestic duties.

British propaganda focused more on things like "Garden Pests and How to Deal with Them," rather than gendered instruction and advertising for American victory gardening.[55] In terms of the food production by colonial populations, however, British propaganda promoted white women as educators and leaders in agricultural production. Illustrations featuring women as heroines in agricultural labor of the colonies characterized a complicated and hegemonic nationalism of the Grow More Food colonial campaigns. The British Food Production Department used its propaganda campaign to show that the negative aspects of food shortages and war damage served as proof of the positive strengths of the empire. Newspapers printed stories about Londoners uniting to create allotment gardens in the areas affected by the blitz. For a variety of reasons, these gardens are curiously telling. First, Londoners planted these bomb crater gardens in the areas affected by the blitz because this land was readily available and was, as a result of the blitz, no more than "slacker land," a name used in the First World War to describe idle land. Second, and perhaps most intriguingly, these gardeners tried to create life in an area marked by destruction and death. This circular pattern of cultivation for the birth of vegetation for the opportunity to make ammunition and supplies that are used in destructive wartime actions that are intended to kill other humans and vegetation, after which other humans will seek to cultivate again, is an interesting cycle of creation and destruction that perhaps deserves more attention.[56]

While the British government relied on conscription of women in national service, the United States used caution when attempting to gain women's support outside the home. While Britain had immediate needs that necessitated all able-bodied people to contribute to their utmost physical capacity, the U.S. government's objective was primarily to develop a program that would "encourage" women to embrace their "traditional" roles as kitchen and household managers—an effort to maintain a sense of middle-class consensus for the coming postwar world. This conservative focus also gave soldiers on the war front a reason for fighting: the protection of white middle-class womanhood and the preservation of American middle-class values. Most women who saved, stored, rationed, and grew their own food in the name of victory were white, middle-class domestics who were married or older than their WLA counterparts. Propaganda of both Britain and the United States played on women's concerns for their children, reminding women of their need to produce for the good of their families while portraying white-middle-class scenes as the ideal.

Whereas both WLA and Victory Garden movements were popular in Britain and the United States, the wartime propaganda illustrates the difference between the two governments' desired outcomes. Campaigns in both nations focused on women, but Britain addressed the serious shortages of the nation while the United States emphasized the responsibility of women to sacrifice and conserve for an abundant future for America and its allies. Internationally, popular media and advertising assisted the propaganda campaigns during the Second World War by helping to promote the cultivation needed to win the war. As the war progressed, American popular media and advertising provided tools to (re)domesticate women so that a postwar society built upon conformity could thrive. The USDA and NFWI simultaneously governing the recruitment of female agricultural labor and, through home demonstrations, reprimanding women for their household wastefulness and inattention meant a shift in social sphere for women. While working-class women now had an important responsibility to support the family, their responsibilities of managing the home and caring for children remained. Thus as women's sphere expanded, so did their responsibilities and society's expectations of them.

The United States and Great Britain promoted cultivation as both a weapon and as a creator of a peaceful postwar world; however, the United States took the power of food it presumed it had over the world and used it as a tool of diplomacy as the war progressed. Cartoons such as Charles Henry Alston's 1943 "*You* can make this kind of ammunition!!" provided humorous yet powerful suggestions about the power of food. The U.S. Office of War Information later produced a 1944 film titled *America's Hidden Weapon* to promote the cultivation of land as the most valuable resource and tool to win the war. In the First World War, Woodrow Wilson and Herbert Hoover sought to use food to solve the food shortages of Britain, but in the Second World War, food was the weapon against the enemy and the path to political hegemony.

Just as Great Britain led the organization of the WLA during the First World War, the United States in the Second World War and beyond attempted to act as the leader in the Victory Garden movement, at the very moment the British Empire was in decline. For the British, a growing dependence upon the colonies for agricultural support meant a greater number of production and conservation programs in the postwar years. Though many of the allotments in England quickly gave way to new commercial and residential development at the war's end, the Grow More Food Campaign continued on for decades in most of the colonies to support the needs of England. Thus for the British, food was a symbol of survival of the empire. For Americans, the victory garden equated the individuality of the gardeners and the abundance of the nation. After the war's end, food continued to be a major issue in the rebuilding of the postwar global society based upon ideas about gender, food, and abundance or lack thereof. The United States held on to the opportunity to use its abundance of food to ensure political hegemony. How that stance played out in the minds and memories of both politicians and the public over the next fifty years says as much about the national and personal identity associated with the campaigns as it does about the events themselves.

Part III.

CULTIVATION AND CULTURAL TRANSCENDENCE

Food is strength, and food is peace, and food is freedom, and food is a helping hand to people around the world whose good will and friendship we want.

—Senator John F. Kennedy, speech in South Dakota, 1960

CHAPTER 7

The Women's Land Army, Victory Gardens, and Cultural Transcendence

For many years on Remembrance Sunday, we have not been asked to be represented. The question is, why not? Do we not deserve to be recognised with pride and honour? Why were we forgotten so easily after we were no longer needed? We were proud then to wear our uniform and serve our country. Those of us who are left are still proud to have belonged to the Women's Land Army, and we will never forget.

—Grace Wallace, Women's Land Army member, BBC People's War Archive

WHEN THE BRITISH AND AMERICAN people who served in the Women's Land Armies (WLAs) or who cultivated victory gardens during the world wars recalled their experiences, they often used words like "change," "growth," and "remembrance."[1] What these words meant to the leaders and to cultivators did not always coincide with what those words meant to the nations they supported. For reformers and leaders of agricultural labor, these words reflected years of personal work to provide political voice for women. For the cultivators of victory, much of the meaning of these words derived from the personal experiences surrounding disbandment and demobilization of the agricultural programs, the transition to postwar society, and the nostalgic attempts to claim space for themselves in the public memory about the war. For the governments of Britain and the United States, these words reflected the development of food as both diplomatic strategy and as a political tool and thus their meanings centered more on policy than on society. Just as reformers and leaders of the leisure classes found limited space in the public memories of women's roles in agriculture, both the cultivators of victory and the governments that persuaded them struggled to find a place for cultivation in the history of wartime service; and the intersection of women, cultivation, and governments created national memories that skewed historical realities. The transition from demobilization to cultural memory occurred by means of consumption, politics, language, art, and gardening practices. This transition is crucial to the history of these movements because how the WLA and the Victory Garden movements are remembered over time profoundly shaped and continues to shape popular culture through social organizations, literature, and a global consumer and political culture.

How, where, who, and for what purpose people in Great Britain and the United States remember this wartime service is critical to completing the analysis of these movements. In contrast to the British, who recall proudly and nostalgically the vital wartime service of the land girls, Americans give little space in their collective, public memory for their WLA recruits, at times pejoratively labeled farmerettes. The United States uprooted the WLA from its collective memory and in its place planted the victory garden as symbol of postwar consensus and of national abundance. Regardless of the aspect of culture (whether consumer or political) wartime cultivation penetrated, it reflected varying degrees of change in personal and national identities among both individuals and governments in a postwar global society.

Demobilization

When the war came to an end, WLA members received the news of the soldiers' return with mixed feelings. Though the women were immensely happy the war was over, many feared the loss of their newly found freedoms and careers. Additionally, amid the celebrations of the war's end, some WLA members felt ignored for their contributions and service. Contributors to *Land Girl Magazine* expressed their disdain for the missing acknowledgment of their service in a simple phrase: "Blow, blow, thou winter wind, thou art not so unkind as man's ingratitude."[2]

Though the demobilization of the food campaigns and WLAs after the First World War brought a welcome end to years of hard labor, it also provided a precedent for future homefront organization during wartime. For Britain, the Ministry of Food realized the importance of the Women's Institutes (WIs) and other women's groups to help relieve the homefront food shortages. Accepting the praise of the government and public, Lady Denman continued to lead the NFWI, bringing rural and urban women of all classes together in education and fellowship. When war loomed again over Europe two decades later, the Ministry of Agriculture remembered the success of English women and the WIs and therefore responded to women's suggestions to re-create the WLA in England three months before Britain went to war again in 1939. For Britain, the position and activism of Denman and the strength of the WIs kept the memory of the WLA strong and positive. Though WLAA leaders often publicly criticized conservative programs designed to reduce waste and tie women to management of the home, in the postwar years childhood hunger took those leaders away from their stances on women's place in labor and led to new attitudes about women as mothers of the nation. In the postwar years, leaders of the WLAA and the Department of Labor bickered over control of women's labor, and the WLA disbanded in 1919. With no standing leadership and no WI to serve as a collective hub of women's education and organization, the memory of the work of reformers and laborers alike faded. Though some WLAA leaders continued to train agricultural laborers after the First World War, there was no WI in the interwar years to serve as a collective hub of women's organization and education, so local county extension agencies under the guidance of the USDA took on most of the responsibility for the recruitment of WLAA workers in the Second World War. Moreover, the USDA recognized after the First World War that war gardens (later termed victory gardens) relieved much of the agricultural burden of the nation and therefore it promoted the development of more urban domestic programs rather than rural farm programs during the Second World War. Additionally, demobilization of the food campaigns seemed like a fruitful lesson in effective homefront efforts and national unity. From that perspective, the rural labor of the women fighting for their place in labor and in politics disappeared from the memory of female war service and in its place stood the efficiency of the kitchen garden. For both Britain and the United States, perceiving demobilization of these programs as only part of a process toward peace minimized social transitions that influenced the personal and cultural memories of the WLA and the Victory Garden movements.

After the demobilization of the WLA in both nations after the First World War, many women felt their service brought greater acceptance of women in labor and a sense of pride for the work accomplished; however the British method of demobilization caused great controversy after the Second World War and remains a disappointment in the memories of many British WLA members. Women confined to the home in both Great Britain and the United States found great relief in the lessened restraint upon their household management as a result of the demobilization of the food campaigns and were for the most part eager to return to prewar ways of home management and life; women who served in the WLAs, however, quickly found themselves at the end of their service with no postwar job placement, no gratuity as payment, and no official appreciation for their services. Many members of the British

WLA at the time of disbandment received only a letter from the Queen as appreciation for their services. As Irene Grimwood, a member of the British WLA, put it, "While I was very proud to have received this letter I was somewhat disappointed not to have been given a gratuity. We left the W.L.A. with just the money we had earned for our last week's work. No more."[3]

Though the British government offered no thanks in the form of economic support, it did publicly praise the WLA for its service. At the end of nearly six years of service during the Second World War, the British WLA invited the land girls to a Christmas party to celebrate and publicly acknowledge the six years of hard labor and sacrifices made for victory. In this public ceremony, a guard of land girls in dress uniforms officially greeted Her Majesty the Queen. Upon arrival of Lady Gertrude Denman, however, the land girls burst into cheers and applause out of their excitement and respect for their director.[4] Though members appreciated that King George VI, Queen Elizabeth, and other officials took interest in the land girls by attending several parades and rallies supporting the work of the WLA, their devotion and gratitude toward their leader, Lady Denman, was obvious.[5]

The uniform of the British WLA was of great significance to the women that served, as many had to turn in clothing ration coupons just to obtain replacement items, and when the WLA disbanded, members were required to give back the uniforms. Despite Denman's very determined and public insistence on treating the members like all other conscripted civilian services by offering gratuity and public appreciation, the British Parliament refused to view the WLA as an equal branch of civilian service. This action toward the laborers left Denman, an organizer of agricultural labor for nearly three decades, devastated by the disrespect. It was only after her virulent protest that the British government allowed the women who served in the British WLA to keep a few minimal pieces of clothing as a token of its appreciation for service. Many women not allowed to keep their uniforms felt very disappointed as they were the only symbols available of the hard work the women performed.[6] Denman resigned out of protest and disgust with the disrespect shown to both the laborers and her long-term leadership. Thus postwar experiences of the WLA workers and the victory gardeners differed and influenced the societal collective memories of their efforts. While leaders and members of the British WLA felt lasting resentment toward disbandment without gratuity or support, disbandment of the American WLA met little public resistance or controversy and was in general symbolic of the war's end and of the peace to come. In fact, the idea of women stepping down from occupations previously held by men in the prewar years was widely accepted across all industries in America at the end of the Second World War. The disbandment of the American WLA in 1947 received little attention from the press and for the most part drew very little attention among Americans at all.

Demobilization of the urban food campaigns of Great Britain and the United States comprised the gradual relaxation of restrictions of food rationing and a reduction of education by home demonstrations. For the British, this easing of restrictions did not come for some time after the war, however, as rationing continued and in some cases tightened after the war's end. For instance, the British Ministry of Food rationed bread in 1946 even though it did not did not ration it during the war. The rationing of sweets did not end until 1953, and the rationing of bananas did not lift until 1954. In short, British food shortages did not cease with the war's end. In addition to the Grow More Food campaign in the colonies, the country turned to the dwindling WLA to continue service until its official disbandment in 1950. With Denman and many of the tenured workers gone in protest over poor treatment, the remaining structure provided minimal support for agricultural production. Despite the continued shortages, the British government publicly lauded the agricultural strength of the nation—King George, a supporter of the WLA, entertained workers from his Sandringham estate after the war's end with a "victory garden party" to celebrate the accomplishments of the nation.[7]

In America, the rationing of foods officially ended in 1946. Though some aspects of rationing, such as restrictions on canned foods, ended shortly after the war, the cultural effects did not. New foods like oleomargarine, cottage cheese, and Kraft Macaroni and Cheese boxed dinners served as substitutes for butter, meat, and cheese, and remained staples in the American diet. As a result of the war, the American consumption of coffee increased in 1945 to the highest per capita rate up to that time.[8] Unfortunately, the abundance of fresh vegetables in the diets of Americans slowly receded along with the restrictions on household management. Despite the reductions of gardens, however, the USDA urged victory gardeners to continue to produce additional quantities of food to aid in the reconstruction of Europe.[9] For urban Americans, the lessening of food restrictions meant decreased interest in producing additional quantities of food at home. The USDA estimated that Americans would continue to increase the number of peacetime gardens as a result of the wartime education campaigns on topics such as balanced diets. The USDA estimated there were about 5 million to 6 million gardens in America before the war and over 21 million during the peak of the Victory Garden campaign in 1943. Near the war's end, the lessening of restrictions such as the rationing of canned vegetables led to a slight decrease in interest in vegetable gardening—the estimated total of gardens was 17.5 million to 18 million in 1945.[10]

Something about wartime gardening enabled women to find new opportunities to discover their own identities through cultivation. In an article about her relationship with a woman to whom victory gardening was an important marker of her identity, Mary Kay Blakely recalled:

> "I have to get home" she told him, carefully folding the remnants of her grilled cheese sandwich into her napkin. "I have a *lot* of things to do," she reported, remembering her awesome list. "I have to plant my tomatoes for one thing." Those tomatoes, I knew, were more than vegetation to her. Her tomato crop was famous in her suburban neighborhood—last year, one plant alone yielded more than a hundred perfect fruits. Every summer, she had the pleasure of distributing the wealth among her neighbors, collecting their thanks and admiration. Tomatoes, in her case, were the key to community, to her sense of place.[11]

Can something as simple as cultivating tomatoes represent one's identity and sense of place? For Blakely, recounting for *Ms. Magazine* in 1987 the personal and cultural meaning that decades of "victory" gardening held for the eighty-four-year-old unnamed woman, it *did* represent those things.

Food as Diplomacy

The concept of food as a diplomatic tool rested not only within governmental offices, but also in everyday entertainment to keep the people of the nation focused on the goal of victory. Parades, theatrical performances, and radio dramas were just some of the ways that Britain and the United States demonstrated their dedication to the wartime cause. Upon examination of the venues, however, a standard theme emerged, one that linked the strength of nations together by a commonality of an interdependency on food and abundance. For governments, the theme was simple—food was diplomacy.

> JOHN (*after pause*): Food . . . it's a weapon. Used as a weapon of *conquest*, it can bring a nation to its knees. Used wisely—generously—food can revive that nation—win the war—write the peace.

> FIRST WOMAN: Ever since the beginning of time, food has determined the fate of men and nations.

> NARRATOR: The whole history of mankind is a history of food. The nations which could produce the most and the best food—or get it from their neighbors—become the strongest nations. They had time to write books—paint pictures—build temples in which to praise God, who had given them such abundance.

FIRST WOMAN: But even the *great* nations learned what it meant to be hungry. They lived until famine struck. Then they disappeared—forgotten. . . .

NARRATOR: The history of mankind has been the story of a struggle against famine. Yet not 'til about a hundred and fifty years ago did men actually dare hope that someday famine might be abolished.

YOUNG MAN: We have a republic now. The land belongs to *us*—the people. And we are learning how to use it to *prevent* famine. Some day, not in your lifetime—perhaps not in mine—but *some day* . . . men and women—all mankind will have enough to eat.[12]

Global food shortages made production of food a stronger tool of foreign diplomacy than it had during the war years. In 1946, Chester C. Davis, chairman of President Truman's Famine Emergency Committee and former administrator of the Agricultural Adjustment Administration, argued that "never before in our time have so many people been living so close to death by starvation." Davis urged Americans to consider the agricultural need of Europeans when deciding whether to continue gardening. He argued the war-ravaged nations of Europe were unable to help themselves with their own food shortages due to drought and decreased industrial production of canned foods and that Americans should try to make every effort to help end the global starvation. Just as the U.S. food administrator Herbert Hoover did after the First World War, Chester C. Davis asked Americans and Canadians to continue the Victory Garden programs so that more food could be sent to aid nations in need.[13] When British Prime Minister Clement Attlee requested help from the United States to supplement the postwar agricultural needs of the nation, U.S. President Harry Truman urged Americans to consider fulfilling global agricultural need as the duty of America. Truman argued that adjustments to a postwar society included fulfilling the "responsibilities and staggering obligations" of world leadership by promoting the continued urban gardening that was so successful during the First and Second World Wars.

In response to the European need, Secretary of State George C. Marshall urged Americans to look at gardening as a tool to spread freedom and success across Europe and said, "I don't speak from a desk in the State Department. . . . I ordered my seeds and settings ten days ago. If the question comes up, 'Do I negotiate or do I hoe, plant, and weed,' my answer is 'I propose to do both.'" He argued that increased home production of food in "Freedom Gardens" should be a vital part of the European Recovery Program and that Americans should take his own personal experiences as an example of how to use food as diplomacy.

When asked about how gardening could truly spread ideas, he replied with an example of how his own gardening activities changed the mind of a Chinese woman whom he and his wife "brought back to this country." While taking a wheelbarrow and a shovel to spread manure on his acreage he engaged in "one of the most remarkable negotiations" with the woman: "Anna spied me with the wheelbarrow. . . . In China probably the lowest form of human life is the man with the wheelbarrow. He is below the man with the ricksha. The situation was utterly repugnant to her. She thought I had lowered and humiliated the position of Secretary of State. Our struggle over the wheelbarrow I settled only by superior strength. She and I both understood the importance of food, but we had a slight difference on the matter of implementation of this principle."[14]

Postwar gardens were not just part of the Marshall Plan; they were also promoted as personal insurance against inflation and tough economic times. Secretary of Agriculture Charles F. Brannan asked Americans in 1951 to plant "Liberty Gardens" to offset the strain on American food budgets. No matter what the name of the garden, the action remained the same: cultivation meant asserting the American identity of abundance to a struggling global community.

Remembrance and Cultural Transcendence

In the years after demobilization of the WLAs and the Victory Garden campaigns, women who cultivated victory shared their experiences with a younger generation. Decades after the war, American Mary Appling stated, "had I known that these remembrances would be of interest to anyone at a later date, I would have recorded them at a time when they were clearer in my mind. As it is, now that I am 81, what I recall as the 'war-impacted life' of one single American woman in the U.S. during World War II may, when added to the accounts of others, give some idea of the diversity of women's experiences on the home front."[15]

In the years after the Second World War, the British WLA evolved into a symbol of both national identity and the strength of British women. After the war, many women privately felt the lack of official political recognition for their labor egregious and disrespectful. In public, however, they did not pursue recourse or revenge because welcoming soldiers home and returning to some sense of a normal life seemed more pressing and important. Many women in the British WLA kept in touch with the friends, coworkers, and farmers they met while volunteering; many remained close friends until death. Such relationships spurred the organizing of reunions of former WLA members to gather together and share memories of the WLA and personal stories. These reunions and gatherings sparked considerable public attention in the press and partly as a response to that, many women wrote and published their memoirs of life as land girls and life on the farm front during the world wars. The popularity of published memoirs increased in the 1970s, corresponding to a worldwide interest in environmental issues that peaked in the 1990s with the public recognition in the press of the accomplishments of the land girls. Despite this interest in the land and those who worked it, however, public attention turned to the domestic women who cultivated for victory, which the nation saw as part and parcel of a larger role of maintaining the household during war. It was not until December 2007 that the British government officially recognized the women for their service and awarded them with badges to commemorate their service to the nation in the Second World War.[16] Exhibits on land girls are now common among local and national history museums of Great Britain where the communities seek to honor the service of the elder women.

The image of the land girl found its way into British consumer culture in the form of collectible dolls, fine china, and such everyday items as notepads, drinking glasses, and posters. Fine china maker Royal Doulton commemorated the WLA by issuing a mug in the shape of a WLA member's face. Another Royal Doulton collectible, the land girl figurine of the Bunnykins collection, serves as part of a collection commemorating British workers of the Second World War (see fig. 7.1). Collectible dolls, mugs, posters, and other memorabilia entered the consumer industry in the 1990s to draw on the nostalgia of the WLA and the symbol of women and cultivation (see figs. 7.2 and 7.3). Regardless of the product sold, the message remained the same: the British land girl is a symbol of the strength and resiliency of women who furthered the survival and stability of Britain.

If art imitates life, then the play *Lilies on the Land* exemplified the public affection for the British WLA. When the production company The Lion's Part announced they intended to produce a play about the WLA, they received in response 140 letters with stories and photos from former land girls. The Lion's Part enlisted the help of former land girls in the creation of the play, which turned out to be a form of reunion and commemoration of the WLA for many of the members. Many contributed to the content and script of the play by offering songs, poems, and even old uniforms. The play was an acclaimed success, not only by professional reviewers, but by the former land

FIGURE 7.1. *(above, left)*
Royal Doulton, *Land Girl*, Bunnykins
collection. Royal Doulton Image supplied by WWRD United Kingdom
Ltd., Stoke on Trent.

FIGURE 7.2. *(left)*
Royal Doulton, *Women's Land Army
Character Mug*. Royal Doulton
Image supplied by WWRD United
Kingdom Ltd., Stoke on Trent.

FIGURE 7.3. *(above, right)*
Royal Doulton, *Women's Land Army
Figure*. Royal Doulton Image sup-
plied by WWRD United Kingdom
Ltd., Stoke on Trent.

girls as well, bringing the nostalgic memory of the land girls forward into the twenty-first century.

Textual and visual representations of land girls increased in the 1990s and 2000s, for example, in Elizabeth Elgin's novel *A Scent of Lavender* (2003), a nostalgic story more focused on romance than wartime service. In this story, an entire town is swept up in the emotion of war, and apparently each other, as volunteers take the opportunity to find new identities in their wartime work and with new acquaintances. The land girl identified in the book struggles with the meaning of patriotism as she falls in love with a conscientious objector.[17] The film *The Land Girls*, based upon Angela Huth's novel of the same name, depicts the story of three young British WLA members—a hairdresser, a Cambridge graduate, and a young girl engaged to a naval officer—who become friends and use the war experience to forge identities for themselves outside of their prewar lifestyles.[18] The film is just as nostalgic as Elgin's novel and similarly focuses on romance. As the women find friendship and love amid the fieldwork, the film does more for our understanding of British nostalgia than of actual land girl experiences. However, this film does depict the changes in the memory of the land girls' service to the nation.

From music and television shows to terminology and labels on consumer products, the American victory garden at the turn of the twenty-first century remains a cultural symbol of domesticity, patriotism, and above all the ability of everyday citizens to utilize and manipulate the land to achieve a common goal. The "victory garden" is a cultural phrase that transcended the Second World War and denotes American cultivation of land, whether growing vegetables as in the war years, or a mixture of vegetables and flowers, as in the prewar and postwar years. After the war, Americans were free to enjoy flower gardening, though many embraced planting both vegetables and flowers as symbols of the American garden of abundance. In September 1945 the employees of the Federal Reserve Bank of New York hosted a Flower and Victory Garden Show, exhibiting flowers to symbolize the reduced food restrictions of wartime and the abundance of their victory gardens. Governor Thomas L. Bailey of Jackson, Mississippi, contributed to the show by flying in one hundred pounds of his victory garden tomatoes along with okra, white squash, small red peppers, and "several kinds of beans" to display and enter into the show contest. Intended to show the abundance of the American garden, Governor Bailey's collection also displayed the regional identity of abundance of the "typically Southern" vegetables to northern gardeners.[19] Leaders of the National Victory Garden Institute urged gardeners "not to rest on their hard-won laurels," but to continue to make gardening part of their everyday lives. This show and others like it represented the general trends of the nation toward gardens as symbols of abundance and recreation instead of necessity.

In the spirit and principle of President Hoover's programs of international food distribution and perhaps reminiscent of Taft's Dollar Diplomacy, Americans continued to increase produce in hopes of cultivating a new world of peace and democracy, to free people from want "everywhere in the world."[20] Americans received mixed and perhaps confusing messages, however, as the USDA, George Marshall, and others urged Americans to continue gardening in a postwar effort to help save the world from the threat of communism by supplying hungry nations with food and aid. By changing the name of the victory garden to a freedom garden or a liberty garden, political leaders hoped to draw the same kind of support to battle world hunger and fight communism as the wartime Victory Garden campaigns. Such plans failed, however, as in the 1950s many Americans grew tired of working to produce garden vegetables for their own kitchens and instead focused on consumption and a life of plenty. This does not mean that victory gardens lay in ruins, however. American gardeners liked the physical exercise and satisfaction of cultivating plants and started growing flowers again instead of vegetables. For many, vegetable gardening just didn't seem to fit with the new postwar ideals of the modern American home. After the war experience, growing one's own vegetables was not a sign of economic prosperity after all, even though one of the war's primary aims was "freedom from want."

These postwar ideals changed as time and circumstance dictated. Gardening, which was once a community effort became a way for modern people to hoard in a greedy society. In the postwar years, the garden evolved from a symbol of political identity to one of personal identity in promoting new suburban neighborhoods where each homeowner could enjoy the personal benefits of a new home, lawn, and garden. No longer did the garden hasten the return of loved ones or feed the hungry children of the world, but rather it symbolized all the abundance of the individual American household. Women were urged in verbal and nonverbal ways to pay more "attention to kitchens" after the war, and the production and consumption of food went hand in hand with that sentiment. The family's economic level was considered higher if the woman stayed at home to raise children than that of families who needed women to work outside the home; therefore, the home in which a woman tended to the garden and kitchen with all its technological advances was at once nostalgic and modernly abundant. By placing the garden in the kitchen domain and consumer culture, a program that once called on women to save the nation now served to tie them to the kitchen and essentially (re)domesticate them in a modern way.[21] In the postwar years, the "call" to women to manage the production of food remained despite evolving ideas about women's place in labor.

Perhaps the most visible cultural remnant of the wartime victory garden is an American national series on public television (PBS) on home gardening, *Crockett's Victory Garden.* Initially aired in 1975, this series hosted by Jim Crockett offered basic information on cultivating both flowers and vegetables.[22] Though the increase in interest in gardening during the 1970s prompted the publication of dozens of manuals on gardening techniques and such television programs as *Crockett's Victory Garden,* American citizens did not seek to end world hunger or even battle rising inflation with the personal vegetable garden. For them, gardening signified psychological therapy and escape from the outside world as well as exercise and above all an aesthetically pleasing landscape of suburbia. These benefits alone inspired Americans to garden, and anyone suggesting otherwise faced insults in the press. The World Bank discussed world hunger and attempted to answer the question "Who will feed the world's hungry?" and on the same day a press release appeared about the series premiere of *Crockett's Victory Garden.* Shortly afterward, the *New York Times* featured a commentary on the world's economic struggles and used the victory garden as an old solution for a modern problem. The editorial featured an illustration of a board game much like Monopoly with a head of lettuce in the center; each surrounding square, on which any Monopoly player might expect a property, contained bugs, shovels, and money among other obstacles to a successful garden. The caption read, "The New Family-Fun Game for Inflation-Fighting Americans and the object of the game was to simply plant the SEED in the GARDEN so that a player grows enough VEGETABLES to win VICTORY over inflation. The excitement of the game is that at each TOSS of the DICE, players court CHANCE and DISASTER as they invest lavish amounts of MONEY, TIME, and HARD LABOR."[23] Gone were the days of patriotic sacrifice on the land. Increasingly the nostalgia of the Victory Garden campaigns of the world wars were a longing for success of the past rather than the revitalizing of actions taken to achieve such goals. Nearly three decades after the war, most Americans still did not want to return to hard labor to help their neighbors in need.

Not every American abandoned their work in victory gardens. Some continued to care for their gardens years after the war and food crises passed. In 1952 about one hundred residents of the Bronx, New York, area tended to an urban half block next to Monteflore, one of the community's hospitals. Together the "city farmers" each paid one dollar to pool for gardening tools and equipment and in return got all the exercise they could handle along with all the vegetables they could eat.[24] From roses and fig trees to corn and grapevines, the gardens contained a wide variety of vegetables. This is but one example of many community activities across the country after the Second World War that continued to produce more food by means of community gardening. The community garden movement did not stem from the Second World War; it was part of a century-long process aimed at reform for the working poor to build character and offer supplemental food resources. In the first half of the century, the community gardens sought to make better citizens through labor on the land and in that sense also make the most efficient use of all available urban lands. School gardens targeted women not as the primary cultivators but as teachers of a younger generation about the virtues of gardening. In the second half of the century, however, community gardens served a more utilitarian purpose as communities sought supplemental food supplies due to high food prices, inflation, and even increased pesticide use.[25]

Once the consumer culture absorbed the victory garden, the term often ceased to act as a noun in the American vernacular and instead functioned as an adjective, a term of production from a bygone era used as a nostalgic descriptor of consumption. The term appears as names of fabric patterns, in a variety of housewares ranging from tablecloths to patio furniture, and as a label of other items of Second World War nostalgia. Even the patriotic historical fiction character and doll Molly McIntire made by the American Girl company wears a victory garden dress during her homefront service. In the consumer culture of the late twentieth and early twenty-first centuries, the victory garden symbolizes women, kitchens, and nostalgia for a consensus long lost.[26]

Y2K and Beyond

In the late twentieth and early twenty-first centuries, calls for victory gardens reflected not only nostalgia, but also changing attitudes about food and abundance. The Victory Seeds Company advertised in 2006 that "history is cyclical, the strong economy of the 1980s and 1990s has begun to weaken, and there are lessons to be learned from the past. It is always a good time to plant your own Victory Garden." In a speech to children of Bancroft Elementary School in March 2009, Michelle Obama promoted the lessons to be learned from proper nutrition. Excitedly, she cheered the students on. "Let's hear it for vegetables," she shouted, eliciting a cheer. "Let's hear it for fruits!," she said to more cheers. Then: "Did I hear a boo?"

Modern calls for the immediate need for cultivation of the land in times of crises are heard in the international and national Victory Garden movements promoted to prevent economic, health, and national disasters surrounding Y2K, world poverty, and to subvert the use of dangerous pesticides and improve general health. In 1999, many people worldwide feared the perceived impending doom of a technology crash at the turn of the millennium known as Y2K. In anticipation of this widely predicted disaster, people stockpiled food, household items, and electric generators for fear that society as they knew it might collapse. The victory garden was seen by people not as a way to save the nation or end world hunger, but as a way to save themselves from the greed of their neighbors. In this every-man-and-woman-for-themselves attitude, people looked to the ways earlier generations lived to teach them to be self-sufficient. Out of this fear, many people returned to the idea of cultivating their own food for survival. Looking to the victory gardens of the world wars, many felt a nostalgic trip down memory lane might bring them closer to self-reliance in the wake of anticipated disaster. Whereas the Victory Garden campaigns of the world wars focused on helping produce for the nation, victory gardens in the Y2K era focused on self-reliance and were based on widespread fear that hoarding and greed by others might deny individuals their opportunity for survival. Though the concept of the victory garden was not new, it was far from an imitation of the original intentions of the campaigns in the first half of the twentieth century. By signing pledges not to hoard, by rationing and recycling what they had, people in the first half of the century focused on obtaining victory for all and starvation for none. Unlike the wartime generations however, people at the end of the century turned to hoarding as a means of psychological satisfaction and comfort in an uncertain world.

In recent years Americans continue to use cultivation and the term "victory garden" in ways that are at once nostalgic and anxious about future economic and political outcomes. Wartime gardening lessened after 1945 as nations gave up patriotic calls for service, yet some women still felt a responsibility to continue as a response to global and personal crises. Amid increasing anxieties over women's responsibilities in new wartime economies, Deborah Holmes, an experienced gardener, wrote an article for *The Old House Web*, an Internet forum for "old house enthusiasts" in which she outlined her modern reasons for planting a victory garden:

> As the mother of two teenage boys, I'm more than a little uneasy about an impending military strike on Iraq, and talk of biological and chemical attacks and terrorism here in America. So I'm going to plant some cabbage . . . and tomatoes, and beans and beets and broccoli and summer squash and onions. . . . Like my parents and grandparents did during World War II, I want to plant a Victory Garden. Americans in 1941 embraced the idea of turning yards, vacant lots, ball fields, parks, and even tiny strips of grass between row houses into fertile ground for vegetables. There's comfort in

growing one's own food, and in the certainty that tiny seedlings will grow into robust plants.[27]

Throughout the article Holmes uses pictures and examples of American war gardeners from the Second World War to encourage others to grow victory gardens in a time of economic and political uncertainty. What she does not suggest, however, is that the modern-day victory gardens should be used for relieving commercial agriculture to feed the troops or to help feed the world's hungry. Gone are the sentiments of international support to aid the needy of the world. What remains is the concept of the victory garden to promote individual Americans' own sense of security and stability.

While early victory gardens of the war years were morale boosters and a way of building community and often involved parades, judging contests, and national displays, many modern-day adaptations shun such ideas as aspects of a bygone era and instead move toward self-preservation. To have a parade or national campaign to promote modern-day survivalist gardening would seem out of balance and out of character to such individuals, for many were both afraid and resentful of a government that could have allowed such a disaster as Y2K to occur in the first place. For survivalists, the war efforts of the world wars were of another generation from a completely different time and mindset, and many recalled the era with nostalgia when selectively referring to the efforts made by their ancestors for survival. Realistically, however, the number of people gardening during the first half of the twentieth century outnumbered the gardeners at the turn of the twenty-first century. Up until 2009, victory gardens planted as nationalistic statements on White House lawns, in community grounds, vacant lots, and in company-owned lands were a thing of the past, or at least were a dying breed. What sprouted in their places were gardens of both leisure and necessity, but almost none attributed a reason for existence to patriotic nationalism.

Early in 2009, Michelle Obama, wife of the newly elected U.S. president Barack Obama, responded to pleas to promote the health benefits of locally grown foods by announcing that she decided to plant a victory garden on the White House lawn (see fig. 7.4). With the help of the White House culinary and gardening staff as well as some eager Washington, D.C., fifth graders, she broke ground for a garden—something not seen in the White House since the days of Eleanor Roosevelt's victory garden during the Second World War.[28] This time the focus was not on feeding the world's hungry or on supplementing food during times of rationing, but on spreading education about the epidemic of obesity and diabetes that threatens children in America and the health benefits of organic, locally grown food. Garden plans include do-

FIGURE 7.4. Joyce N. Boghosian, *First Lady Michelle Obama and White House Horticultur-ist Dale Haney work with kids from Washington's Bancroft Elementary School to break ground for a White House garden*, White House web site, 2009.

nating what food the White House has in abundance to local kitchens that feed the homeless in Washington, D.C. Though the causes of the first ladies differ, both gardens denoted times of economic stress and political uncertainty. Is Michelle Obama's garden an attempt to recall an era when communities banded together for the common good or to represent modern-day attempts at gardening in that it serves a more personal purpose for her as a first lady interested in the health of the country? Only time will tell. Though Obama's garden does represent modern agricultural trends such as locavore and organic gardening movements, it also reflects attitudes about women's responsibilities to feed and care for children's health. Michele Obama's position as first lady brings an expectation to embody what national motherhood looks like. As an educated woman with a successful career, Michelle Obama rounds out the national expectations on motherhood with a public display of caring for children's health as part of her kitchen garden in a way that even Harriot Stanton Blatch would approve of. Though the idea of today's modern White House garden originated from activists Daniel Bowman Simon and Casey Gustowarow and their White House Organic Farm Project, Michelle Obama formed her own personal and political statement with her decision to plant one on the White House lawn. As a mother figure to the nation,

Michelle Obama blends notions of childhood health, locavore movements, and organic gardening into one public display through what some consider "nudge" politics. Thus, she blends many political motives of health and agriculture into very personal motives for mothers of American children.

For millions of American and British people, what started out as political became personal. The cultivation of food changed their perceptions of patriotism, hard work, and their definitions of abundance. Though the people who cultivated for victory in the first half of the twentieth century left their service at the end of the wars, they inspired millions more in the decades following to explore the meaning of sacrifice and the personal benefits of home cultivation. In the latter half of the twentieth century and beyond, cultivation became more of a symbol than an action and though no formal vestiges of the WLA or the wartime food campaigns remain, the British and American national, personal, and collective memories, ideologies, and identities remain.

Epilogue
GARDEN AS METAPHOR

"Women and War" is a headline. . . . But, after all, it is only a headline, for there is nothing to say about women and war. . . . There are no words made for women in time of war. There is only waiting, misery, want, horror, heartbreaking. For the women who are actually suffering, there is no need or use for words. For the women who are only looking on . . . words seem futile, ineffectual, insignificant. . . . The greatest relief to women lies in some sort of definite action which either helps or is intended to help the suffering of someone else. . . . Some of them have gone into the fields to harvest the crops. . . . They are working for the preservation of their homes and their children; for the men who are wounded in battle, for the country which, by accident of birth, is theirs. . . . There is no difference between the women of the different countries. Their men have gone to war. They are left alone with their work and their waiting. They are all brave, busy, silent. . . . For so many years they have borne the wars which men have made. . . . And now, they are bearing it again, and this time it is the worst war of the world. . . . And again they bear it in silence, for after all, there is nothing to say.

—"Women Harvest Crops While Men Folk Fight," *Dallas Morning News*,
21 September 1914, 8

NEVER IS THE PHRASE "actions speak louder than words" more appropriate than when words go unrecognized. From the lens of governmental wartime agencies across the globe during the first half of the twentieth century, women had an image, but no voice. Nations not only used the image of women and cultivation to incite patriotism and promote homefront efforts, but also to tie the cultural image of women to the land to give soldiers a gendered reason to fight for their homeland. In this way, women represented the homeland and were symbolically tied to the land. Land and the cultivation of it were gendered symbols of nationalism. When women organized to fill the agricultural labor needs of their nations, however, they met gendered prejudices and discrimination despite the cultural image of the connections of women to the land. British and American national wartime agencies that promoted victory by using the image of women rarely addressed the individual and collective voices of the women laborers. In retrospect, scholars recognize that had it not been for the strength of women's voices, much of the women's war work in agriculture would not have taken place. Women in fact *did* have much to say about war, politics, and their roles in homefront agricultural efforts. Their voices led to organizational efforts that in turn led to the development of many of the national homefront agricultural programs of the First and Second World Wars. Through women's collective efforts at recruitment, training, and organization, the governments of Britain and the United States raised a labor force in the attempt to solve the international food crises of the first half of the twentieth century. Recognition of that voice, however, was complicated by biases based both upon class and gender as well as the governmental desire to utilize food as a tool of international diplomacy. These events resulted in a transformation of the cultural memory of women in agriculture and the role of women in wartime.

The standardization of agricultural training served as a springboard for the suffrage movement and for reformers seeking a political stage. The very personal choice of agriculture as a wartime service by women served a political purpose of gaining recognition and respect in labor and society. The devastation of the war, however, complicated societal expectations for women, and changing political roles removed agriculture as that springboard for political equality. Instead, the memory of that service served to tie management of food production and the home to the changing expectations for women and led to a dualistic responsibility placed upon them as both laborers and efficient home managers. Women were at once politically equal and socially responsible as mothers to nurture their children through proper nutrition.

Though initially not a topic for a large national campaign, the growing of a "war garden" in one's own home, whether rural or urban, was part and parcel of an efficient and effective patriotic home according to popular belief. With women's responsibility to recycle, ration, and plan came the added responsibility of growing vegetables to protect their children and their nations from hunger. Over time that private cultivation meant personal identity; and generation after generation, women altered that identity to meet their own personal needs. Though many argue that much of the public attitude toward the creation of modern societies and families came during the postwar era in the Cold War push for conformity, the evidence suggests that this promotion occurred even earlier. In select stories and printed publications such as "Making Better Americans," we see how nations used gendered agricultural organizations such as the Women's Land Army in attempts to Americanize immigrants and mold a modern society. One can look even further back in time than the First World War, however, and see these types of societal shaping. Both England and the United States promoted the production of gardens to mold the character of the working poor, and in America, to make immigrants less of a threat to the working class. In this way, the natural environments of nations, when used agriculturally, were tools nations used to achieve progressive goals of social change and modernization.

During the wartime food shortages, nations portrayed women as vital to the nations' future and stability and thus women represented the nation and national values in a variety of ways. One of the first portrayals of women was as a protecting figure or as Mother. By portraying woman as Mother, nations sought to appeal to women's maternal senses and urge them to service, to protect not only their own children but all the soldiers as well. Second, a portrayal of woman as Daughter of the government helped establish the authoritative parental relationship between the government and women. When nations needed to find some method of behavior modification or manipulation of young women, they often depicted them as daughters of the nation, naïve, vulnerable, and in need of protection and guidance from a masculine government (e.g., Uncle Sam) to direct them on how best to serve the nation. Third, portraying woman as Wife illustrated the need to (re)domesticate women near the end of the war so that returning soldiers did not feel threatened and to ensure a return to the comforts of prewar life. With many women taking wartime jobs in factories, nations worried about the demise of the family and the political values it represented (i.e., refuting communism). Last, women often portrayed themselves as Sister because of a most obvious, though perhaps unintentional, transnational exchange of ideas. Women in large part were loyal to their countries and eager to obey calls for consumptive restraint, and they also collaborated with their international sisters and were sympathetic to both their public and private causes. What role women were portrayed as assuming at any given time depended on government needs and women's faith in themselves as reformers, cultivators, and mothers.

The author hopes that this study serves to open new conversations about the implications of class, race, and gender upon wartime cultivation. Did women's efforts in the food campaigns serve as another facet of the fight for women's suffrage? Once governments connected women to the production of food in the national identity, how did that affect the gender roles and norms across nations in the second half of the century? Alternatively, how much influence did the culture of abundance have in shaping other aspects of diplomacy? How else is food used as a political or social motivator? These are questions that cannot be addressed completely in this study, but it is hoped that the analysis and critique here will serve to spark interest for future research into the topic.

What is certain is that for thousands of women, over decades and across oceans, cultivation was closely tied to personal identification. Reformers identified with women's place in labor and used cultivation to liberate women from such limitations. Laborers personally identified with the social constraints upon women and found work on the land both liberating and patriotic. For political purposes, however, cultivation was a weapon to conquer the enemy and women were opportune tools to gain that weapon. Just as women manufactured munitions in the factories, women cultivated weapons in the gardens and fields of America and Great Britain. When scarcity and fear struck both nations, they turned to each other and especially to women to forge a path for national survival. Women in turn used the war as a tool to gain personal liberty and self-awareness. Thus the global wars of the early twentieth century were not merely wars of political allies, nor were they merely wars of women on the homefront; rather they were wars of identity and the cultivation of that identity. For millions of people in the twentieth century, the act of cultivation brought newfound identity and a sense of place within the global political community. Whether it was a world leader urging his people to come to the agricultural aid of their allies, a lady of leisure finding interest in reform, or a young woman setting out on an adventure "snagging turnips and scaling muck," the cultivators of victory helped to change personal and political norms into new opportunities for world leadership and gender equality. What started out as mere political and humanitarian aid evolved into a lasting cultural legacy that forever changed global perceptions of the connections of politics, gender, and cultivation. These memories and the cultural meanings surrounding them are significant and worthy of narration for there *are* indeed words for women and war, provided there are those of us willing to hear and give voice to them.

Whereas gardens at the beginning of the twentieth century were a bridge and pathway between the middle classes and the elite, gardens at the end of the century provided very personal and internal motivation for both American and British women. Throughout the century, women cultivated for social mobility, patriotism, health, and at times for personal gain. Regardless of intent or decade, women viewed agricultural labor and the organization of it as an opportunity to overcome personal obstacles. Through women's very personal actions, nations struggled to form their own global identities based upon the labor of women. In this way, the garden and cultivation were metaphors for identity, both political and personal. Women in war throughout the

twentieth century cultivated more than just food and abundance; they cultivated a sense of self, memories both personal and cultural, and pride for their
contribution to change in a world of turmoil. Just as they planted "tomatoes
where the roses used to grow" women found that they were planted as leaders
in food production—in a place where only men used to grow. In the fields of
their homelands, food was ammunition and women were the cultivators—the
cultivators of victory.

NOTES

Introduction: Gardening in the New Century

Epigraph: Gilbert Mills, Ted Rolfe, and Billy Faber, "There'll Be Tomatoes Where the Roses Used to Grow" (New York: Arrow Music, 1945). This song was sent to the War Food Administration Publicity Department to be used "free of royalties" for the war effort.

1. For further analysis of the significance of women's national and international organization for wartime agricultural production, see Dorthea Abbott, *Librarian in the Land Army* (Stratford-Upon-Avon: D. Abbott, 1984); Kate Adie, *Corsets to Camouflage: Women and War* (London: Hodder and Stoughton, 2004); Diane Bardsley and Miklos Soltesz, *Land Girls: In a Man's World, 1939–1946* (Dunedin, NZ: University of Otago Press, 2000); Amy Bentley, *Eating for Victory: Food Rationing and the Politics of Domesticity* (Urbana: University of Chicago, 1998); Susan Briggs, *The Home Front: War Years in Britain, 1939–1945* (London: George Weidenfeld and Nicolson Ltd., 1975); Stephanie A. Carpenter, *On the Farm Front: The Women's Land Army in World War II* (DeKalb: Northern Illinois University Press, 2003); Melissa Hardie, *Digging for Memories: The Women's Land Army in Cornwall* (Penzance, Cornwall: Hypatia Trust, 2006); Gervas Huxley, *Lady Denman, G. B. E.* (London: Chatto and Windus, 1962); Inver Primary School, *Alisa Munro, Land Army* (Hamilton: SLIC, 2006), http://www.wardetectives .info/projects/wardetectives/wewillremember/inveoo52.htm; Peter King, *Women Rule the Plot: The Story of the 100 Year Fight to Establish Women's Place in Farm and Garden* (London: Duckworth, 1999); Laura J. Lawson, *City Bountiful: A Century of Community Gardening in America* (Berkeley: University of California Press, 2005); Penny Martelet, "The Women's Land Army, World War I," in *Clio Was a Woman: Studies in the History of American Women*, ed. Mabel E. Deutrich and Virginia Cardwell Purdy (Washington,

D.C.: Howard University Press, 1980), 135–45; Bob Powell and Nigel Westacott, *The Women's Land Army, 1939–1950* (Stroud: Sutton Publishing, 2000); Nicola Tryer and Rosemary Davies, *They Fought in the Fields: The Women's Land Army: The Story of a Forgotten Victory* (Oxford: ISIS Audio Books, 2002); Carol Twinch, *Women on the Land* (Cambridge: Lutterworth Press, 1990); Elaine Weiss, *The Fruits of Victory: The Women's Land Army of America in the Great War* (Dulles: Potomac Books, 2008).

2. For more discussion on the culture of abundance, see Bentley, *Eating for Victory*, 142–70; Lizabeth Cohen, *A Consumer's Republic: The Politics of Mass Consumption in Post-war America* (New York: Vintage Books, 2003), 1–15; Thomas Hine, *I Want That! How We All Became Shoppers: A Cultural History* (New York: Harper Collins, 2002), 3–40; Robert M. Collins, *More: The Politics of Economic Growth in Postwar America* (New York: Oxford University Press, 2000), 14–39; David Morris Potter, *People of Plenty: Economic Abundance and the American Character* (Chicago: University of Chicago Press, 1954).

3. For more information on how the wartime food shortages altered British culture, see Susan Bordo, "Hunger as Ideology," in *Eating Culture*, ed. Ron Scapp and Brian Seitz (Albany: SUNY Press, 1998); John Burnett, *England Eats Out: A Social History of Eating Out in England from 1830 to the Present* (Harlow: Pearson, 2004); Reay Tannahill, *Food in History* (New York: Stein and Day Publishers, 1973), 323, 326–27, 373, 376–78; Arnold Palmer, *Moveable Feasts: A Reconnaissance of the Origins and Conse-quences of Fluctuations in Meal-Times with Special Attention to the Introduction of Luncheon and Afternoon Tea* (London: Oxford University Press, 1952); C. Anne Wilson, *Food and Drink in Britain* (Chicago: Academy of Chicago Publishers, 1991); Roy C. Wood, *The Sociology of the Meal* (Edinburgh: Edinburgh University Press, 1995).

4. Harriot Stanton Blatch, *Mobilizing Woman-Power* (New York: Womans Press, 1918), 66.

5. Lady Gertrude Denman, "Introduction," in *Land Girl: A Manual for Volunteers in the Women's Land Army*, ed. W. E. Shewell-Cooper (London: English Universities Press, printing date unknown), iii.

Chapter 1. Ladies of Leisure and Women of Action

Epigraph: Harriot Stanton Blatch, *Mobilizing Woman-Power* (New York: Womans Press, 1918), 102.

1. Colin Bingham. *The Affairs of Women: A Modern Miscellany* (Sydney: Currawong, 1969), 134.

2. Daniel T. Rodgers, *Atlantic Crossings: Social Politics in a Progressive Age* (Cambridge, Mass.: Harvard University Press, 1998); Daniel De Leon, "Lady Warwick," *People* (New York) 9, no. 21 (20 August 1899): 1.

3. For more discussion of the transnational cultural exchange of ideas in the international women's movement see Leila J. Rupp, *Worlds of Women: The Making of an International Women's Movement* (Princeton, N.J.: Princeton University Press, 1997). A further analysis can also be found in Geoffrey C. Ward and Ken Burns, *Not for Ourselves Alone: The Story of Elizabeth Cady Stanton and Susan B. Anthony* (New York: Alfred A. Knopf, 1999).

4. Kathy Peiss, *Cheap Amusements: Working Class Women and Leisure in Turn-of-the-Century New York* (Philadelphia: Temple University Press, 1986), esp. chaps. 1 and 2.

5. Rupp, *Worlds of Women*. For more information on the rise of women's clubs as forms of political and social reform, see Bessie Louise Pierce, "The Political Pattern of Some Women's Organizations," *Annals of the American Academy of Political and Social Science* (May 1935): 50, 58; Erika A. Kuhlman, *Petticoats and White Feathers: Gender Conformity, Race, the Progressive Peace Movement, and the Debate over War, 1895–1919* (Westport, Conn.: Greenwood Press, 1997).

6. This drop in percentages of women can also be attributed to the dropping economic success of agriculture as an occupation in general. British studies in 1910 suggested that one of the highest percentages of male pauperism was found in the occupation of agriculture. See "A Statistical Survey of the Problems of Pauperism," *Journal of the Royal Statistical Society* 74 (December 1910), British National Archives, ref. PRO 30/69/1864.

7. Harriet Stanton Blatch Papers, 1907–1915, Library of Congress, MSS12997, boxes 1–13.

8. Report on the International Women's Council from the *Times* (London), June 1899, cited in Peter King, *Women Rule the Plot: The Story of the 100 Year Fight to Establish Women's Place in Farm and Garden* (London: Duckworth, 1999), 12–16.

9. *Times* (London), May and June 1899.

10. Max Pemberton, "Mrs. Cornwallis-West as a Reigning Beauty," *Weekly Dispatch* (London), 7 January 1917, 5. Countess Warwick's influence on the people of England was quite profound as seen in a song composed in 1892 by an admirer Harry Dacre titled "Daisy Bell," known best for the phrase "Daisy, Daisy / give me your answer do / I'm half crazy / all for the love of you."

11. Frances Evelyn Maynard Warwick, *Life's Ebb and Flow* (New York: Morrow and Co., 1929).

12. "Brilliant Gathering at Hertford House," *Daily News* (London), 23 June 1900, 3.

13. Warwick, *Life's Ebb and Flow*. Lady Warwick's serious devotion to the socialist ideal was debated and doubted by members of the socialist party in America in Daniel De Leon, "Lady Warwick," *People* (New York) 9, no. 21 (20 Aug. 1899): 1.

14. King, *Women Rule the Plot*, 8.

15. "Lady Warwick on 'Man's Opportunity,'" *Daily News* (London), 28 May 1900, 8.

16. *Daily News* (London), 28 May 1900, 6.

17. Records relating to the Warwick hostel, WAR 5/1, Reading Museum of English Rural Life, Reading, England, British National Archives.

18. Details of Countess Warwick's proposed agricultural scheme can be found in both the *Land Magazine*, Christmas edition, 1897, and *Times* (London), 17 August 1898.

19. Report on the First Annual Meeting of the Lady Warwick Agricultural Association, WAR 5/1, Reading Museum of English Rural Life, Reading, England, British National Archives; republished in King, *Women Rule the Plot*, 16–17.

20. *Times* (London), 17 August 1898; see also King, *Women Rule the Plot*.

21. Records relating to the Warwick hostel, WAR 5/1, Reading Museum of English Rural Life, Reading, England, British National Archives.

22. Women's Agricultural and Horticultural International Union leaflet, 15 March 1900, quoted in King, *Women Rule the Plot*, 18.

23. Mrs. Chamberlain, paper read at Women's Institute at Grosvenor Crescent, London, November 1900, quoted in King, *Women Rule the Plot*, 19; more information on the preoccupation of management in agriculture can be found in Alun Howkins, *The Death of Rural England: A Social History of the Countryside Since 1900* (London: Routledge, 2003), 7–35.

24. For more information on the development of the Women's Institute, see Maggie Andrews, *The Acceptable Face of Feminism* (London: Lawrence and Wishart, 1997); Gervas Huxley, *Lady Denman, G. B. E.* (London: Chatto and Windus, 1962).

Chapter 2. The Land Girls

1. For more information on the percentages of women in agricultural employment, see Samuel J. Hurwitz, *State Intervention in Great Britain: A Study of Economic and Social Response, 1914–1919* (New York: Columbia University Press, 1949); "Letter from the Board of Agriculture and Fisheries to Local Councils Urging Them to Take Control of Land and Use It to Grow Food," December 1916, Ministry of Agriculture Files, British National Archives, PRO ref: 48/219. Hurwitz argues women made the smallest employment gains in the field of agriculture, where the total number of female agricultural workers climbed from 80,000 in 1914 to 113,000 in 1918 and represented in 1918 approximately only "37%" of the workers in agriculture; however Hurwitz's citations conflict with the Ministry of Agriculture report citing women in agriculture increased from 190,000 to 228,000. Though the figures differ somewhat, both represent the increase in women's work in agriculture to be the lowest among other fields such as industry, commerce, and transportation. Hurwitz does not include that "domestic" service in fact saw the least "gains": there was a marked decrease during the war of 400,000 women, according to the Board of Trade figures cited by the War Cabinet Committee in 1918.

2. For a more detailed discussion of the strategies of supply blockades, see C. Paul Vincent, *The Politics of Hunger: The Allied Blockade of Germany, 1915–1919* (Athens, Ohio: Ohio University Press, 1985).

3. Susan R. Grayzel, *Women's Identities at War: Gender, Motherhood and Politics in Britain and France During the First World War* (Chapel Hill: University of North Carolina Press, 1999), chap. 3; Susan Kingsley Kent, *Gender and Power in Britain, 1640–1990* (New York: Routledge, 1999), 257–310. For a more broad discussion of the role of food in shaping female identity in the twentieth century, see Amy Bentley, *Eating for Victory* (Urbana: University of Chicago, 1998).

4. "Women's Farm and Garden Union," *Common Cause* (London), 19 July 1915, 188.

5. "10,000 Women Wanted at Once," *Weekly Dispatch* (London), 1 April 1917, 8.

6. Letter from Meriel Talbot, *Times* (London), quoted in Peter King, *Women Rule*

the Plot (London: Duckworth, 1999), 7; "10,000 Women Wanted at Once," *Weekly Dispatch* (London), 1 April 1917, 8.

7. "10,000 Women Wanted At Once," 8.

8. "To Britain's Women Workers: 30,000 Pairs of Stockings—Free," *Daily News* (London), 16 December 1918, 6. For more discussion on the importance of the British uniform as compared with the liberation it brought, see Bob Powell and Nigel Westacott, *The Women's Land Army, 1939–1950* (Stroud: Sutton, 2000), 5–7. For more on the "threatening" nature of the uniform, see Alun Howkins, *The Death of Rural England* (London: Routledge, 2003), 31–32.

9. For more discussion about the role of women workers in late nineteenth- and early twentieth-century Britain, see: Nicola Verdon, *Rural Women Workers in Nineteenth-Century England: Gender, Work and Wages* (Suffolk: Boydell Press, 2002); Ellen Jordan, *The Women's Movement and Women's Employment in Nineteenth-Century Britain* (New York: Routledge, 1999); Robert Colls, *Identity of England* (New York: Oxford University Press, 2002), 108–39.

10. "The Land Army at Work," *Daily News* (London), 10 October 1918, 4.

11. For more on the struggles of women and agriculture, see Joan M. Jensen, *With These Hands: Women Working on the Land* (Old Westbury, U.K.: Feminist Press, 1981).

12. Oral interview of Mary Lees, ID number 506, Imperial War Museum, London. Recorded 30 November 1974; "Trained Farm Girls. Obstinate Farmers' Refusal to Pay Them," *London Daily Mail*, 12 May 1917, 3.

13. "Senate Passes Food Control Bill," *New York Times*, 9 August 1917, 1; "The Food Administration Bill," *New York Times*, 4 June 1917, 10.

14. "16,000 Women to Aid City Food Campaign," *New York Times*, 1 October 1917, 15; Herbert Hoover, *Herbert Hoover: An American Epic: Famine in Forty-Five Nation Organization Behind the Front, 1914–1923* (Chicago: Henry Regency Co., 1960), 59; Frank M. Surface and Raymond L. Bland, *American Food in the World War and Reconstruction Period* (Stanford: Stanford University Press, 1931), vii, 189.

15. "C. D. Gibson's Committee for Patriotic Posters," *New York Times*, 20 January 1918, 63.

16. Penny Martelet, "The Women's Land Army, World War I," in *Clio Was a Woman: Studies in the History of American Women*, ed. Mabel E. Deutrich and Virginia Cardwell Purdy (Washington, D.C.: Howard University Press, 1980), 136–45.

17. Martelet, "Women's Land Army," 136–37; Stephanie Carpenter, *On the Farm Front: The Women's Land Army in World War II* (DeKalb: Northern Illinois University Press, 2003), chap. 1.

18. "Plan Land Army Work: Women from Sixteen States Meet to Consider Harvest Program," *New York Times*, 26 June 1918.

19. "Girl Laborers on Small Farms at $2 a Day," *New York Times*, 3 February 1918.

20. "Land Army Praised, President Writes in Appreciation of Women's Farm Work," *New York Times*, 11 April 1918.

21. "Land Army Incorporates," *New York Times*, 24 May 1918; "Plan Land Army

Work: Women from Sixteen States Meet to Consider Harvest Program," *New York Times*, 26 June 1918; Carpenter, *On the Farm Front*, chap. 1; Martelet, "Women's Land Army," 137–44.

22. Women's Land Army of America, *Handbook of Standards* (Washington, D.C.: National Board of the Women's Land Army of America, 1919). For a continued discussion on the role of gender biases and farm labor, see King, *Women Rule the Plot*; Donald B. Marti, *Women on the Grange: Mutuality and Sisterhood in Rural America, 1866–1920* (New York: Greenwood Press, 1991).

23. "City Girl as Farm Worker—Her Own Story," *New York Times*, 24 February 1918; "Girl Laborers on Small Farms at $2 a Day," *New York Times*, 3 February 1918; Martelet, "Women's Land Army," 142.

24. Emma L. George Papers, 1915–1920, Library of Congress, Washington, D.C., Miscellaneous Manuscripts Collection, box 1, folder 1.

25. Sophia Smith Collection of Papers, College Archives of Smith College, Northampton, Mass., box 130; Martelet, "Women's Land Army," 136–37.

26. Training Brochure, Women's Land Army Training Camp, Emma L. George Papers, 1915–1920, Library of Congress, Washington, D.C., Miscellaneous Manuscripts Collection, box 1, folder 1.

27. Women's Land Army of America Inc., Progress Report, Emma L. George Papers, 1915–1920, Library of Congress, Washington, D.C., Miscellaneous Manuscripts Collection, box 1, folder 1.

28. Carpenter, *On the Farm Front*, 15–34; Women's Land Army of America, *Handbook of Standards*.

29. Women's Land Army of America, *Handbook of Standards*, 10.

30. Ibid., 9.

31. "New Jersey Land Army Opens Cooperative Farm to Train Women Workers," Emma L. George Papers, 1915–1920, Library of Congress, Washington, D.C., Miscellaneous Manuscripts Collection, box 1, folder 1.

32. Helen Kennedy Stevens, WLAA member, *New York Times*, 24 February 1918.

33. "Barnard Girls to Go to Farm Camp," *New York Times*, 9 May 1918; Martelet, "Women's Land Army," 136–37.

34. Women's Land Army of America, *Handbook of Standards*, 10.

35. Ibid.

36. "Girl Laborers on Small Farms at $2 a Day," *New York Times*, 3 February 1918.

37. "City Girl as Farm Worker—Her Own Story," *New York Times*, 24 February 1918.

38. Carpenter, *On the Farm Front: The Women's Land Army in World War II* (DeKalb: Northern Illinois University Press, 2003), 15–34.

39. Women's Land Army of America, *Handbook of Standards*.

40. "Mrs. Whitman in Land Army," *New York Times*, 3 September 1918, 8.

41. *Republic*, 11 January 1919.

42. Martelet, "Women's Land Army," 144–45.

43. Emma L. George Papers, 1915–1920, Library of Congress, Washington, D.C., Miscellaneous Manuscripts Collection, box 1, folder 1.

44. "Working Song," Emma L. George Papers, 1915–1920, Library of Congress, Washington, D.C., Miscellaneous Manuscripts Collection, box 1, folder 1.

45. "Fighting Song of the Farmerettes," Emma L. George Papers, 1915–1920, Library of Congress, Washington, D.C., Miscellaneous Manuscripts Collection, box 1, folder 1.

46. "American Farmerette Song," Emma L. George Papers, 1915–1920, Library of Congress, Washington, D.C., Miscellaneous Manuscripts Collection, box 1, folder 1.

47. King, *Women Rule the Plot*, 5–20; Carpenter, *On the Farm Front*, 15–34.

48. "Women on the Farms," *New York Times*, 29 July 1918.

49. Emma L. George Papers, 1915–1920, Library of Congress, Washington, D.C., Miscellaneous Manuscripts Collection, box 1, folder 1.

50. "Helping to Make Americans," National War Garden Commission, Emma L. George Papers, 1915–1920, Library of Congress, Washington, D.C., Miscellaneous Manuscripts Collection, box 1, folder 1.

51. Harriot Stanton Blatch, *Mobilizing Woman-Power* (New York: Womans Press, 1918), chaps. 9–12; Women's Land Army of America, *Handbook of Standards*; Marilyn Irvin Holt, *Linoleum, Better Babies, and the Modern Farm Woman, 1890–1930* (Albuquerque: University of New Mexico Press, 1995), 13–64.

52. "Finest Harvest for 50 Years," *Daily News* (London), 20 August 1918, 5.

53. "Record Wheat Crop: Official Reports from the Districts," *Daily News* (London), 7 September 1918, 5; and "Finest Harvest for 50 Years," *Daily News* (London), 20 August 1918, 5.

54. "Gathering in the Harvest," *Daily News* (London), 21 August 1918, 3.

55. "The Prisoner's 'Joke,'" *Daily News* (London), 20 August 1918, 5.

56. "Woolrich Girls Return Home," *Daily News* (London), 27 November 1918, 3.

57. "Women and the Election," *Daily News* (London), 16 November 1918, 6.

Chapter 3. Sowing the Seeds of Victory

Epigraph: Harriot Stanton Blatch, *Mobilizing Woman-Power* (New York: Womans Press, 1918), 146–49.

1. Frank V. DuMond, "Liberty Sowing the Seeds of Victory," 1917, Poster and Print Collection, POS-US.D84, no. 1 (C size), Library of Congress, Washington, D.C.; "Food Supply Is Much Increased," *Wray Rattler*, 29 August 1918; "War Garden Party in Park," *New York Times*, 22 May 1917.

2. Charles Lathrop Pack, *The War Garden Victorious: Its War Time Need and Its Economic Value in Peace* (Washington, D.C.: National War Garden Commission and Lippincott Co., 1919); chaps. 1 and 10; Laura J. Lawson, *City Bountiful* (Berkeley: University of California Press, 2005), 126; Amy Bentley, *Eating for Victory* (Urbana; University of Chicago, 1998), 7.

3. *Punch, or the London Charivari* 152 (30 May 1917): 352.

4. Kathleen Burk, *Britain, America, and the Sinews of War, 1914–1918* (Boston: George Allen and Unwin, 1985), 5; Benjamin Horace Hibbard, *Effects of the Great War upon Agriculture in the United States and Great Britain* (New York: Oxford University Press, 1919), 168–69.

5. Benjamin Horace Hibbard, *Effects of the Great War*, 192–93.

6. Jay Winter and Jean-Louis Robert, *Capital Cities at War: Paris, London, Berlin, 1914–1919* (Cambridge: Cambridge University Press, 1997), 307–9.

7. Samuel J. Hurwitz, *State Intervention in Great Britain* (New York: Columbia University Press, 1949), 100, 106, 151–53, 158, 215–16, 250, 267; Hibbard, *Effects of the Great War*, 193.

8. Hurwitz, *State Intervention in Great Britain*, 195; Susan Briggs, *The Home Front: War Years in Britain, 1939–1945* (London: American Heritage Publishing Co., 1975), intro.; Marjorie and C. H. B. Quennell, *A History of Everyday Things in England* (London: B. T. Batsford, 1918), 24, 39–41, 176–77, 114, 210; Miles Hadfield, *A History of British Gardening* (London: John Murray, 1979); Karen Sayer, "The English Cottage Garden," *Country Cottages: A Cultural History* (Manchester: Manchester University Press, 2000), 79–112. Also see George W. Johnson, *A History of English Gardening* (New York: Garland Publishing, 1982).

9. "Songs of Food Production," *Punch, or the London Charivari* 152, 30 May 1917, 355.

10. *Times* (London), 18 November 1916, 9; Hibbard, *Effects of the Great War*, 192–94.

11. Hibbard, *Effects of the Great War*, 192–94.

12. For more about British gardens and national identity, see Sayer, *Country Cottages*, 126–28.

13. Pack, *War Garden Victorious*, chap. 1.

14. For more discussion on the land as metaphor and land as nationalism, see Phillip Bull, *Land, Politics, and Nationalism* (New York: St. Martin's Press, 1996), 54–115.

15. "Position of Girl Clerks in Whitehall," *Daily News* (London), 14 November 1918, 2.

16. "Questions Every Woman Is Asking," *Weekly Dispatch* (London), 19 August 1917, 7.

17. Pack, *War Garden Victorious*, chap. 2; Lawson, *City Bountiful*, 136–37.

18. Pack, *War Garden Victorious*, chap. 2.

19. "Questions Every Woman Is Asking," *Weekly Dispatch* (London), 19 August 1917, 7.

20. "Theatreland Gossip," *Weekly Dispatch* (London), 21 October 1917, 6.

21. Hibbard, *Effects of the Great War*, 168–82; P. W. Wilson, "Over There," *Daily News* (London), 3 October 1918, 4.

22. "A Great Achievement: Brilliant Results of the Land Campaign," *News of the World* (London), 26 May 1918, 1.

23. "Lord Mayor's Pageant: Procession that Will Live in History," *Daily News* (London), 11 November 1918, 7.

24. "Lord Mayor's Pageant: Procession that Will Live in History," *Daily News* (London), 11 November 1918, 7.

25. *Garden Magazine* 25, no. 4 (May 1917): 220.

26. Frank M. Surface and Raymond L. Bland, *American Food in the World War and Reconstruction Period: Operations of the Organizations under the Direction of Herbert Hoover 1914 to 1924* (Stanford, N.J.: Stanford University Press, 1931), 3–5; Lawson, *City Bountiful*, 144–69; Lawrence E. Gelfand, *Herbert Hoover, the Great War, and Its Aftermath, 1914–1923* (Iowa City: University of Iowa Press, 1979).

27. "Says Food Vultures Rob East Side Poor," *New York Times*, 15 February 1918.

28. Pack, *War Garden Victorious*, 1.

29. Ibid., 2.

30. Charles Lathrop Pack, "Making a Nation of Garden Cities," *Garden Magazine* 27, no. 4 (May 1918): 7.

31. Ibid.; Lawson, *City Bountiful*, 170–203. For more about the decline in farms and how it related internationally, see Benjamin H. Hibbard, *Effects of the Great War* (New York: Oxford University Press, 1919), esp. chap. 1.

32. For more information about the San Francisco celebration, see Lawson, *City Bountiful*, 117. For information on Marion and other cities and their community efforts, see Pack, *War Garden Victorious*.

33. Pack, *War Garden Victorious*, chap. 4.

34. "Schools Aiding War Charities," *New York Times*, 30 September 1917.

35. "War Garden Seeds Scarce and Costly," *New York Times*, 27 January 1918.

36. Pack, *War Garden Victorious*, chap. 4; Lawson, *City Bountiful*, 289.

37. Pack, "Making a Nation of Garden Cities," 183.

38. Pack, *War Garden Victorious*, 18 (my emphasis). For more information about how gardening had "come to stay," see "Food Supply Much Increased," *Wray Rattler*, 29 August 1918.

39. Lawson, *City Bountiful*, 93–143.

40. "Helping to Make Americans," National War Garden Commission, Emma L. George Papers, 1915–1920, Miscellaneous Manuscripts Collection, Library of Congress, Washington, D.C., box 1, folder 1.

41. Lawson argues in *City Bountiful* that the nation experimented with gardening as a community and social reform mechanism for decades, such as in the implementation of school gardens and community gardens in poorer urban areas, so when the call came for gardening as an expression of patriotism and national strength, citizens answered the call with eagerness and enthusiasm.

42. For more information on the ideas of land as Americanization during the First World War, see the Emma L. George, 1915–1920, Library of Congress, Miscellaneous Manuscripts Collection, Library of Congress, Washington, D.C.

43. Pack, *War Garden Victorious*, 8.

44. "Says Food Vultures Rob East Side Poor," *New York Times*, 15 February 1918.

45. Lawson, *City Bountiful*, chap. 6; Pack, *War Garden Victorious*, chap. 9.

46. "War Garden Fete Toll a Vegetable: Throng in Washington Square," *New York Times*, 23 May 1917; "War Garden Party in Park," *New York Times*, 22 May 1917.

47. "War Garden Fete Toll a Vegetable: Throng in Washington Square," *New York Times*, 23 May 1917; "War Garden Party in Park," *New York Times*, 22 May 1917.

48. Pack, *War Garden Victorious*, chap. 2.

49. Surface and Bland, *American Food in the World War and Reconstruction Period*, 4–22.

50. Lawson, *City Bountiful*, 125.

51. Lawson, *City Bountiful*, 141, 156–57, 170–71; Pack, *War Garden Victorious*, 31.

52. Pack, *War Garden Victorious*, 22.

53. See Hibbard, *Effects of the Great War*, 100, for a slightly different discussion about Wilson's rejection of laissez-faire policy. Hibbard argues that the president did what was necessary in rejecting laissez-faire, but one might argue that if Wilson was truly interested in action to solve the problem, he would have created the Food Administration *before* the United States made declarations of war.

4. The Aftermath of War: Gender and Agriculture in the Interwar Years

Epigraph: Harriot Stanton Blatch, *A Woman's Point of View: Some Roads to Peace* (New York: Womans Press, 1920), 17.

1. Harriot Stanton Blatch, *Woman's Point of View*, 59–60.

2. Ibid., 31.

3. Ibid., 55.

4. Ibid., 50.

5. Ibid., 68, 55.

6. Ibid., 145.

7. Jane Robinson, "There's More to the WI than Jam and 'Jerusalem,'" *Telegraph* (London), 16 October 2011.

8. Joseph Stalin, "To the Chairman of the Board of the All-Union Centre of Machine and Tractor Stations. To All Machine and Tractor Stations," *Works: Volume 13, July 1930–January 1934* (Moscow: Foreign Languages Publishing House, 1954), 50–51.

9. Nick Cullather, "Miracles of Modernization: The Green Revolution and the Apotheosis of Technology," *Diplomatic History* 28, no. 2 (April 2004): 227–54; Alun Howkins, *Death of Rural England* (London: Routledge, 2003), chaps. 2 and 3.

10. "The Peace Loaf," *Daily News* (London), 21 November 1918, 7; also see Howkins, *Death of Rural England*, chap. 3.

11. Carol Helstosky, *Garlic and Oil: Food and Politics in Italy* (New York: Berg, 2004), chaps. 4 and 5.

12. For more information on the significance of food and urban cultivation during the Second World War, see Amy Bentley, *Eating For Victory* (Urbana: University of Illinois, 1998); Susan Briggs, *The Home Front: War Years* (New York: American Heritage, 1975); Helstosky, *Garlic and Oil*; Peter King, *Women Rule the Plot* (London: Duckworth, 1999); Laura J. Lawson, *City Bountiful* (Berkeley: University of California Press, 2005).

13. Harriot Stanton Blatch, *A Woman's Point of View*, 76.

Chapter 5. "A Call to Farms"

Epigraph: Joan Snelling, *A Land Girl's War* (Ipswich: Old Pond Publishing, 2004), 7.

1. Snelling, *A Land Girls War*, chaps. 1–2, 15.

2. A good resource for art depicting the unsettling nature of the First World War and the uneasiness and fear of a Second World War is Tim Cross, *The Lost Voices of World War I: An Anthology of Writers, Poets, and Playwrights* (Iowa City: University of Iowa Press, 1989).

3. Nancy McLennan, "Women's Farm Unit Gains Backing Here," *New York Times*, 10 December 1942, 32.

4. Gervas Huxley, *Lady Denman, G. B. E.* (London: Chatto and Windus, 1962).

5. "Correspondence with Committee Members: Lady Denman," 1942, records of the Ministry of Housing and Local Government, Committee on Land Utilisation in Rural Areas, National Archives, Kew, catalogue reference 95294/15/4.

6. Lady Gertrude Denman, "Introduction," in *Land Girl: A Manual*, W. E. Shewell-Cooper (London: English Universities Press, Ltd., 1940); for more information about the instructional pamphlets and advertisements, see Susan Briggs, *The Home Front: War Years in Britain 1939–1945* (New York: American Heritage, 1975).

7. Denman, "Introduction."

8. Queen Elizabeth, transcript of speech to Land Army at the Mansion House on 7 December 1945, *Land Girl* 6, no. 10 (January 1946): 1.

9. Ibid.

10. For more discussion on how the experience of the land girls influenced their personal relationships, see Pauline Cole, *Transition to Arcady: A Story of Two Years Spent in the Women's Land Army—'47 to '49* (Ilfracombe: Arthur H. Stockwell, 2001); Marjorie M. Dean, *The Women's Land Army and Me* (Victoria Park: Association for the Blind of Washington, 1997), chap. 11; Peggy Grayson, *Buttercup Jill* (Ipswich: Farming Press, 1994); Irene Grimwood, *Land Girls at the Old Rectory* (Ipswich: Old Pond Publishing, 2000); Anne Hall, *Land Girl* (Bradford-Upon-Avon: Ex-Libris Press, 1993); Shirley Joseph, *If Their Mothers Only Knew* (London: Faber and Faber, 1946); Joan Snelling, *Land Girl's War*; and Doreen Strange, *A Land Girl's Diary: Burnham 1948* (Maidenhead: Burnham Historians, 1999).

11. Violet Cowley, *Over My Shoulder* (Ilfracombe: Stockwell, 1985), 48.

12. Denman, "Introduction"; letter from Meriel Talbot, *Times* (London), 1941, quoted in Bob Powell and Nigel Westacott, *The Women's Land Army, 1939–1950* (Stroud: Sutton Publishing, 2000), 7; "10,000 Women Wanted at Once," *Weekly Dispatch* (London), 1 April 1917, 8.

13. Irene Grimwood, *Land Girls at the Old Rectory* (Ipswich: Old Pond Publishing, 2000), 9, 10.

14. Hall, *Land Girl*, 8–31.

15. Ibid., 20.

16. Ibid., 19–31.

17. Snelling, *A Land Girl's War*, 19; Cowley, *Over My Shoulder*.

18. Briggs, *Home Front*, 129–46.

19. *The Land Girl* 6, no. 10 (January 1946): 6.

20. Ibid., 5.

21. "Queen Entertains Land Army," *New York Times*, 4 July 1943, 13.

22. Queen Elizabeth, transcript of speech to Land Army, 1.

23. Nancy McLennan, "Women's Farm Unit Gains Backing Here," *New York Times*, 10 December 1942, 32.

24. Ibid.

25. "New Action by President," *New York Times*, 27 March 1943, 1; Stephanie A. Carpenter, *On the Farm Front: The Women's Land Army in World War II* (DeKalb: Northern Illinois University Press, 2003), 35–54.

26. "Senate Passes Bill for Land Migrants," *New York Times*, 9 April 1943, 1; "$26,100,000 Voted for Land Army," *New York Times*, 17 April 1943, 1.

27. "The Winter Soldiers of the Women's Land Army," *Prologue* 25 (1993): 355, 357; "Women's Land Army of America," *Prologue* 25 (1993): 349; "Women's Land Army," *Prologue* 25 (1993): 347–58; "Will Head Women in New Crop Corps," *New York Times*, 13 April 1943, 22.

28. Carpenter, *On the Farm Front*, 4, 55.

29. "Will Head Women in New Crop Corps," *New York Times*, 13 April 1943, 22.

30. Bess Furman, "Land Army Seeks 800,000 Women: Rise of 200,000 from Last Year Is Needed," *New York Times*, 17 May 1944, 22; "Will Discuss Farm Aid," *New York Times*, 30 September 1943, 18.

31. Carpenter, *On the Farm Front*, 46, 50.

32. "Will Discuss Farm Aid," *New York Times*, 30 September 1943, 18.

33. M. C. Wilson, "Feminine Land Army: Plans in the Making Would Put City Women on Farms to Help Feed Forces," *New York Times*, 28 February 1943, 13 (X)

34. "Seeks 400,000 Women: Land Army Hopes to Get Half the Quota Needed for Farms," *New York Times*, 11 March 1944, 17.

35. Wilson, "Feminine Land Army," 13 (X).

36. "Will Head Women in New Crop Corps," *New York Times*, 13 April 1943, 22.

37. This argument is the central theme in Amy Bentley, *Eating for Victory* (Urbana: University of Illinois Press, 1998). Also see "Women's Land Army Newsletter," *Prologue* 25 (1993): 354, 356, 358.

38. Wilson, "Feminine Land Army," 13 (X).

39. *The Women's Land Army of the U.S. Crop Corps* (1944), reprinted in Judy Barrett Litoff and David C. Smith, ed., "Women and Farm Work," *American Women in a World at War: Contemporary Accounts from World War II* (Wilmington, Del.: Scholarly Resources, 1997), 206.

40. Wilson, "Feminine Land Army," 13 (X).

41. "City Folk Respond to Farmers' Appeals: Land Army on Move to Help Grow Food," *New York Times*, 20 June 1944, 22.

42. Katherine Jellison, *Entitled to Power: Farm Women and Technology, 1913–1963* (Chapel Hill: University of North Carolina Press, 1993), 132.

43. For a further discussion of race and rationality, see Carpenter, *On the Farm Front*, 135–47.

44. Lucy Greenbaum, "At the Front with Our Land Army," *New York Times*, 4 July 1943, 12 (SM).

45. Ibid.

46. Ibid.

47. "Miss Edge Aids on Farm," *New York Times*, 16 August 1944, 13.

48. Wilson, "Feminine Land Army," 13 (X).

49. "Co-eds Form 'Land Army,'" *New York Times*, 25 December 1942, 20.

50. "Land Army Course Begun by Women," *New York Times*, 10 February 1942, 22.

51. Ibid.

52. "Will Head Women in New Crop Corps," *New York Times*, 13 April 1943, 22.

53. Greenbaum, "At the Front with Our Land Army," 12 (SM).

54. "Land Army Described: Head of Women's Program Also Shows Model of Uniform," *New York Times*, 11 May 1943, 18.

55. "Will Head Women in New Crop Corps," 22.

56. "Land Army Described," *New York Times*, 11 May 1943, 18; "Lack of Denim Hits Farm Uniform Plan," *New York Times*, 13 May 1943; "Women Enrolled in New Land Army: Recruits Include Future Wave and Housewife," *New York Times*, 26 May 1943, 26.

57. "Land Army Rally Volunteers Praised by Leader at Rally Here for Their Service to Farms," *New York Times*, 7 February 1945, 18.

58. Minutes, Farm Labor Conference, College Station, Texas, 28 November 1944, Western History Collection, Denver Public Library, 5.

59. Rebecca Sharpless, *Fertile Ground, Narrow Choices: Women on Texas Cotton Farms, 1900–1940* (Chapel Hill: University of North Carolina Press, 1999), 160, 166–67.

60. Dorothy Schneider and Carl J. Schneider, *American Women in the Progressive Era 1900–1920* (New York: Facts on File, 1993), 119; Sharpless, *Fertile Ground, Narrow Choices*, 161.

61. Shirley Threlfo, *The Australian Women's Land Army, 1942–1945* (Paterson: Paterson Historical Society, 1997); "For Women's Land Army," *New York Times*, 31 July 1942, 18.

62. Marion Kelsey, *Victory Harvest: Diary of a Canadian in the Women's Land Army, 1940–1944* (Montreal: McGill-Queen's University Press, 1997).

63. Diane Bardsley and Miklos Soltesz, *The Land Girls* (Dunedin: University of Otago Press, 2000), iv.

64. Bardsley, *The Land Girls*, 6.

65. Ibid., insert.

66. Ibid., 7.

67. Nancy McLennan, "Women's Farm Unit Gains Backing Here," *New York Times*, 10 December 1942, 32.

68. Furman, "Land Army Seeks 800,000 Women," 22.

69. Briggs, *Home Front*, 171; "Lady Denman, 69, of Land Army Dies," *New York Times*, 3 June 1954, 27; Ministry of Food, Women's Land Army, Index to Service Records of the Second World War, 1939–1948, National Archives, Kew.

70. Powell and Westacott, *Women's Land Army*, 123; Ministry of Food, Women's Land Army, Index to Service Records of the Second World War, 1939–1948, National Archives, Kew.

Chapter 6. Freedom from Want:
The Role of the Victory Garden in the Second World War

1. Elizabeth Borgwardt, *A New Deal for the World: America's Vision for Human Rights* (Cambridge, Mass.: Harvard University Press, 2005); Lloyd Gardner, *Spheres of Influence: The Great Powers Partition Europe, from Munich to Yalta* (Chicago: Ivan R. Dee Publisher, 1993); Amy Bentley, *Eating for Victory: Food Rationing and the Politics of Domesticity* (Urbana: University of Illinois, 1998), 143–70; Susan Briggs, *The Home Front* (London: George Weidenfeld and Nicolson, Ltd., 1975), 160–63, 169–83.

2. Dorothy Dunbar Bromley, "Women Work for Their Country," *Woman's Home Companion*, December 1941, 82.

3. Laura J. Lawson, *City Bountiful* (Berkeley: University of California Press, 2005), 171–73.

4. "Mobilization Guide," 6, RG 16, box 1, file 1, United States Department of Agriculture Food Campaign Files, National Archives, Washington, D.C.

5. "Fact Sheet," RG 16, box 1, file 1, United States Department of Agriculture Food Campaign Files, National Archives, Washington, D.C.

6. "Food Fights for Freedom," 7, RG 16, box 1, file 1, United States Department of Agriculture Food Campaign Files, National Archives, Washington, D.C.

7. "Fact Sheet," RG 16, box 1, file 1, United States Department of Agriculture Food Campaign Files, National Archives, Washington, D.C.

8. "Fact Sheet," RG 16, box 1, file 1, United States Department of Agriculture Food Campaign Files, National Archives, Washington, D.C.; script for film *Food Fights for Freedom*, p. 4, RG 16, box 1, file 1, United States Department of Agriculture Food Campaign Files, National Archives, Washington, D.C.

9. Script for film *Food Fights for Freedom*, p. 4, RG 16, box 1, file 1, United States Department of Agriculture Food Campaign Files, National Archives, Washington, D.C.

10. Campaign Fact Sheets, United States Department of Agriculture Food Campaign Files, box 1, folder 7, National Archives, Washington, D.C.

11. Bentley, *Eating for Victory*, 9.

12. For a more in-depth discussion of the significance of household management to the identity of American women in the Second World War, see Bentley, *Eating for Victory*.

13. J. Edgar Hoover, "Mothers . . . Our Only Hope," *Woman's Home Companion*, January 1944, 20.

14. Rosalyn Baxandall and Elizabeth Ewen, *Picture Windows: How the Suburbs*

Happened (New York: Basic Books, 2000), 78–82; James Madison Wood, "Should We Draft Mothers?," *Woman's Home Companion,* January 1944, 21.

15. United States Department of Agriculture Food Campaign Files, box 1, folder 7, National Archives, Washington, D.C.

16. Campaign File Fact Sheets, RG 16, box 1, file 1 and box 1, file 7, United States Department of Agriculture Food Campaign Files, National Archives, Washington, D.C.

17. "Training Guide," 3–4, RG 16, box 1, file 1, United States Department of Agriculture Food Campaign Files, National Archives, Washington, D.C.

18. "Eat Your Way to Beauty" in *Health for Victory Meal Planning Guide,* 25–30, April 1944, RG 16, box 1, file 21, United States Department of Agriculture Food Campaign Files, National Archives, Washington, D.C.

19. Nancy A. Walker, *Women's Magazines 1940–1960: Gender Roles and the Popular Press* (Boston: Bedford St. Martin's, 1998), 1–25.

20. "Things to Do," RG 16, box 1, file 1, United States Department of Agriculture Food Campaign Files, National Archives, Washington, D.C.

21. Ibid.

22. Dianne Savage, *Broadcasting Freedom: Radio, War, and the Politics of Race, 1938–1948,* (Chapel Hill: University of North Carolina, 1999), 168-69; Lawson, *City Bountiful,* 78.

23. Lawson, *City Bountiful,* 80–81.

24. Bentley, *Eating for Victory,* 120–21, 48.

25. For more information on the role of the OWI in shaping homefront campaigns, see Alan Winkler, *The Politics of Propaganda;* Alan Winkler, "The Homefront Experience During World War II," OAH *Magazine of History* 16, no. 3 (spring 2002): 3–4.

26. Ruth D. Balcomb, "College Days Without Men," in *Women of the Homefront: World War II Recollections of 55 Americans,* ed. Pauline Parker (Jefferson: McFarland and Company, Inc., 2002), 39–46.

27. Anona Stoetzel Kuehne, "Growing Up in Wartime," in Parker, *Women of the Homefront,* 47–52.

28. Virginia Raymond Ott, "I'd Rather Have Joined the WAC," in Parker, *Women of the Homefront,* 178–80.

29. Mary L. Appling, "Behind the Combat," in Parker, *Women of the Homefront,* 205–11.

30. Sara Mae Weidmaier, as told to Pauline E. Parker, in Parker, *Women of the Homefront,* 212–15.

31. Parker, *Women of the Homefront,* 212–15.

32. Script for film *Food Fights for Freedom,* 7, RG 16, box 1, file 1, United States Department of Agriculture Food Campaign Files, National Archives, Washington, D.C.

33. Hunter Reynolds, "Get Out and Dig, Dig, Dig" (Chicago: Skokie Music Co., 1943), RG 16, box 9, file: "Get Out and Dig, Dig, Dig," Food Campaign Files, United States Department of Agriculture, National Archives, Washington, D.C.

34. W. R. Williams and Howard Peterson, *"Mistress Mary Quite Contrary" Has a Vict'ry Garden Now* (Chicago: W. Rossiter, 1943).

35. Winston Churchill, *National Allotments Journal* (autumn 1940): 3; as quoted in Lesley Acton, "Dig for Victory: World War II campaign to Grow More Food," *Newsgrape*, 5 December 2011, http://www.newsgrape.com/a/dig-for-victory/#_edn20.

36. Barbara Anne Salter, "The Germans at the End of the Garden," World War II People's War Archive, 28 January 2006; World War II People's War is an online archive of wartime memories contributed by members of the public and gathered by the BBC. The archive can be found at http://bbc.co.uk/ww2peopleswar.

37. Briggs, *Home Front*.

38. Charles Lathrop Pack, *The War Garden Victorious* (Washington, D.C.: National Victory Garden Commission, 1919).

39. James M. Erdmann, *Leaflet Operations in the Second World War: The Story of the How and Why of the 6,500,000,000 Propaganda Leaflets Dropped on Axis Forces and Homelands in the Mediterranean and European Theaters of Operations* (Denver: Denver Instant Printing, 1969), 2, 214–15.

40. "Where the Nazi's Sowed Death, a Londoner and His Wife Have Sown Life-Giving Vegetables in a London Bomb Crater," ARC Identifier 196480, National Archives, Washington, D.C.

41. Nagendranahath Gangulee, *The Battle of the Land: An Account of the Food Production Campaign in Wartime Britain* (London: Lindsay Drummond, 1943), 70.

42. Briggs, *Home Front*, 146.

43. Anne Hall, *Land Girl: Her Story of Six Years in the Women's Land Army, 1940–1946* (Bradford on Avon: Ex Libris Press, 1993); David Trenbirth, "The Germans at the End of Our Birmingham Garden," World War II People's War Archive, 16 November 2005, http://www.bbc.co.uk/history/ww2peopleswar/stories/51/a7032151.shtml. Additional detail on prisoner gardens is found in Kenneth Helphand, *Defiant Gardens: Making Gardens in Wartime* (San Antonio, Tex.: Trinity University Press, 2008).

44. Trenbirth, "Germans at the End of Our Birmingham Garden."

45. Marguerite Patten, "Mother's Wartime Garden," World War II People's War Archive, 29 June 2005, http://www.bbcattic.org/ww2peopleswar/stories/25/a4304125.shtml.

46. Alma Heeley, "The Day a Pilot Dropped in My Garden," World War II People's War Archive, 24 August 2005, http://www.bbc.co.uk/history/ww2peopleswar/stories/41/a5288141.shtml.

47. "Machine Gunning at the Bottom of the Garden," World War II People's War Archive, 27 August 2005, http://www.bbc.co.uk/history/ww2peopleswar/stories/62/a5353562.shtml.

48. Alice Freeman, "German in the Garden," World War II People's War Archive, 11 June 2004, http://www.bbc.co.uk/history/ww2peopleswar/stories/53/a2733653.shtml.

49. Olive Creek, "A Plane at the Bottom of My Aunt's Garden," World War II

People's War Archive, 19 September 2005, http://www.bbc.co.uk/history/ww2 peopleswar/stories/76/a5807676.shtml.

50. Nicholas Pronay, Clive Coultass, and Frances Thorpe, *British Official Films in the Second World War* (Oxford: Clio Press, 1980), 1:44.

51. "The Factory in a Garden," World War II People's War Archive, 29 December 2005.

52. Ibid.

53. Humphrey Jennings and Harry Watt, *London Can Take It*, British Ministry of Information, INF 6, folder no. CFU 201, British National Archives, 1940.

54. "Food Fights for Freedom," 7, RG16, box 1, file 1, United States Department of Agriculture Food Campaign Files, National Archives, Washington, D.C.

55. "Garden Pests and How to Deal with Them," *Dig for Victory Leaflet,* no. 16, British Ministry of Agriculture.

56. For an interesting discussion of creation of gardens in the literal presence of combat, see Ketzel Levine, "Tending 'Defiant Gardens' During Wartime," *Morning Edition*, National Public Radio, 26 May 2006, http://www.npr.org/templates/story/story.php?storyId=5435131.

Chapter 7. The Women's Land Army, Victory Gardens, and Cultural Transcendence

1. Grace Wallace, World War II People's War Archive, 17 November 2004, http://www.bbc.co.uk/history/ww2peopleswar/stories/91/a3287991.shtml; Violet Cowley, *Over My Shoulder* (Ilfracombe: Arthur H. Stockwell, 1985), 109; E. M. Barraud, "We Will Remember This," *Tail Corn* (London: Chapman and Hall, 1948), 182; Peggy Grayson, *Buttercup Jill* (Ipswich: Farming Press, 1994), 148–53.

2. *Land Girl Magazine*, quoted in Anne Hall, *Land Girl* (Bradford-Upon-Avon: Ex Libris Press, 1993), 141.

3. Irene Grimwood, *Land Girls at the Old Rectory* (Ipswich: Old Pond Publishing, 2000), 85; Joan Snelling, *A Land Girl's War* (Ipswich: Old Pond Publishing, 2004), 92; Hall, *Land Girl*, 141; Bob Powell and Nigel Westacott, *The Women's Land Army* (Stroud: Sutton Publishing, 2000), 113–26.

4. Powell and Westacott, *Women's Land Army*, 123.

5. Snelling, *Land Girl's War*, 92; Powell and Westacott, *Women's Land Army*, 115, 123.

6. Some former land girls recall no formal recognition at all, not even in the form of the official Queen's letter to the WLA members, and did not know of such recognition until years later. See Snelling, *Land Girl's War*, 92.

7. "King George Entertains Tenants," *New York Times*, 14 July 1946, 9.

8. Jane Holt, "Best Way to Make Coffee," *New York Times*, 5 August 1945, 80.

9. "'46 Victory Gardens Are Believed Certain," *New York Times*, 23 August 1945, 26.

10. "Topics of the Times," *New York Times*, 28 August 1945, 18; "'46 Victory Gardens Are Believed Certain," 26; "Fact Sheet," 1944, RG 16, box 1, file 1, United States

Department of Agriculture Food Campaign Files, National Archives, Washington D.C.

11. Mary Kay Blakely, "An Old Woman's Victory Garden," *Ms. Magazine*, September 1987.

12. Radioscript, "Food Makes History," 1943, USDA Food Campaign Files, National Archives, Washington, D.C.

13. "Truman Aide Fears Wide Starvation," *New York Times*, 24 March 1946, 22; "Asks 20,000,000 Victory Gardens," *New York Times*, 30 March 1946, 11; "News of Food: Methods of Conserving Wheat and Oils to Help Hungry Abroad Are Suggested," *New York Times*, 15 April 1946, 24.

14. Bess Furman, "Marshall Calls for Freedom Gardens," *New York Times*, 3 February 1948.

15. Mary L. Appling, "Behind the Combat," in *Women of the Homefront: World War II Recollections of 55 Americans*, ed. Pauline Parker (Jefferson: McFarland and Company, Inc., 2002), 205.

16. British Department of Environment, Food and Rural Affairs, www.defra.gov/uk; also see Grimwood, *Land Girls at the Old Rectory*, 87–90; Powell and Westacott, *Women's Land Army*, 8, 127. More information on the various reunions of the British WLA can be found at: http://www.wartimememories.co.uk/womenslandarmy.html.

17. Elizabeth Elgin, *A Scent of Lavender* (London: Harper Collins Publishers, 2003).

18. Dir. David Leland, *The Land Girls* (1998).

19. "Reserve Bank Aides Hold Garden Show," *New York Times*, 7 September 1945, 19; "Flower Show to Open," *New York Times*, 6 September 1945, 21; "Victory Gardeners Display Their Wares," *New York Times*, 14 September 1945, 19; "Green Thumb Prizes Awarded," *New York Times*, 23 November 1945, 20; "New Lawns and Old," *New York Times*, 9 September 1945, 57; "Contest, Tours and Show," *New York Times*, 5 May 1946, X18.

20. Excerpt from President Franklin D. Roosevelt, "Four Freedoms" speech delivered to U.S. Congress 6 January 1941.

21. Mary Roche, "California Homes Shown in Exhibits," *New York Times*, 5 January 1946, 10. For more discussion on consumer culture in the war era, also see Amy Bentley, *Eating for Victory* (Urbana: University of Illinois, 1998); Thomas Hine, *I Want That: How We All Became Shoppers, a Cultural History* (New York: Harper Collins, 2002); Stephanie Coontz, *The Way We Never Were: American Families and the Nostalgia Trap* (New York: Basic Books, 2000).

22. "Television This Week," *New York Times*, 25 May 1975, 129.

23. Glenn Collins, "Endpaper: The New Family-Fun Game for Inflation-Fighting Americans," *New York Times*, 25 May 1975.

24. "City's $1 Farmers Reap Skimpy Crop: It's a Bit Under Par, Hospital Group Says, Blaming it on Weather," *New York Times*, 30 August 1952, 15.

25. For an excellent and thorough look at community gardening throughout the twentieth century, see Laura J. Lawson, *City Bountiful* (Berkeley: University of California Press, 2005).

26. Amy Bentley, "Rationing Is Good Democracy," in *Eating for Victory,* 9–29.

27. This article and the forum discussed above can be located online, see Deborah Holmes, "Victory Gardens," *Old House Web,* http://www.oldhouseweb.com/gardening.

28. "Michelle Obama to Create an Organic 'Victory' Garden at the White House," *Guardian,* 20 March 2009; "Obamas to Plant Vegetable Garden at White House," *New York Times,* 20 March 2009; "Politics in Spades," Why the Obama Veg Patch Matters," *New York Times,* 24 March 2009.

BIBLIOGRAPHY

Primary Sources

ARCHIVAL COLLECTIONS

Blatch, Harriot Stanton, Papers, 1907–1915. Miscellaneous Manuscript Collection, Library of Congress, Washington, D.C.

British Ministry of Agriculture. Textual records of campaigns to promote Women's Land Army and the creation of Victory "War" Gardens. British National Archives, Kew.

Butterfield, President Kenyon L. Women's Committee on Food Conservation Files, 1917–1918. Selected Records Related to Women's Education, University of Massachusetts.

Canadian Department of Agriculture. Textual records of campaigns to promote Women's Land Army and the creation of Victory Gardens, Ottawa.

Denman, Lady Gertrude, Papers, 1939–1946. Liddell Hart Centre for Military Archives, King's College, London.

Farm Labor Conference. Minutes, College Station, Texas. November 1944, Western History Collection, Denver Public Library.

George, Emma L., Papers, 1915–1920. Miscellaneous Manuscripts Collection, Library of Congress, Washington, D.C.

Lees, Mary. Oral Interview. Recorded 30 November 1974. ID number 506, Imperial War Museum, London.

Smith, Estelle T. The Home Demonstration Report of Mrs. Estelle T. Smith, Special Collections Research Center, North Carolina State University Digital Collection. www.lib.ncsu.edu/resolver/1840.6/1005.

Smith, Sophia, Collection of Papers. College Archives of Smith College, Northampton, Massachusetts.

United States Department of Agriculture. Food Campaign Files. RG 16, National Archives, Washington, D.C.

United States Department of Agriculture. Food Campaign Files. Textual Records, National Archives, College Park, Maryland.

Warwick hostel records. WAR 5/1, Reading Museum of English Rural Life, Reading, England. British National Archives.

PERSONAL MEMOIRS AND PRIMARY TEXTS

Ayling, Keith. *Calling All Women.* New York: Harper and Brothers, 1942.

Balcomb, Ruth D. "College Days Without Men." In *Women of the Homefront: World War II Recollections of 55 Americans,* edited by Pauline E. Parker. Jefferson, N.C.: McFarland and Company, Inc., 2002.

Barrington, Brendan, ed. *The Wartime Broadcasts of Francis Stuart, 1942–1945.* Dublin: Lilliput Press, 2000.

Barraud, E. M. *Set My Hand Upon the Plough.* Worcester: Littlebury, 1946.

———. *Tail Corn.* London: Chapman and Hall, 1948.

Bates, Martha. *Snagging Turnips and Scaling Muck: The Women's Land Army in Westmoreland.* Edited by Anne Bonney. Kendal: Helm, 2001.

Biles, Roy E. *The Modern Garden Book.* Chicago: J. G. Ferguson, 1941.

Blatch, Harriot Stanton. *Mobilizing Woman-Power.* New York: Womans Press, 1918.

———. *A Woman's Point of View: Some Roads to Peace.* New York: Womans Press, 1920.

Burdett, James H. *The Victory Garden Manual.* Chicago: Ziff-Davis, 1943.

Cole, Pauline. *Transition to Arcady: A Story of Two Years Spent in the Women's Land Army —'47 to '49.* Ilfracombe: Arthur H. Stockwell, 2001.

Cowley, Violet. *Over My Shoulder.* Ilfracombe: Arthur H. Stockwell, 1985.

Davis-Goff, Annabel. *This Cold Country.* New York: Harcourt, 2002.

Dodd, Helen. *The Healthful Farmhouse.* Boston: Whitcomb and Barrows, 1911.

Elgin, Elizabeth. *A Scent of Lavender.* London: HarperCollins, 2003.

Entwistle, Mary. *Land Army Girl.* Leamington Spa: Drewfern, 1990.

Everett, T. H., and Edgar J. Clissold. *Victory Backyard Gardens: Simple Rules for Growing Your Own Vegetables.* Racine: Whitman Publishing Company, 1942.

Foy, Ellis. *Peaceful Wartime.* Edinburgh: Pentland Press, 1999.

Gangulee, Nagendranahath. *The Battle of the Land: An Account of the Food Production Campaign in Wartime Britain.* London: Lindsay Drummond, 1943.

Gast, Ross A. *Vegetables in the California Garden: Victory Garden Edition.* Los Angeles: Murray and Gee, Inc., 1943.

Geere, Marjorie. *Reminiscences of a Land Girl in Witham.* Witham: Poulter, 1987.

Gillham, Mary E. *Town Bred, Country Nurtured: A Naturalist Looks Back Fifty Years.* Cardiff: M. E. Gillham, 1998.

Gray, Affleck. *Timber!* Edited by Uiga Robertson and John Robertson. East Linton: Tuckwell, European Ethnological Research Centre, 1998.

Grayson, Peggy. *Buttercup Jill.* Ipswich: Farming Press, 1994.

Green, Michael, and Evelyn Dunbar. *A Book of Farmcraft.* London: Longman, 1942.

Grimwood, Irene. *Land Girls at the Old Rectory.* Ipswich: Old Pond Publishing, 2000.

Hall, Anne. *Land Girl: Her Story of Six Years in the Women's Land Army, 1940–1946.* Bradford-Upon-Avon: Ex-Libris Press, 1993.

Harris, Carol. *Women at War, 1939–1945: The Home Front.* Gloucestershire: Sutton, 2000.

Harrison, Tom, and Charles Madge, eds. *War Begins at Home by Mass Observation.* London: Chatto and Windus, 1940.

Hoover, J. Edgar. "Mothers . . . Our Only Hope." *Woman's Home Companion*, January 1944, 20.

Humphreys, Helen. *The Lost Garden.* London: Bloomsbury, 2004.

Iddon, Jean. *Fragrant Earth.* London: Epworth Press, 1947.

Jacques, Jacqueline. *Someone to Watch over Me.* Long Preston: Magna Story Sound, 1999.

Johns, Elise. *Dappled Sunlight: A Land Girl's Story.* Ilfracombe: Arthur H. Stockwell, 1998.

Joseph, Shirley. *If Their Mothers Only Knew.* London: Faber and Faber, 1946.

Kelsey, Marion. *Victory Harvest: Diary of a Canadian in the Women's Land Army, 1940–1944.* Montreal: McGill-Queen's University Press, 1997.

Knappett, Rachael. *Pullett on the Midden.* London: Michael Joseph, 1946.

———. *Wait Now.* London: Country Book Club, 1953.

Kuehne, Anona Stoetzel. "Growing Up in Wartime." In *Women of the Homefront: World War II Recollections of 55 Americans,* edited by Pauline Parker. Jefferson: McFarland and Company, Inc., 2002.

Leland, David. *The Land Girls* (1998).

Macklin, Mary P. *The Fourth Service: Ex-Australian Women's Land Army, World War II.* Maryborough: Mary Patricia Macklin, 2001.

Mant, Joan. *All Muck, No Medals.* Lewes: Book Guild, 1994.

Mist, Eleen. *Aw-Ahhr! Experiences in the Women's Land Army.* Penzance: United Writers, 1992.

Morgan, Christopher. *Castle, Kit Bag and Cattle Truck: The Australia Women's Land Army at Abercrombie House, Bathurst.* Manly: Runciman Press, 2001.

Morgan, Gwenda. *The Diary of a Land Girl, 1939–1945.* Risbury: Whittington Press, 2002.

Nicholson, Harold. *The War Years: Diaries and Letters, 1939–1945.* New York: William Collins Sons and Co., 1967.

Ott, Virginia Raymond. "I'd Rather Have Joined the WAC." In *Women of the Homefront: World War II Recollections of 55 Americans,* edited by Pauline Parker. Jefferson, North Carolina: McFarland and Company, Inc., 2002.

Pack, Charles Lathrop. *The War Garden Victorious: Its War Time Need and Its Economic Value in Peace.* Philadelphia: National War Garden Commission and Lippincott Co., 1919.

Palmer, Arnold. *Movable Feasts: A Reconnaissance of the Origins and Consequences of Fluctuations in Meal-Times with Special Attention to the Introduction of Luncheon and Afternoon
Tea.* London: Oxford University Press, 1952.

Paton Walsh, Jill, and Dorothy L. Sayers. *A Presumption of Death.* New York: St.
Martin's Press, 2003.

Putnam, Jean-Marie, and Lloyd C. Cosper. *Gardens for Victory.* New York: Harcourt
Brace and Co., 1942.

Rawlings, Geoffrey. *Tolcarne Merock.* Penzance: United Writers, 2002.

Roberts, Irene. *Walker Street.* London: Piatkus, 1997.

Roosevelt, Franklin D. Annual Message to Congress ["Four Freedoms" speech],
January 6, 1941. Records of the United States Senate, SEN 77A-H1, Record Group
46, National Archives.

Sackville-West, V. *The Women's Land Army.* London: Michael Joseph, 1944.

Savage, Barbara Dianne. *Broadcasting Freedom: Radio, War, and the Politics of Race,
1938–1948.* Chapel Hill: University of North Carolina Press, 1999.

Seymour, E. L. D. *The New Garden Encyclopedia: Victory Garden Edition.* New York:
W. M. Wise and Co., 1943.

Shewell-Cooper, W. E. *Land Girl: A Manual for Volunteers in the Women's Land Army.*
London: English Universities Press, n.d.

Snelling, Joan. *A Land Girl's War.* Ipswich: Old Pond Publishing, 2004.

Squires, Mary. *An Army in the Fields.* London: Minerva, 2000.

Stevenson, James. *Don't You Know There's a War On?* New York: Greenwillow Books,
1992.

Strange, Doreen. *A Land Girl's Diary: Burnham 1948.* Maidenhead: Burnham Historians, 1999.

Surface, Frank M., and Raymond L. Bland. *American Food in the World War and Reconstruction Period: Operations of the Organizations under the Direction of Herbert Hoover,
1914 to 1924.* Stanford: Stanford University Press, 1931.

Terkel, Studs. *The Good War: An Oral History of World War Two.* New York: Pantheon
Books, 1984.

Thornton, Margaret. *Don't Sit Under the Apple Tree.* Long Preston: Magna, 2004.

Timber Corps Members. *Meet the Members.* Bristol: Bennett Bros., 1945.

Tresham, Leslie. "My Experience as an Emergency Farm Worker." In *Women's Land
Army, Extension Farm Labor Program, 1943, 1944, 1945,* United States Department of
Agriculture Extension Service. Washington, D.C.: United States Department of
Agriculture, 1945.

Turner, Norah. *In Baggy Brown Breeches and a Cowboy Hat.* Rainham: Meresborough
Books, 1992.

Wells, Irene. *My Life in the Land Army.* Alcester: Williams, 1984.

Whitmee, Jeanne. *Pride of Peacocks.* Whitey Bay: Tyne and Wear Soundings, 2004.

Whitton, Barbara. *Green Hands.* London: Faber and Faber, 1953.

Wilding, Frances. *Land Girl at Large.* London: Paul Elek, 1972.

Williams, Irene. *Life After the Land Army.* Alecester: Williams, 1993.

Williams, Mavis. *Lumber Jill: Timber Corps.* Bradford-Upon-Avon: Ex Libris Press, 1994.

NEWSLETTERS

Common Cause, 1915.

Grower Talks, 1943–1944.

Northwest Gardens and Homes, 1942.

MISCELLANEOUS MEDIA

British Ministry of Agriculture. Posters, films, and other visual media to promote Women's Land Army and the creation of Victory Gardens.

Canadian Department of Agriculture. Posters and other visual media to promote Women's Land Army and the creation of Victory Gardens.

Crown Film Unit. *Words for Battle.* Video recording. Sponsored by the British Ministry of Information, 1941.

Dean, Marjorie M. *The Women's Land Army and Me.* Sound recording. Victoria Park: Association for the Blind of Washington, 1997.

Ealing Studios. *Salvage with a Smile.* Video recording. Sponsored by the British Ministry of Information for the British Ministry of Agriculture, 1940.

Jennings, Humphrey, and Harry Watt. *London Can Take It.* Video recording. Sponsored by the British Ministry of Information, 1940.

Library of Congress Poster and Print Collection. Posters and other visual media. Library of Congress, Washington, D.C.

Merton Park. *More Eggs from Your Hens.* Video recording. Sponsored by the British Ministry of Information for the British Ministry of Agriculture, 1941.

National Film and Sound Archive. *Home Front: Australia's World War II Newsreels.* Video recording. Australia National Library, Canberra, 1998.

NBC. Promotional newsreels depicting both the Victory Garden and Women's Land Army campaigns [various].

Royal Statistical Society. "A Statistical Survey of the Problems of Pauperism." *Journal of the Royal Statistical Society* 74 (December 1910), British National Archives, ref. PRO 30/69/1864.

Spectator [Short Films]. *Dig for Victory.* Video recording. Sponsored by the British Ministry of Agriculture and the British Ministry of Information, 1942.

Stalin, Joseph. "To the Chairman of the Board of the All-Union Centre of Machine and Tractor Stations. To All Machine and Tractor Stations." *Works: Volume 13, July 1930–January 1934.* Moscow: Foreign Languages Publishing House, 1954.

United States Department of Agriculture. Posters and other visual media. National Archives, Washington, D.C.

———. Radio and film scripts and recordings for the promotion of the Food Campaigns [various, untitled]. National Archives, Washington, D.C.

Secondary Sources

Abbott, Dorothea. *Librarian in the Land Army*. Stratford-upon-Avon: D. Abbott, 1984.

Adie, Kate. *Corsets to Camouflage: Women and War*. London: Hodder and Stoughton, 2004.

Anderson, Benedict. *Imagined Communities: Reflections on the Origin and Spread of Nationalism*. London: Verso, 1983.

Anderson, Bonnie S. *Joyous Greetings: The First International Women's Movement, 1830–1860*. Oxford: Oxford University Press, 2000.

Andrews, Maggie. *The Acceptable Face of Feminism*. London: Lawrence and Wishart, 1997.

Antrobus, Stewart. *We Wouldn't Have Missed It for the World: The Women's Land Army in Bedfordshire, 1939–1950*. Copt Hewick: Book Castle Publishing, 2008.

Bardsley, Diane, and Miklos Soltesz. *Land Girls: In a Man's World, 1939–1946*. Dunedin, NZ: University of Otago Press, 2000.

Barrington, Brandon, ed. *The Wartime Broadcasts of Francis Stuart, 1942–1944*. Dublin: Lilliput Press, 2000.

Baxandall, Rosalyn, and Elizabeth Ewen. *Picture Windows: How the Suburbs Happened*. New York: Basic Books, 2000.

Bennett, Sue. *Five Centuries of Women and Gardens*. London: National Portrait Gallery, 2000.

Bentley, Amy. *Eating for Victory: Food Rationing and the Politics of Domesticity*. Urbana: University of Illinois, 1998.

Bingham, Colin. *The Affairs of Women: A Modern Miscellany*. Sydney: Currawong, 1969.

Bordo, Susan. "Hunger as Ideology." In *Eating Culture*, edited by Ron Scapp and Brian Seitz. Albany: SUNY Press, 1998.

Borgwardt, Elizabeth. *A New Deal for the World: America's Vision for Human Rights*. Cambridge, Mass.: Harvard University Press, 2005.

Bradshaw, Rita. *Always I'll Remember*. London: Headline, 2005.

Briggs, Susan. *The Home Front: War Years in Britain, 1939–1945*. New York: London: George Weidenfeld and Nicolson Ltd., 1975.

Bull, Phillip. *Land, Politics, and Nationalism*. New York: St. Martin's Press, 1996.

Burk, Kathleen. *Britain, America, and the Sinews of War, 1914–1918*. Boston: George Allen and Unwin, 1985.

Burnett, John. *England Eats Out: A Social History of Eating Out in England from 1830 to the Present*. Harlow: Pearson, 2004.

Carpenter, Stephanie A. *On the Farm Front: The Women's Land Army in World War II*. DeKalb: Northern Illinois University Press, 2003.

Cohen, Liz. *A Consumer's Republic: The Politics of Mass Consumption in Postwar America*. New York: Vintage Books, 2003.

Collins, Robert M. *More: The Politics of Economic Growth in Postwar America*. New York: Oxford University Press, 2000.

Colls, Robert. *Identity of England*. New York: Oxford University Press, 2002.

Coontz, Stephanie. *The Way We Never Were: American Families and the Nostalgia Trap.* New York: Basic Books, 2000.

Crosby, Alfred W. *Ecological Imperialism: The Biological Expansion of Europe, 900–1900.* Cambridge: Cambridge University Press, 2004.

Cross, Tim. *The Lost Voices of World War I: An Anthology of Writers, Poets, and Playwrights.* Iowa City: University of Iowa Press, 1989.

Cullather, Nick. "Miracles of Modernization: The Green Revolution and the Apotheosis of Technology." *Diplomatic History* 28, no. 2 (April 2004): 227–54.

Deutrich, Mabel E., and Virginia Cardwell Purdy, ed. *Clio Was a Woman: Studies in the History of American Women.* Washington, D.C.: Howard University Press, 1980.

Dombrowski, Nicole Ann, ed. *Women and War in the Twentieth Century: Enlisted with or without Consent.* New York: Garland, 1999.

Dunlap, Thomas R. *Nature and the English Diaspora: Environment and History in the United States, Canada, Australia and New Zealand.* New York: Cambridge University Press, 1999.

Erdmann, James M. *Leaflet Operations in the Second World War: The Story of the How and Why of the 6,500,000,000 Propaganda Leaflets Dropped on Axis Forces and Homelands in the Mediterranean and European Theaters of Operations.* Denver: Denver Instant Printing, 1969.

Foner, Eric. *The Story of American Freedom.* New York: W. W. Norton, 1998.

Garden, Donald. *Australia, New Zealand, and the Pacific: An Environmental History.* Santa Barbara: ABC-Clio, 2005.

Gardner, Lloyd. *Spheres of Influence: The Great Powers Partition Europe, from Munich to Yalta.* Chicago: Ivan R. Dee Publisher, 1993.

Gelfand, Lawrence E. *Herbert Hoover, the Great War, and Its Aftermath, 1914–1923.* Iowa City: University of Iowa Press, 1979.

Goldsmith, Barbara. *Other Powers: The Age of Suffrage, Spiritualism, and the Scandalous Victoria Woodhull.* New York: Random House, 1998.

Grayzel, Susan R. *Women's Identities at War: Gender, Motherhood and Politics in Britain and France During the First World War.* Chapel Hill: University of North Carolina Press, 1999.

Hadfield, Miles. *A History of British Gardening.* London: John Murray, 1979.

Hardie, Melissa. *Digging for Memories: The Women's Land Army in Cornwall.* Penzance, Cornwall: Hypatia Trust, 2006.

Harrison, Tom. *Living Through the Blitz.* London: Collins, 1976.

Hays, Samuel P. *Conservation and the Gospel of Efficiency: The Progressive Conservation Movement, 1890–1920.* Pittsburgh: University of Pittsburgh Press, 1999.

Helstosky, Carol. *Garlic and Oil: Food and Politics in Italy.* New York: Berg, 2004.

Hibbard, Benjamin Horace. *Effects of the Great War upon Agriculture in the United States and Great Britain.* New York: Oxford University Press, 1919.

Hine, Thomas. *I Want That! How We All Became Shoppers: A Cultural History.* New York: Harper Collins, 2002.

Hinton, James. *Women, Social Leadership, and the Second World War.* Oxford: Oxford University Press, 2002.

Hobsbawm, E. J. *Nations and Nationalism Since 1780: Programme, Myth and Reality.* Cambridge: Cambridge University Press, 1990.

Holt, Marilyn Irvin. *Linoleum, Better Babies, and the Modern Farm Woman, 1890–1930.* Albuquerque: University of New Mexico Press, 1995.

Howkins, Alun. *The Death of Rural England: A Social History of the Countryside Since 1900.* London: Routledge, 2003.

Humphreys, Helen. *The Lost Garden.* New York: Norton, 2002.

Hurwitz, Samuel J. *State Intervention in Great Britain: A Study of Economic Control and Solid Response, 1914–1919.* New York: Columbia University Press, 1949.

Huth, Angela. *Land Girls.* New York: St. Martin's Press, 1996.

Huxley, Gervas. *Lady Denman, G. B. E.* London: Chatto and Windus, 1962.

Inver Primary School. *Alisa Munro, Land Army.* Hamilton: SLIC, 2006. http://www .wardetectives.info/projects/wardetectives/wewillremember/inve0052.htm.

Jensen, Joan M. *With These Hands: Women Working on the Land.* Old Westbury: Feminist Press, 1981.

Johnson, George W. *A History of English Gardening.* New York: Garland, 1982.

Jones, Martin. *Feast: Why Humans Share Food.* Oxford: Oxford University Press, 2007.

Jordan, Ellen. *The Women's Movement and Women's Employment in Nineteenth-Century Britain.* New York: Routledge, 1999.

Kent, Susan Kignsley. *Gender and Power in Britain, 1640–1990.* New York: Routledge, 1999.

King, Peter. *Women Rule the Plot: The Story of the 100 Year Fight to Establish Women's Place in Farm and Garden.* London: Duckworth, 1999.

Knighton, Joyce. *Land Army Days: Cinderellas of the Soil.* Bolton: Aurora, 1994.

Korthals, Michiel. *Before Dinner: Philosophy and Ethics of Food.* Nowell: Springer, 2004.

Kuhlman, Erika A. *Petticoats and White Feathers: Gender Conformity, Race, the Progressive Peace Movement, and the Debate over War, 1895–1919.* Westport, Conn.: Greenwood Press, 1997.

Lang, Caroline. *Keep Smiling Through: Women in the Second World War.* Cambridge: Cambridge University Press, 1989.

Laughlin, Margaret. "The Woman's Land Army: 1918–1920." *Social Education* 58, no. 2 (1994): 85–88.

Laurie, Clayton. *The Propaganda Warriors: America's Crusade against Nazi Germany.* Lawrence: University of Kansas Press, 1996.

Lawson, Laura J. *City Bountiful: A Century of Community Gardening in America.* Berkeley: University of California Press, 2005.

Litoff, Judy Barrett, and David C. Smith. *Since You Went Away: World War II Letters from American Women on the Home Front.* New York: Oxford University Press, 1991.

———, eds. *American Women in a World at War: Contemporary Accounts from World War II.* Wilmington, Del.: SR Books, 1997.

Lysaght, Patricia, ed. *Food and Celebration: From Fasting to Feasting.* Dublin: University College Dublin, 2002.

Macklin, Mary. *The Fourth Service: Ex Australian Women's Land Army, World War II.* Maryborough: Mary Patricia Macklin, 2001.

Martelet, Penny. "The Women's Land Army, World War I." In Deutrich and Purdy, *Clio Was a Woman.*

Merchant, Carolyn. *Reinventing Eden: The Fate of Nature in Western Culture.* New York: Routledge, 2003.

Montgomerie, Deborah. *The Women's War.* Auckland: Auckland University Press, 2001.

Nelson, G. K. *Countrywomen on the Land.* Stroud: Sutton, 1992.

Norwood, Vera. *Made from This Earth: American Women and Nature.* Chapel Hill: University of North Carolina Press, 1993.

Pack, Charles Lathrop. "Making a Nation of Garden Cities." *Garden Magazine,* May 1918.

Paton-Walsh, Margaret. *Our War Too: American Women against the Axis.* Lawrence: University Press of Kansas, 2002.

Peiss, Kathy. *Cheap Amusements: Working Class Women and Leisure in Turn-of-the-Century New York.* Philadelphia: Temple University Press, 1986.

Potter, David Morris. *People of Plenty: Economic Abundance and the American Character.* Chicago: University of Chicago Press, 1954.

Powell, Bob, and Nigel Westacott. *The Women's Land Army, 1939–1950.* Stroud: Sutton Publishing, 2000.

Price, Jennifer. *Flight Maps: Adventures with Nature in Modern America.* New York: Basic Books, 1999.

Pronay, Nicholas, Clive Coultass, and Frances Thorpe. *British Official Films in the Second World War.* Oxford: Clio Press, 1980.

Quennell, Marjorie, and C. H. B. *A History of Everyday Things in England.* London: B. T. Batsford, 1918.

Riley, Glenda. *Women and Nature: Saving the "Wild" West.* Lincoln: University of Nebraska Press, 1999.

Rodgers, Daniel T. *Atlantic Crossings: Social Politics in a Progressive Age.* Cambridge, Mass.: Harvard University Press, 1998.

Roseman, Mindy Jane. "The Great War and Modern Motherhood: La Maternité and the Bombing of Paris." In Dombrowski, *Women and War in the Twentieth Century.*

Rupp, Leila J. *Worlds of Women: The Making of an International Women's Movement.* Princeton, N.J.: Princeton University Press, 1997.

Sautter, R. Craig, and Edward M. Burke. *Inside the Wigwam: Chicago Presidential Conventions 1860–1996.* Chicago: Wild Onion Books, 1996.

Sayer, Karen. "The English Cottage Garden." *Country Cottages: A Cultural History.* Manchester: Manchester University Press, 2000.

Scapp, Ron, and Brian Seitz, ed. *Eating Culture.* Albany: SUNY Press, 1998.

Schneider, Dorothy, and Carl J. Schneider. *American Women in the Progressive Era 1900–1920.* New York: Facts on File, 1993.

Schulman, Holly Cowan. *The Voice of America: Propaganda and Democracy, 1941–1945.* Madison: University of Wisconsin Press, 1990.

Sharpless, Rebecca. *Fertile Ground, Narrow Choices: Women on Texas Cotton Farms, 1900–1940.* Chapel Hill: University of North Carolina Press, 1999.

Shaw, Do. *Back to the Land.* London: Oberon, 2002.

Shukert, Elfrieda Berthiaume, and Barbara Smith Scibetta. *War Brides of World War II.* Novato, Calif.: Presidio Press, 1988.

Steel, Philip. *Land Girl (My War).* London: Hodder Wayland, 2003.

Stenton, Michael. *Radio London and Resistance in Occupied Europe: British Political Warfare, 1939–1943.* Oxford: Oxford University Press, 2000.

Stewart, Mart A. *"What Nature Suffers to Grow": Life, Labor, and Landscape on the Georgia Coast, 1680–1920.* Athens: University of Georgia Press, 1996.

Summerfield, Penny. *Women Workers in the Second World War.* London: Croom Helm, 1984.

Tannahill, Reay. *Food in History.* New York: Stein and Day Publishers, 1973.

Thomas, Keith. *Man and the Natural World: A History of the Modern Sensibility.* New York: Pantheon Books, 1983.

Thomas, Maurice. *Do You Remember What Granny Told You about the Women's Land Army.* Abthorpe: R. J. Chapman, 1999.

Thomson, Bob. *The New Victory Garden.* In *The Victory Garden: The Essential Companion, Three Complete Volumes in One,* by James W. Wilson, Bob Thomson, and Thomas Wirth. New York: Black Dog and Leventhal, 1990.

Threlfo, Shirley. *The Australian Women's Land Army, 1942–1945: The Experiences of Mabs Keppie.* Paterson: Paterson Historical Society, 1997.

Tillet, Iris. *The Cinderella Army.* London: Michael Joseph, 1988.

Tresham, Leslie. "My Experience as an Emergency Farm Worker." In Rupp, "Women in Farm Work," *Worlds of Women.*

Tryer, Nicola, and Rosemary Davies. *They Fought in the Fields: The Women's Land Army: The Story of a Forgotten Victory.* Oxford: ISIS Audio Books, 2002.

Twinch, Carol. *Women on the Land.* Cambridge: Lutterworth Press, 1990.

Verdon, Nicola. *Rural Women Workers in Nineteenth-Century England: Gender, Work and Wages.* Suffolk: Boydell Press, 2002.

Vincent, C. Paul. *The Politics of Hunger: The Allied Blockade of Germany, 1915–1919.* Athens, Ohio: Ohio University Press, 1985.

Walker, Nancy A. *Women's Magazines 1940–1960: Gender Roles and the Popular Press.* Boston: Bedford St. Martin's, 1998.

Ward, Geoffrey C., and Ken Burns. *Not for Ourselves Alone: The Story of Elizabeth Cady Stanton and Susan B. Anthony.* New York: Alfred A. Knopf: 1999.

Warwick, Frances Evelyn Maynard. *Life's Ebb and Flow.* New York: Morrow and Co., 1929.

Watson, James L., and Melissa L. Caldwell, eds. *The Cultural Politics of Food and Eating: A Reader*. Malden: Blackwell Publishing, 2005.

Weatherford, Doris. *American Women and World War II*. New York: Facts on File, 1990.

Weiss, Elaine. *The Fruits of Victory: The Women's Land Army of America in the Great War*. Dulles: Potomac Books, 2008.

White, Cynthia L. *Women's Magazines, 1693–1968*. London: Michael Joseph, 1970.

Williams, Mari A. *A Forgotten Army: Female Munitions Workers of South Wales, 1939–1945*. Cardiff: University of Wales Press, 2002.

Wilson, C. Anne. *Food and Drink in Britain: From the Stone Age to the 19th Century*. Chicago: Academy Chicago Publishers, 1991.

Wilson, James W. *Masters of the Victory Garden*. In *The Victory Garden: The Essential Companion, Three Complete Volumes in One*, by James W. Wilson, Bob Thomson, and Thomas Wirth. New York: Black Dog and Leventhal, 1990.

Winkler, Alan. *The Politics of Propaganda*. New Haven: Yale University Press, 1978.

Winter, Jan, and and Jean-Louis Robert. *Capital Cities at War: Paris, London, Berlin, 1914–1919*. Cambridge: Cambridge University Press, 1997.

Wirth, Thomas. *The Victory Garden Landscape Guide*. In *The Victory Garden: The Essential Companion, Three Complete Volumes in One*, by James W. Wilson, Bob Thomson, and Thomas Wirth. New York: Black Dog and Leventhal, 1990.

Wood, Roy C. *The Sociology of the Meal*. Edinburgh: Edinburgh University Press, 1995.

Yellin, Emily. *Our Mother's War: American Women at Home and at the Front during World War II*. New York: Free Press, 2004.

Zeiger, Susan. *In Uncle Sam's Service: Women Workers with the American Expeditionary Force, 1917–1919*. Ithaca: Cornell University Press, 1999.

INDEX

suffragettes: activism, 21–24; American
adoption of the label, 59; association
with farmerette label, 59; England,
21, 23; Millicent Fawcett, 95; Sylvia
Pankhurst, 17
suffragists, 15–17, 21, 58–59, 99
symbolism: of food, 68, 133, 148, 153, 157,
160, 163, 187; of war gardens 64, 65,
83–86, 141, 151; of women in wartime
agriculture, 184–186. *See also* image;
sphere, women's; tractors

Talbot, Merial, 34, 36–37, 75, 97. *See also*
Women's Land Army (Britain)
Tennessee Valley Authority (TVA), 103. *See
also* Roosevelt, Franklin, D.
Texas: agricultural traditions, 125–27;
newspaper reports, 126; Vina Cochran,
126
theatrical productions, 75, 146. *See also*
radio, use of
Time, 138
tobacco, 123
tomatoes. *See* vegetables
tractors, 102, 110, 120–21
training (Britain): gardening, 2, 101–2, 150,
155; numbers, 6; occupational results of,
28; pre–First World War discussions,
25–28, 30, 35; Roland Prothero, 35;
WLA (First World War), 35, 37, 40–41,
43, 60, 101; WLA (Second World War),
110, 112–14, 184. *See also* Warwick, Lady
Frances Evelyn "Daisy" Maynard Grenville, Countess of; Wilkins, Louisa
training (United States): Food Administration, 68, 117; gardening, 2, 101–2,
138–39; male agriculturalists, 103; Mel
Werner, 122; numbers, 48; price of,
48; WLA (Second World War), 115–16,
118–19, 122–24, 184; WLAA (First World
War) 24, 43–44, 46, 48, 50–52, 57. *See
also* school programs; Stevens, Helen
Kennedy

training (New Zealand), 129
transportation, 40, 68, 78, 80, 118, 124,
192n1
turnips. *See* vegetables

uniforms. *See* clothing
United Nations, 118, 131
Uncle Sam, 134, 185
United States Crop Corps, 117, 119, 137
United States Employment Service, 43, 51,
118. *See also* Blatch, Harriot Stanton
urban demographics. *See* rural vs. urban
demographics
United States School Garden Army, 87. *See
also* school programs

vacant lot gardening: First World War, 1,
58, 68, 74, 83; Second World War, 150,
179, 180
vegetables: beans, 1, 52, 137, 149, 154,
175, 179; beets, 121, 179; broccoli, 179;
cabbage, 179; carrots, 106, 137, 149;
cauliflower, 149; corn, 57, 61, 113, 124,
149, 177; lettuce, 124, 156, 177; onions,
179; peppers, 175; potatoes, 1, 56, 78,
149; radish, 149; squash, 149, 175, 179;
tomatoes, 1, 56, 145, 149, 154, 156, 170,
175, 179, 187, 189; turnips, 186, 210
Vermont, 15, 48
Victory Garden campaign: campaign
organization 134–136; housewife
training and support, 139–40, 146, 152;
Lillian Crawford Addis, 146; modern
nostalgia about, 179–84; new American
vernacular, 178; public opinion about,
156; recruitment of school teachers, 140,
178; results of, 135, 169; symbolism of,
141, 151. *See also* Appling, Mary; Dewar,
Ruth McCord; food campaigns; Kuehne,
Anona Stoetzl; Ott, Virginia Raymond
Victoria, Queen of the United Kingdom of
Great Britain and Ireland, 17